EVOLVE

STUDENT'S BOOK

with Digital Pack

Ben Goldstein and Ceri Jones

4

CAMBRIDGE
UNIVERSITY PRESS

CAMBRIDGE
UNIVERSITY PRESS & ASSESSMENT

Shaftesbury Road, Cambridge CB2 8EA, United Kingdom

One Liberty Plaza, 20th Floor, New York, NY 10006, USA

477 Williamstown Road, Port Melbourne, VIC 3207, Australia

314–321, 3rd Floor, Plot 3, Splendor Forum, Jasola District Centre, New Delhi – 110025, India

103 Penang Road, #05–06/07, Visioncrest Commercial, Singapore 238467

Cambridge University Press & Assessment is a department of the University of Cambridge.

We share the University's mission to contribute to society through the pursuit of education, learning and research at the highest international levels of excellence.

www.cambridge.org
Information on this title: www.cambridge.org/9781009237550

First published with Digital Pack 2022

20 19 18 17 16 15 14

Printed in Brazil by Forma Certa Grafica Digital LTDA

A catalogue record for this publication is available from the British Library

ISBN 978-1-009-23082-7 Student's Book with eBook
ISBN 978-1-009-23755-0 Student's Book with Digital Pack
ISBN 978-1-009-23756-7 Student's Book with Digital Pack A
ISBN 978-1-009-23757-4 Student's Book with Digital Pack B
ISBN 978-1-108-40901-8 Workbook with Audio
ISBN 978-1-108-40874-5 Workbook with Audio A
ISBN 978-1-108-41194-3 Workbook with Audio B
ISBN 978-1-108-40518-8 Teacher's Edition with Test Generator
ISBN 978-1-108-41071-7 Presentation Plus
ISBN 978-1-108-41204-9 Class Audio CDs
ISBN 978-1-108-40795-3 Video Resource Book with DVD
ISBN 978-1-009-23065-0 Full Contact with Digital Pack

Additional resources for this publication at www.cambridge.org/evolve

ACKNOWLEDGMENTS

The *Evolve* publishers would like to thank the following individuals and institutions who have contributed their time and insights into the development of the course:

Maria Araceli Hernández Tovar, Instituto Tecnológico Superior de San Luis Potosí, Capital, Mexico; Kayla M. Briggs, Hoseo University, South Korea; Lenise Butler, Laureate, Mexico; Aslı Derin Anaç, İstanbul Bilgi University, Turkey; Roberta Freitas, IBEU, Rio de Janeiro, Brazil; José Manuel Cuin Jacuinde, Coordinación de Lenguas Extranjeras del Instituto Tecnológico de Morelia, Mexico; Thomas Christian Keller, Universidad de las Américas, Chile; Daniel Lowe, Lowe English Services, Panama; Ivanova Monteros, Universidad Tecnológica Equinoccial, Ecuador; Daniel Nowatnick, USA; Diego Ribeiro Santos, Universidade Anhembi Morumbi, São Paulo, Brazil; Jason Williams, Notre Dame Seishin University, Japan; Matthew Wilson, Miyagi University, Japan; Yudy Rios, Universidad Pedagógica Nacional, Colombia

To our student contributors, who have given us their ideas and their time, and who appear throughout this book:

Andres Ramírez, Mexico; Alessandra Avelar, Brazil; Nicolle Juliana Torres Sierra, Colombia; Ouattara Maryne Soukeina, USA; Seung Geyong Yang, South Korea; Tayra Laritza Lacayo Sanchez, Honduras.

And special thanks to Katy Simpson, teacher and writer at *myenglishvoice.com*

Authors' Acknowledgments:

A special thanks to all the editorial team, particularly Dena Daniel, whose patience and professionalism helped make this project a pleasure to work on.

The authors and publishers acknowledge the following sources of copyright material and are grateful for the permissions granted. While every effort has been made, it has not always been possible to identify the sources of all the material used, or to trace all copyright holders. If any omissions are brought to our notice, we will be happy to include the appropriate acknowledgements on reprinting and in the next update to the digital edition, as applicable.

Text

p. 54: Logo of Social Bite. Copyright © Social Bite Fund. Reproduced with kind permission; p. 55: Logo of World Wildlife Fund. Copyright © 1986 Panda symbol WWF – World Wide Fund for Nature. Reproduced with kind permission; p. 55: Logo of Doctors Without Borders. Copyright © Doctors Without Borders/Médecins Sans Frontières (MSF). Reproduced with kind permission; p. 60: Text about The City Repair Project. Reproduced with kind permission of The City Repair.

Photographs

B = Below, BC = Below Centre, BG = Background, BL = Below Left, BR = Below Right, CL = Centre Left, CR = Centre Right, TC = Top Centre, TL = Top Left, TR = Top Right.

The following photographs are sourced from Getty Images.

p. xvi (TR): asiseeit/E+; p. xvi (BL): vlada_maestro/iStock/Getty Images Plus; p. 1, p. 36 (BR): Chris Ryan/Caiaimage; p. 2 (photo a): Nicola Tree/The Image Bank; p. 2 (photo b): PeopleImages/iStock/Getty Images Plus; p. 3 (photo c): Sigrid Gombert/Cultura; p. 3: artpartner-images/Photographer's Choice; p. 4: Klaus Vedfelt/Taxi; p. 5: DivVector/DigitalVision Vectors; p. 6, p. 21 (CR), p. 53: Hero Images; p. 7: Paul Archuleta/FilmMagic; p. 8: sturti/E+; p. 9: Joe Raedle/Getty Images News; pp. 10, 20, 30, 42, 52, 62, 74, 84, 94, 106, 116, 126: Tom Merton/Caiaimage; p. 10 (tourist): Andrew Peacock/Lonely Planet Images; p. 11: nedomacki/iStock/Getty Images Plus; p. 12: Neilson Barnard/Getty Images Entertainment; p. 13: Mint Images RF; p. 14 (barbeque): Teresa Miller/EyeEm; p. 14 (boil): UllrichG/iStock/Getty Images Plus; p. 14 (chop): Chris Cole/DigitalVision; p. 14 (stir): tzahiV/iStock/Getty Images Plus; p. 14 (fry): Dorling Kindersley; p. 14 (rinse): Sidekick/iStock/Getty Images Plus; p. 15: ma-k/E+; p. 16: Maskot; p. 17: EddieHernandezPhotography/iStock/Getty Images Plus; p. 18 (photo 1): Foodcollection RF; p. 18 (photo 2): KyleNelson/E+; p. 20, p. 30 (couple), p. 104 (TL): Westend61; p. 21: Anouk de Maar/Cultura; p. 22 (TR): vgajic/E+; p. 23: Nomad/E+; p. 24: Ezra Bailey/Taxi; p. 25: Jan Sandvik/EyeEm; p. 26: Rudolf Vlcek/Moment Open; p. 27: NoDerog/iStock/Getty Images Plus; p. 28 (TL): Víctor Del Pino/EyeEm; p. 28 (TC): Maximilian Stock Ltd./Photolibrary; p. 28 (TR): inhauscreative/E+; p. 29: Logorilla/DigitalVision Vectors; p. 30 (CL): Hussein Fardin Fard/EyeEm; p. 30 (CR): Chalabala/iStock/Getty Images Plus; p. 32: Zigy Kaluzny-Charles Thatcher/The Image Bank; p. 33: Maremagnum/Photolibrary; p. 35: SERGEI SUPINSKY/AFP; p. 36 (BL): Fotos International/Archive Photos; p. 36 (BC): Ethan Miller/Getty Images Entertainment; p. 36 (TR): BANARAS KHAN/AFP; p. 38: djedzura/iStock/Getty Images Plus; p. 40 (cowboy): Vicki Jauron, Babylon and Beyond Photography/Moment; p. 40 (photo a): Creative Crop/Photodisc; p. 40 (photo b): Miguel Schincariol/AFP; p. 42 LauriPatterson p. 43: LuminaStock/iStock/Getty Images Plus; p. 47: Jo-Ann Richards/First Light; p. 48: Henn Photography/Cultura; p. 50: fotofrog/iStock/Getty Images Plus; p. 51: Jordan Siemens/Taxi; p. 52 (man): GeorgeRudy/iStock/Getty Images Plus; p. 52 (woman): pablocalvog/iStock/Getty Images Plus; p. 56: AndreyPopov/iStock/Getty Images Plus; p. 58: skynesher/iStock/Getty Images Plus; p. 59: Johner Images; p.62 (CL): Phil Clarke Hill/In Pictures; p. 62 (TL): Mario Tama/Getty Images News; p. 64: UpperCut Images; p. 65: Antonio_Diaz/iStock/Getty Images Plus; p. 66: Matt Cardy/Getty Images News; p. 69: Jasmin Awad/EyeEm; p. 70 (photo 1): Fotosearch; p. 70 (photo 2): Zac Macaulay/Cultura/Getty Images Plus; p. 72 (emoji): Pingebat/iStock/Getty Images Plus; p. 72 (TR): Christophe Morin/IP3/Getty Images News; p. 74 (smartphone): Tim Robberts/The Image Bank; p. 74 (concert): Isabella Torreallba/EyeEm; p. 75: PATRICK KOVARIK/AFP; p. 77 (BL): Stephane Godin/Biosphoto; p. 77 (BR): hardyuno/iStock/Getty Images Plus; p. 77: Roderick Chen/All Canada Photos; p. 80 (photo 1): Jessica Peterson; p. 80 (photo 2): Eduard Titov/Moment; p. 81: David Arky; p. 82 (TL): Klaus Vedfelt/The Image Bank; p. 82 (TR): Cultura Exclusive/Moof; p. 83: John Fedele/Blend Images; p. 84: Jonathan Kitchen/DigitalVision; p. 85 (stop sign): Dallas Stribley/Lonely Planet Images; p. 85 (BR): Bernard Van Berg/EyeEm; p. 88 (TL): Dave Walsh/VW Pics/UIG; p. 88 (TC): Philippe Marion/Moment; p. 88 (TR): Grant Faint/The Image Bank; p. 88 (carriages): Charles Phelps Cushing/ClassicStock/Archive Photos; p. 90: Peter Muller/Cultura; p. 91: Richard Baker/In Pictures; p. 93: Andersen Ross/Blend Images; p. 94 (TL): baranozdemir/iStock/Getty Images Plus; p. 94 (TC): Creatas/Getty Images Plus; p. 96: Dev Carr/Cultura; p. 97: National Geographic; p. 98 (army): holgs/E+; p. 98 (microwave): Bettmann; p. 99: Hinterhaus Productions/DigitalVision; p. 100 (TL): Kevin Winter/Getty Images Entertainment; p. 100 (TR): Allsport/Hulton Archive; p. 101 (BL): Debra Bardowicks/Oxford Scientific; p. 101 (BC): Image Source; p. 101 (BR): Peter Cade/The Image Bank; p. 102 (TC): Yagi-Studio/E+; p. 102 (TR): Kyle Monk/Blend Images; p. 103: WendellandCarolyn/iStock/Getty Images Plus; p. 104 (TR): Henrik Weis/DigitalVision; p. 105: Michael Schwalbe/EyeEm; p. 106 (fire): Moritz Witter/EyeEm; p. 106 (hieroglyphics): Raffi Maghdessian; p. 106 (syringe): AtomicCupcake/DigitalVision Vectors; p. 106 (corn): Diane Labombarbe/DigitalVision Vectors; p. 106 (laptop): hudiemm/DigitalVision Vectors; p. 106 (atom): bortonia/DigitalVision Vectors; p. 107: Alija/iStock/Getty Images Plus; p. 108 (BG): johns0114/johns0114; p. 108 (CR): Elliott Kaufman/Corbis; p. 108 (TL): LWA/Dann Tardif/Blend Images; p. 108 (Lee): YinYang/E+; p. 108 (Allie): moodboard/Getty Images Plus; p. 110 (carrot): rimglow/iStock/Getty Images Plus; p. 110 (cheese): vikif/iStock/Getty Images Plus; p. 110 (honey): Miro Vrlik/EyeEm; p. 111: VladGans/E+; p. 112 (spray): Madmaxer/iStock/Getty Images Plus; p. 112 (candle): Blanchi Costela/Moment; p. 112 (patch): Fahroni/iStock/Getty Images Plus; p. 113 (photo 1): ljpat/iStock/Getty Images Plus; p. 113 (photo 2): kevinjeon00/E+; p. 113 (photo 3): DarioEgidi/iStock/Getty Images Plus; p. 114: metamorworks/iStock/Getty Images Plus; p. 115: VCG/Getty Images News; p. 116: Anton Petrus/Moment; p. 117: Allan Baxter/Photographer's Choice; p. 118 (photo a): Mark Edward Atkinson/Tracey Lee/Blend Images; p. 118 (photo b): Sladic/iStock/Getty Images Plus; p. 118 (photo c), p. 74 (girl): KidStock/Blend Images; p. 119: Rhydian Lewis/Photographer's Choice; p. 120: Barbara Ferra Fotografia/Moment; p. 121 (rollerskates): Peathegee Inc/Blend Images; p. 121 (console): Andy Crawford/Dorling Kindersley; p. 121 (tireswing): sarahwolfephotography/Moment Open; p. 122: SeventyFour/iStock/Getty Images Plus; p. 124 (photo a): PEDRO PARDO/AFP; p. 124 (photo b): altrendo images; p. 124 (photo c): Paul Park/Moment; p. 124 (photo d): Jupiterimages/Stockbyte; p. 126: Eddy LEMAISTRE/Corbis Sport.

Below photographs are sourced from other libraries:

p. 45 (Manuela Saenz): Colport/Alamy Stock Photo; p. 60: © Anton Legoo, Portland Street Art Alliance; p.61: ©VERDEVERTICAL. Reproduced with kind permission; p. 76: © Tasmania 360/Loic Le Guilly; p. 92: © Tim Griffith (photographer) and LMS (architects). Reproduced with permission; p. 94 (TR): keith morris/Alamy Stock Photo; p. 128: image anorak/Alamy Stock Photo.

Front cover photography by Alija/E+/Getty Images.

Illustrations by Ana Djordjevic (Astound US) pp. 86, 157, 159; Mark Duffin (ODI) p. 68; Lyn Dylan (Sylvie Poggio) pp. 157, 159; David Eaton (ODI) pp. 14–15; 290 Sean (KJA Artists) p. 87.

Audio production by CityVox, New York.

EVOLVE

SPEAKING MATTERS

EVOLVE is a six-level American English course for adults and young adults, taking students from beginner to advanced levels (CEFR A1 to C1).

Drawing on insights from language teaching experts and real students, EVOLVE is a general English course that gets students speaking with confidence.

This student-centered course covers all skills and focuses on the most effective and efficient ways to make progress in English.

Confidence in teaching.
Joy in learning.

Better Learning WITH EVOLVE

Better Learning is our simple approach where insights we've gained from research have helped shape content that drives results. Language evolves, and so does the way we learn. This course takes a flexible, student-centered approach to English language teaching.

Meet our student contributors

Videos and ideas from real students feature throughout the Student's Book.

Our student contributors describe themselves in three words.

SEUNG GEYOUNG YANG

Happy, creative
Myongji University, South Korea

ANDRES RAMÍREZ FABIAN

Friendly, happy, funny
Instituto Tecnológico de Morelia, México

OUATTARA MARYNE SOUKEINA

Friendly, perfectionist, creative
Educational Language Services, USA

ALESSANDRA AVELAR

Creative, positive, funny
Faculdade ICESP, Águas Claras, Brazil

TAYRA LARITZA LACAYO SANCHEZ

Tenacious, oustanding, curious
La universidad global de Honduras

NICOLLE JULIANA TORRES SIERRA

Passionate, Friendly, committed
Centro Colombo Americano, Colombia

Student-generated content

EVOLVE is the first course of its kind to feature real student-generated content. We spoke to over 2,000 students from all over the world about the topics they would like to discuss in English and in what situations they would like to be able to speak more confidently.

The ideas are included throughout the Student's Book and the students appear in short videos responding to discussion questions.

INSIGHT

Research shows that achievable speaking role models can be a powerful motivator.

CONTENT

Bite-sized videos feature students talking about topics in the Student's Book.

RESULT

Students are motivated to speak and share their ideas.

"It's important to provide learners with interesting or stimulating topics."

Teacher, Mexico (Global Teacher Survey, 2017)

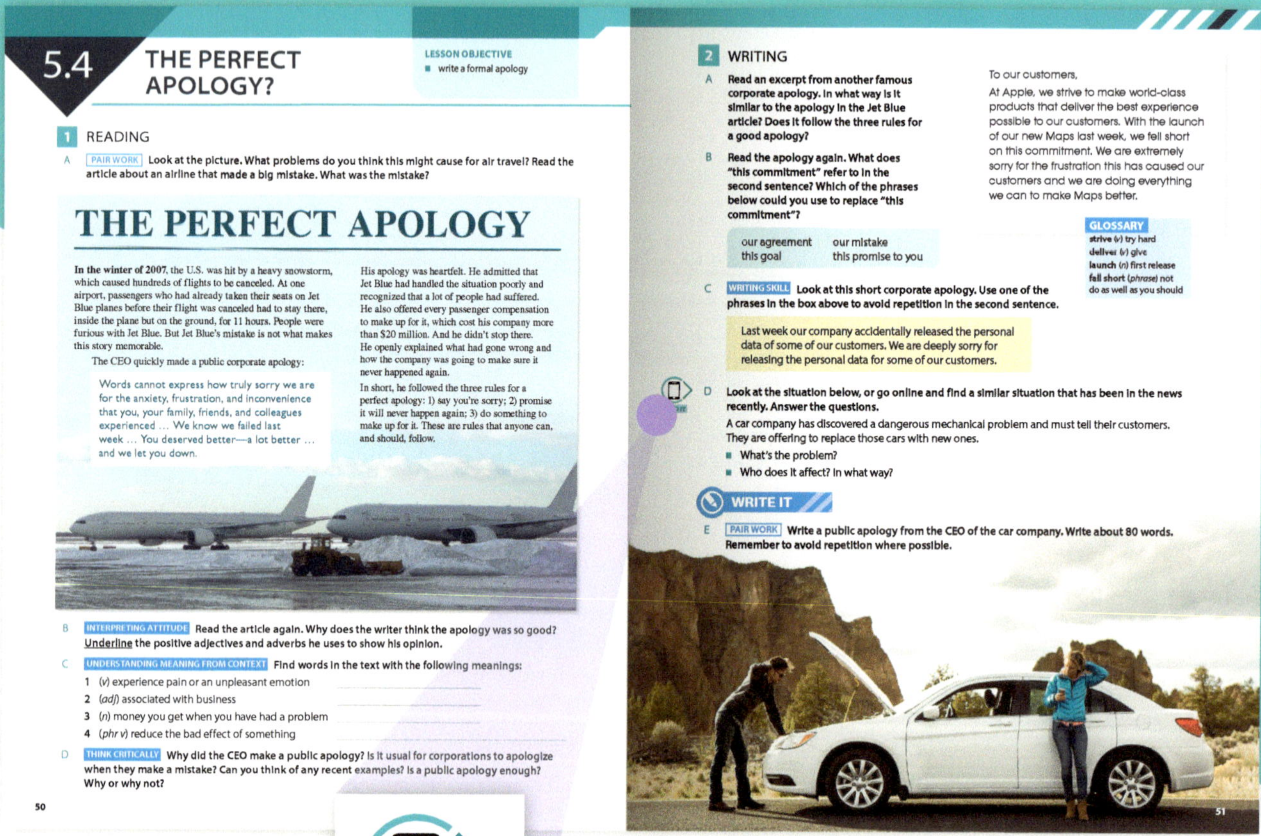

5.4 THE PERFECT APOLOGY?

LESSON OBJECTIVE
- write a formal apology

1 READING

A PAIR WORK Look at the picture. What problems do you think this might cause for air travel? Read the article about an airline that made a big mistake. What was the mistake?

THE PERFECT APOLOGY

In the winter of 2007, the U.S. was hit by a heavy snowstorm, which caused hundreds of flights to be canceled. At one airport, passengers who had already taken their seats on Jet Blue planes before their flight was canceled had to stay there, inside the plane but on the ground, for 11 hours. People were furious with Jet Blue. But Jet Blue's mistake is not what makes this story memorable.

The CEO quickly made a public corporate apology:

> Words cannot express how truly sorry we are for the anxiety, frustration, and inconvenience that you, your family, friends, and colleagues experienced … We know we failed last week … You deserved better—a lot better … and we let you down.

His apology was heartfelt. He admitted that Jet Blue had handled the situation poorly and recognized that a lot of people had suffered. He also offered every passenger compensation to make up for it, which cost his company more than $20 million. And he didn't stop there. He openly explained what had gone wrong and how the company was going to make sure it never happened again.

In short, he followed the three rules for a perfect apology: 1) say you're sorry; 2) promise it will never happen again; 3) do something to make up for it. These are rules that anyone can, and should, follow.

B INTERPRETING ATTITUDE Read the article again. Why does the writer think the apology was so good? Underline the positive adjectives and adverbs he uses to show his opinion.

C UNDERSTANDING MEANING FROM CONTEXT Find words in the text with the following meanings:

1 (*v*) experience pain or an unpleasant emotion ______
2 (*adj*) associated with business ______
3 (*n*) money you get when you have had a problem ______
4 (*phr v*) reduce the bad effect of something ______

D THINK CRITICALLY Why did the CEO make a public apology? Is it usual for corporations to apologize when they make a mistake? Can you think of any recent examples? Is a public apology enough? Why or why not?

50

2 WRITING

A Read an excerpt from another famous corporate apology. In what way is it similar to the apology in the Jet Blue article? Does it follow the three rules for a good apology?

> To our customers,
>
> At Apple, we strive to make world-class products that deliver the best experience possible to our customers. With the launch of our new Maps last week, we fell short on this commitment. We are extremely sorry for the frustration this has caused our customers and we are doing everything we can to make Maps better.

GLOSSARY
strive (*v*) try hard
deliver (*v*) give
launch (*n*) first release
fall short (*phrase*) not do as well as you should

B Read the apology again. What does "this commitment" refer to in the second sentence? Which of the phrases below could you use to replace "this commitment"?

our agreement	our mistake
this goal	this promise to you

C WRITING SKILL Look at this short corporate apology. Use one of the phrases in the box above to avoid repetition in the second sentence.

> Last week our company accidentally released the personal data of some of our customers. We are deeply sorry for releasing the personal data for some of our customers.

D Look at the situation below, or go online and find a similar situation that has been in the news recently. Answer the questions.

A car company has discovered a dangerous mechanical problem and must tell their customers. They are offering to replace those cars with new ones.

- What's the problem?
- Who does it affect? In what way?

WRITE IT

E PAIR WORK Write a public apology from the CEO of the car company. Write about 80 words. Remember to avoid repetition where possible.

51

FIND IT

Find it

INSIGHT

Research with hundreds of teachers and students across the globe revealed a desire to expand the classroom and bring the real world in.

CONTENT

Find it are smartphone activities that allow students to bring live content into the class and personalize the learning experience with research and group activities.

RESULT

Students engage in the lesson because it is meaningful to them.

Designed for success

8.4 **DIGITAL DETOX**

LESSON OBJECTIVE
- write a comment about a podcast

1 LISTENING

A PAIR WORK **Look at the pictures. What are the main differences between the two situations? Which one do you think shows a more positive use of mobile technology? Why?**

B 2.20 LISTEN FOR ATTITUDE **Listen to an extract from a podcast about mobile technology. What is a "digital detox"? How do the two speakers, Tim and Kayla, feel about the idea? Would you ever consider a digital detox?**

C 2.20 PAIR WORK **Read the extracts. Who do you think said each one? Write *T* (Tim) or *K* (Kayla). How do you know? Listen again to check your answers.**

1 I love my phone too much! ___
2 I would never do that, not for a million dollars! ___
3 You don't always have to share everything. ___
4 What's wrong with sharing? ___
5 It's so important that we know what's going on in the world. ___
6 I could be doing something better. ___
7 I am very happy with my 24/7, always connected life. ___

INSIDER ENGLISH

The phrase *not for a million dollars* is often used to show strong dislike for an idea.

I'd never give up my phone – not for a million dollars!

D CRITICAL THINKING **Who do you agree with more? Do you think people need to learn how to control their use of digital devices? Do you think a digital detox is the best way? Can you think of other ways?**

2 PRONUNCIATION: Listening for emphasis

A 2.21 Listen to the extracts from ...
1 A digital detox, me? Are you kiddi...
2 I'm glad you stepped up, Tim, bec...
3 We did it in this cabin out in the fo...

B Choose the correct words to compl...
When a speaker wants to add empha... *shorter / longer.*

82

INSIDER ENGLISH

The phrase *not for a million dollars* is often used to show strong dislike for an idea.

I'd never give up my phone – not for a million dollars!

Pronunciation

INSIGHT

Research shows that only certain aspects of pronunciation actually affect comprehensibility and inhibit communication.

CONTENT

EVOLVE focuses on the aspects of pronunciation that most affect communication.

RESULT

Students understand more when listening and can be clearly understood when they speak.

Insider English

INSIGHT

Even in a short exchange, idiomatic language can inhibit understanding.

CONTENT

Insider English focuses on the informal language and colloquial expressions frequently found in everyday situations.

RESULT

Students are confident in the real world.

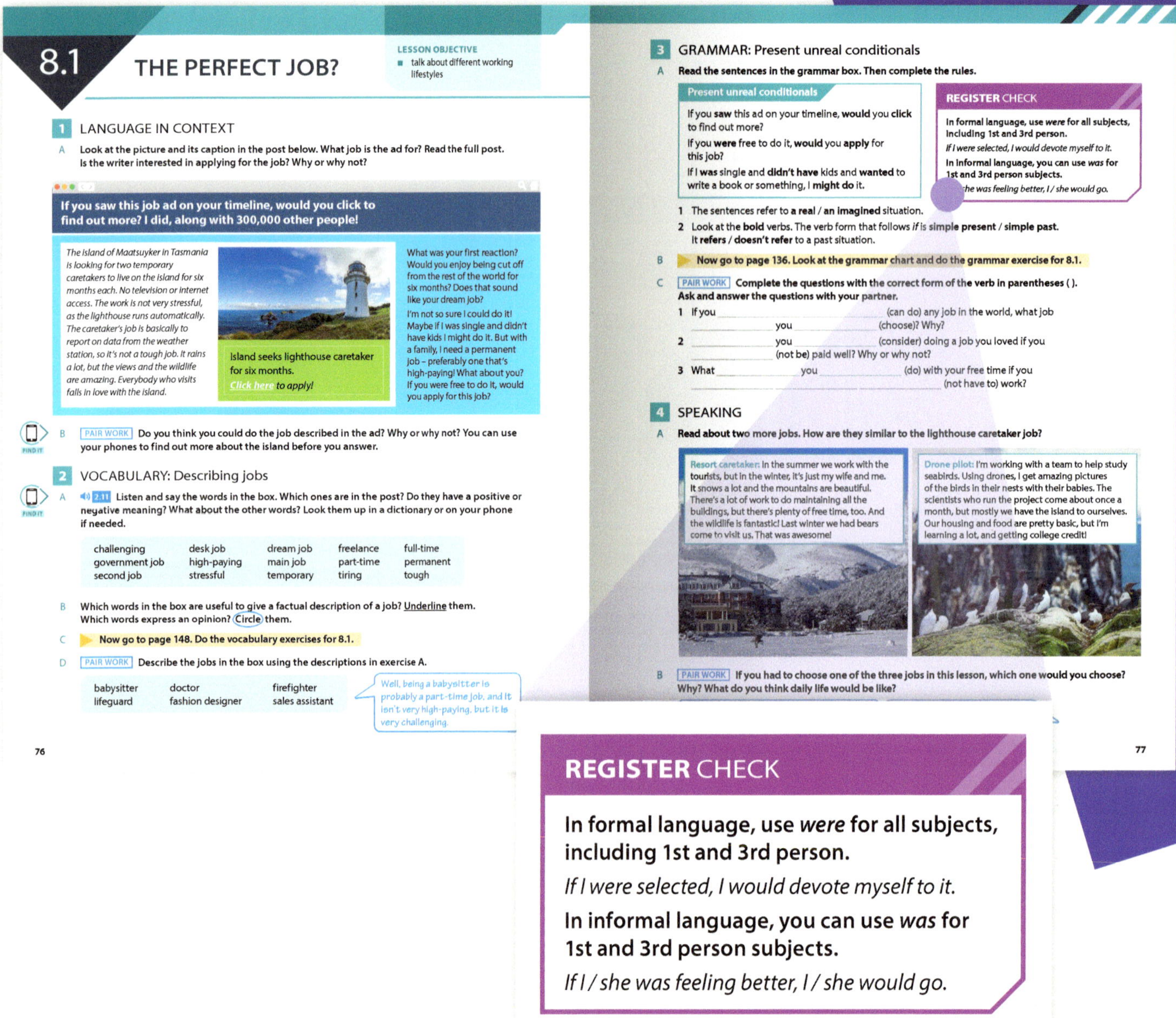

8.1 THE PERFECT JOB?

LESSON OBJECTIVE
- talk about different working lifestyles

1 LANGUAGE IN CONTEXT

A Look at the picture and its caption in the post below. What job is the ad for? Read the full post. Is the writer interested in applying for the job? Why or why not?

If you saw this job ad on your timeline, would you click to find out more? I did, along with 300,000 other people!

The island of Maatsuyker in Tasmania is looking for two temporary caretakers to live on the island for six months each. No television or internet access. The work is not very stressful, as the lighthouse runs automatically. The caretaker's job is basically to report on data from the weather station, so it's not a tough job. It rains a lot, but the views and the wildlife are amazing. Everybody who visits falls in love with the island.

Island seeks lighthouse caretaker for six months. *Click here to apply!*

What was your first reaction? Would you enjoy being cut off from the rest of the world for six months? Does that sound like your dream job? I'm not so sure I could do it! Maybe if I was single and didn't have kids I might do it. But with a family, I need a permanent job – preferably one that's high-paying! What about you? If you were free to do it, would you apply for this job?

B PAIR WORK Do you think you could do the job described in the ad? Why or why not? You can use your phones to find out more about the island before you answer.

2 VOCABULARY: Describing jobs

A 2.11 Listen and say the words in the box. Which ones are in the post? Do they have a positive or negative meaning? What about the other words? Look them up in a dictionary or on your phone if needed.

challenging	desk job	dream job	freelance	full-time
government job	high-paying	main job	part-time	permanent
second job	stressful	temporary	tiring	tough

B Which words in the box are useful to give a factual description of a job? Underline them. Which words express an opinion? Circle them.

C Now go to page 148. Do the vocabulary exercises for 8.1.

D PAIR WORK Describe the jobs in the box using the descriptions in exercise A.

babysitter	doctor	firefighter
lifeguard	fashion designer	sales assistant

Well, being a babysitter is probably a part-time job, and it isn't very high-paying, but it is very challenging.

76

3 GRAMMAR: Present unreal conditionals

A Read the sentences in the grammar box. Then complete the rules.

Present unreal conditionals

If you **saw** this ad on your timeline, **would** you **click** to find out more?
If you **were** free to do it, **would** you **apply** for this job?
If I **was** single and **didn't have** kids and **wanted** to write a book or something, I **might do** it.

REGISTER CHECK
In formal language, use *were* for all subjects, including 1st and 3rd person.
If I were selected, I would devote myself to it.
In informal language, you can use *was* for 1st and 3rd person subjects.
If I / she was feeling better, I / she would go.

1 The sentences refer to **a real / an imagined** situation.
2 Look at the **bold** verbs. The verb form that follows *if* is **simple present / simple past**. It **refers / doesn't refer** to a past situation.

B Now go to page 136. Look at the grammar chart and do the grammar exercise for 8.1.

C PAIR WORK Complete the questions with the correct form of the verb in parentheses ( ). Ask and answer the questions with your partner.

1 If you ________ (can do) any job in the world, what job ________ you ________ (choose)? Why?
2 ________ you ________ (consider) doing a job you loved if you ________ (not be) paid well? Why or why not?
3 What ________ you ________ (do) with your free time if you ________ (not have to) work?

4 SPEAKING

A Read about two more jobs. How are they similar to the lighthouse caretaker job?

Resort caretaker: In the summer we work with the tourists, but in the winter, it's just my wife and me. It snows a lot and the mountains are beautiful. There's a lot of work to do maintaining all the buildings, but there's plenty of free time, too. And the wildlife is fantastic! Last winter we had bears come to visit us. That was awesome!

Drone pilot: I'm working with a team to help study seabirds. Using drones, I get amazing pictures of the birds in their nests with their babies. The scientists who run the project come about once a month, but mostly we have the island to ourselves. Our housing and food are pretty basic, but I'm learning a lot, and getting college credit!

B PAIR WORK If you had to choose one of the three jobs in this lesson, which one would you choose? Why? What do you think daily life would be like?

77

REGISTER CHECK

In formal language, use *were* for all subjects, including 1st and 3rd person.

If I were selected, I would devote myself to it.

In informal language, you can use *was* for 1st and 3rd person subjects.

If I / she was feeling better, I / she would go.

Register check

INSIGHT

Teachers report that their students often struggle to master the differences between written and spoken English.

CONTENT

Register check draws on research into the Cambridge English Corpus and highlights potential problem areas for learners.

RESULT

Students transition confidently between written and spoken English and recognize different levels of formality as well as when to use them appropriately.

"The presentation is very clear and there are plenty of opportunities for student practice and production."

Jason Williams, Teacher, Notre Dame Seishin University, Japan

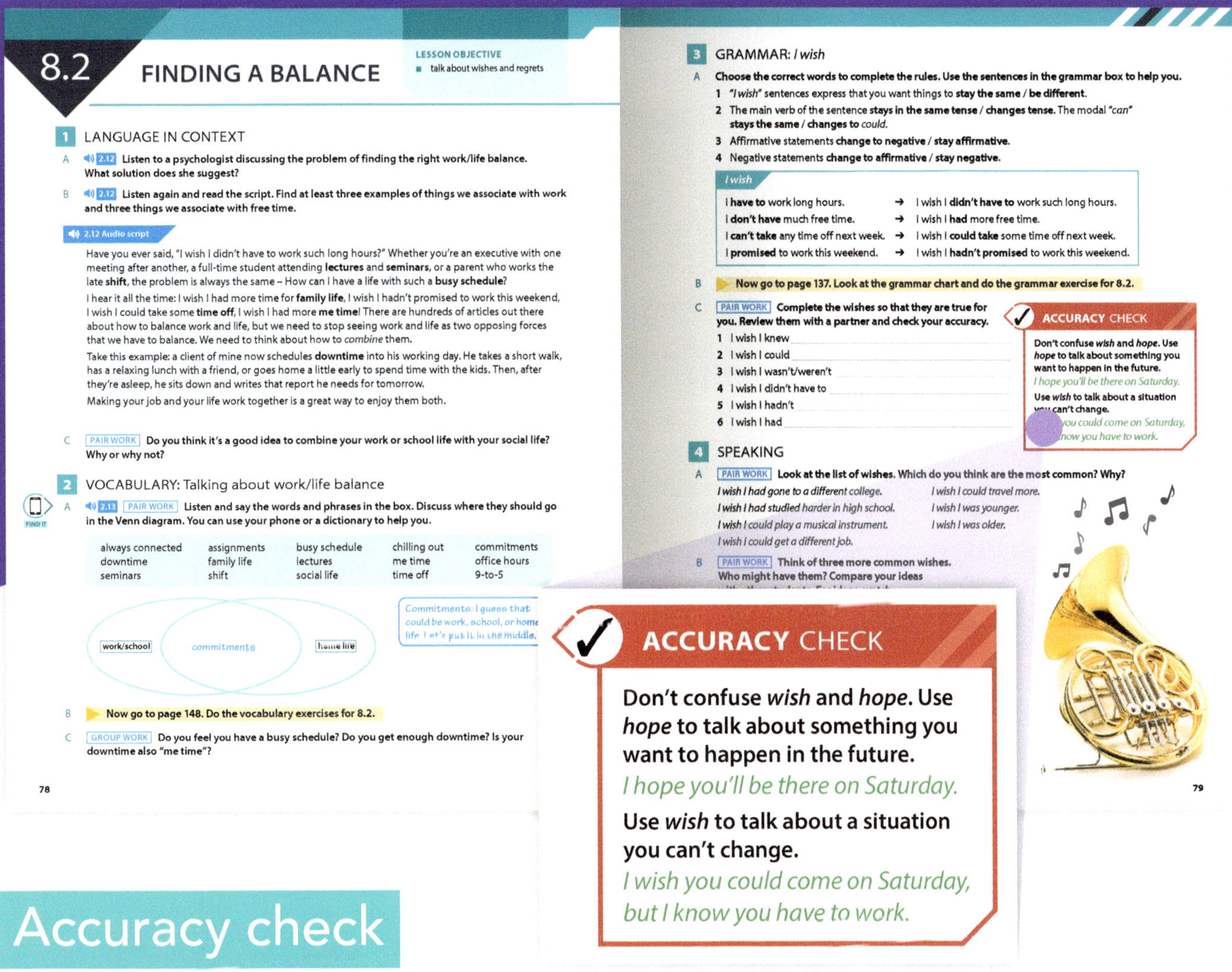

8.2 FINDING A BALANCE

LESSON OBJECTIVE
- talk about wishes and regrets

1 LANGUAGE IN CONTEXT

A 2.12 Listen to a psychologist discussing the problem of finding the right work/life balance. What solution does she suggest?

B 2.12 Listen again and read the script. Find at least three examples of things we associate with work and three things we associate with free time.

2.12 Audio script

Have you ever said, "I wish I didn't have to work such long hours?" Whether you're an executive with one meeting after another, a full-time student attending **lectures** and **seminars**, or a parent who works the late **shift**, the problem is always the same – How can I have a life with such a **busy schedule**?

I hear it all the time: I wish I had more time for **family life**, I wish I hadn't promised to work this weekend, I wish I could take some **time off**, I wish I had more **me time**! There are hundreds of articles out there about how to balance work and life, but we need to stop seeing work and life as two opposing forces that we have to balance. We need to think about how to *combine* them.

Take this example: a client of mine now schedules **downtime** into his working day. He takes a short walk, has a relaxing lunch with a friend, or goes home a little early to spend time with the kids. Then, after they're asleep, he sits down and writes that report he needs for tomorrow.

Making your job and your life work together is a great way to enjoy them both.

C PAIR WORK Do you think it's a good idea to combine your work or school life with your social life? Why or why not?

2 VOCABULARY: Talking about work/life balance

A 2.13 PAIR WORK Listen and say the words and phrases in the box. Discuss where they should go in the Venn diagram. You can use your phone or a dictionary to help you.

always connected	assignments	busy schedule	chilling out	commitments
downtime	family life	lectures	me time	office hours
seminars	shift	social life	time off	9-to-5

work/school — commitments — home life

Commitments: I guess that could be work, school, or home life. Let's put it in the middle.

B Now go to page 148. Do the vocabulary exercises for 8.2.

C GROUP WORK Do you feel you have a busy schedule? Do you get enough downtime? Is your downtime also "me time"?

78

3 GRAMMAR: *I wish*

A Choose the correct words to complete the rules. Use the sentences in the grammar box to help you.

1 "*I wish*" sentences express that you want things to **stay the same / be different**.
2 The main verb of the sentence **stays in the same tense / changes tense**. The modal "*can*" **stays the same / changes to** *could*.
3 Affirmative statements **change to negative / stay affirmative**.
4 Negative statements **change to affirmative / stay negative**.

I wish

I **have to** work long hours.	→	I wish I **didn't have to** work such long hours.
I **don't have** much free time.	→	I wish I **had** more free time.
I **can't take** any time off next week.	→	I wish I **could take** some time off next week.
I **promised** to work this weekend.	→	I wish I **hadn't promised** to work this weekend.

B Now go to page 137. Look at the grammar chart and do the grammar exercise for 8.2.

C PAIR WORK Complete the wishes so that they are true for you. Review them with a partner and check your accuracy.

1 I wish I knew
2 I wish I could
3 I wish I wasn't/weren't
4 I wish I didn't have to
5 I wish I hadn't
6 I wish I had

4 SPEAKING

A PAIR WORK Look at the list of wishes. Which do you think are the most common? Why?

I wish I had gone to a different college. *I wish I could travel more.*
I wish I had studied harder in high school. *I wish I was younger.*
I wish I could play a musical instrument. *I wish I was older.*
I wish I could get a different job.

B PAIR WORK Think of three more common wishes. Who might have them? Compare your ideas

79

ACCURACY CHECK

Don't confuse *wish* and *hope*. Use *hope* to talk about something you want to happen in the future.

I hope you'll be there on Saturday.

Use *wish* to talk about a situation you can't change.

I wish you could come on Saturday, but I know you have to work.

Accuracy check

INSIGHT

Some common errors can become fossilized if not addressed early on in the learning process.

CONTENT

Accuracy check highlights common learner errors (based on unique research into the Cambridge Learner Corpus) and can be used for self-editing.

RESULT

Students avoid common errors in their written and spoken English.

You spoke. We listened.

Students told us that speaking is the most important skill for them to master, while teachers told us that finding speaking activities which engage their students and work in the classroom can be challenging.

That's why EVOLVE has a whole lesson dedicated to speaking: Lesson 5, *Time to speak*.

Time to speak

INSIGHT

Speaking ability is how students most commonly measure their own progress, but is also the area where they feel most insecure. To be able to fully exploit speaking opportunities in the classroom, students need a safe speaking environment where they can feel confident, supported, and able to experiment with language.

CONTENT

Time to Speak is a unique lesson dedicated to developing speaking skills and is based around immersive tasks which involve information sharing and decision making.

RESULT

Time to speak lessons create a buzz in the classroom where speaking can really thrive, evolve, and take off, resulting in more confident speakers of English.

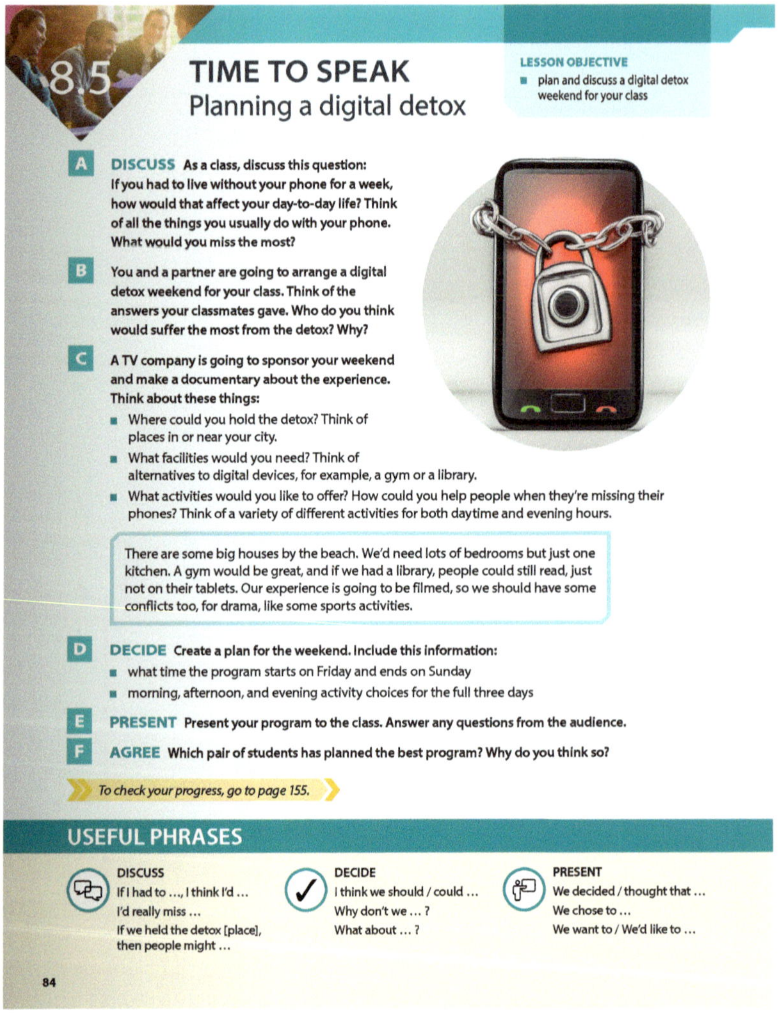

8.5 TIME TO SPEAK
Planning a digital detox

LESSON OBJECTIVE
- plan and discuss a digital detox weekend for your class

A **DISCUSS** As a class, discuss this question:
If you had to live without your phone for a week, how would that affect your day-to-day life? Think of all the things you usually do with your phone. What would you miss the most?

B You and a partner are going to arrange a digital detox weekend for your class. Think of the answers your classmates gave. Who do you think would suffer the most from the detox? Why?

C A TV company is going to sponsor your weekend and make a documentary about the experience. Think about these things:
- Where could you hold the detox? Think of places in or near your city.
- What facilities would you need? Think of alternatives to digital devices, for example, a gym or a library.
- What activities would you like to offer? How could you help people when they're missing their phones? Think of a variety of different activities for both daytime and evening hours.

There are some big houses by the beach. We'd need lots of bedrooms but just one kitchen. A gym would be great, and if we had a library, people could still read, just not on their tablets. Our experience is going to be filmed, so we should have some conflicts too, for drama, like some sports activities.

D **DECIDE** Create a plan for the weekend. Include this information:
- what time the program starts on Friday and ends on Sunday
- morning, afternoon, and evening activity choices for the full three days

E **PRESENT** Present your program to the class. Answer any questions from the audience.

F **AGREE** Which pair of students has planned the best program? Why do you think so?

To check your progress, go to page 155.

USEFUL PHRASES

DISCUSS
If I had to …, I think I'd …
I'd really miss …
If we held the detox [place], then people might …

DECIDE
I think we should / could …
Why don't we … ?
What about … ?

PRESENT
We decided / thought that …
We chose to …
We want to / We'd like to …

84

Experience Better Learning with EVOLVE: a course that helps both teachers and students on every step of the language learning journey.

Speaking matters. Find out more about creating safe speaking environments in the classroom.

EVOLVE unit structure

Unit opening page

Each unit opening page activates prior knowledge and vocabulary and immediately gets students speaking.

Lessons 1 and 2

These lessons present and practice the unit vocabulary and grammar in context, helping students discover language rules for themselves. Students then have the opportunity to use this language in well-scaffolded, personalized speaking tasks.

Lesson 3

This lesson is built around a functional language dialogue that models and contextualizes useful fixed expressions for managing a particular situation. This is a real world strategy to help students handle unexpected conversational turns.

Lesson 4

This is a combined skills lesson based around an engaging reading or listening text. Each lesson asks students to think critically and ends with a practical writing task.

Lesson 5

Time to speak is an entire lesson dedicated to developing speaking skills. Students work on collaborative, immersive tasks which involve information sharing and decision making.

CONTENTS

Functional language	Listening	Reading	Writing	Speaking
■ Meet someone you don't know; introduce someone to others **Real-world strategy** ■ Respond to an introduction		**Flipping your job interview** ■ An article on interview skills	**A comment** ■ A comment on an article ■ Agreeing and disagreeing	■ Talk about a new activity ■ Talk about personal achievements ■ Describe your personal qualities ■ Play an introduction game **Time to speak** ■ Ask and answer interview questions
■ Make, accept, and refuse offers in social situations **Real-world strategy** ■ Acknowledge an acceptance	**Cool food** ■ A conversation between friends		**A report** ■ The results of a survey about eating habits ■ Reporting research results	■ Talk about fusion foods ■ Discuss ideas to avoid food waste ■ Explain a favorite recipe ■ Offer food and drink to others **Time to speak** ■ Present a restaurant rescue plan
■ Make an apology and explain what happened **Real-world strategy** ■ Respond to an apology		**Buyer beware!** ■ Short stories about good and bad online shopping experiences	**A product review** ■ Product reviews ■ Expressing opinions about product features	■ Discuss things money can't buy ■ Talk about quality of life ■ Talk about relative value ■ Talk about a past apology **Time to speak** ■ Repair a customer relationship
■ Exchange and discuss opinions about possible actions **Real-world strategy** ■ Make opinions more emphatic	**Building a brand** ■ A news report about a local company that went global		**A response** ■ A social media post ■ Writing about reasons and consequences	■ Talk about all the signs we see ■ Speculate about a picture ■ Talk about viral stories ■ Give and support opinions **Time to speak** ■ Create and present an ad
■ React to problems and try to find a solution **Real-world strategy** ■ Accepting bad news		**The perfect apology** ■ An article about corporate apologies	**An apology** ■ A letter of apology from a company ■ Using referents to avoid repetition	■ Discuss good storytellers ■ Tell someone's life story ■ Tell the story of a change of plans ■ Act out situations with bad news **Time to speak** ■ Connect events to tell the story
■ Make, refuse, and accept offers of help **Real-world strategy** ■ Imposing on somebody	**Painting safer streets** ■ A podcast about a community art project		**A report** ■ A report on a community project ■ Using quotes as support	■ Talk about acts of kindness ■ Discuss charity organizations ■ Discuss helping others ■ Make offers of help to strangers **Time to speak** ■ Discuss helping your community

	Learning objectives	Grammar	Vocabulary	Pronunciation
Unit 7 Can we talk?	■ Discuss messaging apps ■ Discuss written vs. spoken communication ■ Recount conversations and stories ■ Write an email in formal and informal register ■ Conduct a survey	■ Reported statements ■ Reported questions	■ Describing communication ■ Communicating online	■ Saying /s/ or /z/ at the end of a word
Unit 8 Lifestyles	■ Talk about different work lifestyles ■ Talk about wishes and regrets ■ Talk through options to reach a decision ■ Write a comment about a podcast ■ Plan a digital detox weekend	■ Present unreal conditionals ■ *I wish*	■ Describing jobs ■ Talking about work/life balance	■ Saying the vowel sounds /ɜ/ and /u/ ■ Listening for emphasis
Unit 9 Yes, you can!	■ Talk about rules and regulations ■ Discuss rules and regulations in the past ■ Make generalizations ■ Write a letter of complaint ■ Discuss improvements to your town	■ Prohibition, permission, obligation (present) ■ Prohibition, permission, obligation (past)	■ Talking about places ■ Talking about rules	■ Saying /d/ at the beginning of a word
	Review 3 (Review of Units 7–9)			
Unit 10 What if . . . ?	■ Speculate about events in the past ■ Talk about alternatives and possibilities ■ Keep your listener engaged ■ Write comments in an online discussion ■ Debate the most influential discovery or invention in history	■ Past unreal conditionals ■ Modals of past probability	■ Talking about discoveries ■ Discussing right and wrong	■ Saying long and short vowel sounds ■ Listening for weak words
Unit 11 Contrasts	■ Discuss college life ■ Discuss scientific facts ■ Discuss alternatives and give recommendations ■ Write a comment presenting an argument ■ Present a proposal to solve a problem	■ Gerund and infinitive after *forget, remember, stop* ■ Causative verbs *help, let, make*	■ Talking about college education ■ Talking about science	■ Stressing long words
Unit 12 Looking back	■ Describe a special photo and the story behind it ■ Discuss childhood memories ■ Recall and share past experiences ■ Write a summary and response about pets ■ Recall and discuss a national moment	■ Adding emphasis ■ Substitution and referencing	■ Talking about the senses ■ Describing memories	■ Saying consonant clusters ■ Listening for transitions
	Review 4 (Review of Units 10–12)			
	Grammar charts and practice, pages 129–140	**Vocabulary exercises, pages 141–152**		

Functional language	Listening	Reading	Writing	Speaking
■ Recount conversations and stories to another person **Real-world strategy** ■ Get back on track		**The emoji code** ■ An article about how social media is changing language	**Emails** ■ Short emails to a friend and coworker ■ Changing language to match register	■ Talk about when not to use your phone ■ Talk about social media apps ■ Talk about the way you prefer to communicate ■ Tell and react to stories **Time to speak** ■ Talk about your attitudes to social media
■ Talk through options; encouraging actions **Real-world strategy** ■ Offer a warning	**Digital detox** ■ A podcast debating the benefits of a digital detox		**A comment** ■ A response to two comments ■ Referencing another argument in your writing	■ Discuss the work-lifestyle connection ■ Talk about unusual jobs ■ Talk about wishes and regrets ■ Offer advice and discuss options **Time to speak** ■ Plan a digital detox
■ Make generalizations **Real-world strategy** ■ Give contrasting information		**The story of the ramp** ■ An article about the independent living movement	**A message** ■ A complaint about a business ■ Communicating attitude	■ Talk about street art and graffiti ■ Talk about rules for work or school ■ Talk about unusual laws from the past ■ Talk about different customs and cultures **Time to speak** ■ Discuss how to make life easier for people with special needs
■ Keep your listener engaged **Real-world strategy** ■ Show interest in a story	**I can't live without it!** ■ A podcast about the impact different inventions have had on our lives		**A comment** ■ A comment on the podcast ■ Using words and phrases for similarity and contrast	■ Share photobombing stories ■ Talk about hypothetical past events ■ Speculate about the past events that led to current situations ■ Tell and react to a story about something that is hard to believe **Time to speak** ■ Discuss significant inventions and discoveries in human history
■ Discuss alternatives and respond to suggestions **Real-world strategy** ■ Give a personal recommendation		**Embrace the technological revolution? Not me!** ■ An opinion piece about technological advances	**A response** ■ A response to an opinion piece ■ Transition phrases	■ Talk about appearances ■ Describe an event you'll never forget ■ Talk about folk remedies ■ Role play giving recommendations **Time to speak** ■ Reach a compromise to resolve a problem
■ Recall a memory **Real-world strategy** ■ Share experiences	**Man's best friend?** ■ A student debate about the relationship between humans and dogs		**A summary and response** ■ A summary of and response to an opinion ■ Linking contrasting ideas	■ Test your memory and compare results ■ Tell the story behind a photo ■ Discuss childhood memories ■ Retell a personal story **Time to speak** ■ Share your experience of a national moment

CLASSROOM LANGUAGE

PAIR WORK AND GROUP WORK

1.02 Choosing roles

How should we start?

Why don't you be … and I'll be …

Who wants to present for our group?

Understanding the task

So what are we supposed to do?

I'm not really sure.

Should we ask the teacher?

Asking for more time

Sorry, we're not done yet. We need a few more minutes.

Completing a task

OK. So are we done with this part?

I think so. What's next?

TALKING TO THE TEACHER

Discussing assignments

When is … due?

Can I email … to you?

Discussing a missed class

I was out on … Can you tell me what I missed?

Asking for explanations

Can you tell us what we're supposed to do again?

Can you explain that again? I didn't understand.

Preparing for a text/exam

Will this be on the test?

Will we review this before the test?

UNIT OBJECTIVES

- talk about personal achievements
- talk about qualities that employers look for
- make and respond to introductions
- write a comment on a blog post
- practice a job interview

AND WE'RE OFF!

1

START SPEAKING

A Look at the picture. Where is the man? What is he about to do? How do you think he feels? Why?

B PAIR WORK Think of a new activity you are about to start or that you have started recently (a new job, a new sport, a new course, etc.). What is it? How do you feel about it? For ideas, watch Andres's video.

C GROUP WORK Report three things your partner told you to your group.

Do you feel the same as Andres?

1.1 THIS IS ME!

LESSON OBJECTIVE
- talk about personal achievements

1 LANGUAGE IN CONTEXT

A

B

C

A PAIR WORK **Look at the pictures and describe the three people. Then read the blog post, which is a response to a social media challenge, "Five things about me." Which person wrote it? Why do you think that?**

FIVE THINGS ABOUT ME

Here is my answer to the latest blog challenge!
(If I **get 1,000 likes**, my boss will donate $1,000 to charity. So please like my list!)

1. Every year I **set myself a goal** of learning a new skill. I've done a lot of different things. Last year I learned to play chess. This year I've been learning computer animation and design.
2. People tell me I **have a great sense of humor**, and I love to **tell jokes**!
3. A few years ago, while I was working at a summer camp, a girl came screaming out of her cabin because she saw a huge spider on her bed. I hate spiders, but I **faced my fear**, went in there, and caught that spider. I felt so brave! 😉
4. I'm saving money to open a small studio where I can teach art classes. I've always wanted to **run my own business.** I love **working with my hands**, and I want to do something I can really **take pride in.**
5. This year I'm going to **run a marathon.** I don't want to **win a medal** or **break a record** or anything. I just want to finish! I'm sure I can **rise to the challenge**!

2 VOCABULARY: Describing accomplishments

A 1.03 **Read the post again and find the right verb to complete the expressions. Listen and check.**

1	______ pride in something	5	______ to a challenge	9	______ your fear
2	______ a goal for yourself	6	______ a marathon	10	______ a medal
3	______ a sense of humor	7	______ a business	11	______ a record
4	______ with your hands	8	______ a lot of likes	12	______ a joke

B **Now go to page 141. Do the vocabulary exercises for 1.1.**

C PAIR WORK **Complete the sentences as many times as possible using the expressions in exercise A. Then compare your sentences with a partner. How many things do you have in common?**

1 I have never …
2 I would/wouldn't like to …

I have never told a joke in English.

D PAIR WORK **Imagine you are going to do the blog challenge. What five pieces of information would you choose to share?**

3 GRAMMAR: Tense review (simple and continuous)

A **Complete the descriptions of different tenses. Use the sentences in the grammar box to help you.**

Which tense describes …

1 past experiences with no specific past time given? *present perfect*
2 an action in progress in the past? ______
3 a completed action in the past? ______
4 a habit or repeated action in the present? ______
5 an action in progress in the present? ______
6 an action that started sometime in the past and is still continuing? ______

Simple and continuous tenses

simple present	Every year I **set** myself a goal of learning a new skill.
present continuous	I'**m saving** money to open a small studio.
simple past	I **faced** my fear, **went** in there, and **caught** that spider.
past continuous	I **was working** in a summer camp when it happened.
present perfect	I'**ve done** a lot of different things.
present perfect continuous	This year I'**ve been learning** computer animation.

B **Now go to page 129. Look at the grammar chart and do the grammar exercise for 1.1.**

C **Choose five time expressions from the box and write sentences that are true for you.**

at the moment	at 8 o'clock this morning	never	every day
last year	for the last three months	now	once a week
since I was a child	when I got home	yesterday	

It was raining when I left the house this morning.

D GROUP WORK **Read your sentences to your group. How many of your sentences are the same or similar?**

4 SPEAKING

A PAIR WORK **Read the sentences and discuss which ones are true for you. If they are false, explain why.**

1 I won a medal when I was in high school.
2 I've been studying English for more than 10 years.
3 I once got more than 100 likes for a post on social media.
4 I'm saving money to go on vacation next year.
5 I have never been afraid of anything.

B GROUP WORK **Report back to the class on the five things you learned about your partner.**

Juan runs marathons, and he's won five medals for running. He's been studying English for three years. He doesn't like social media, so he's never …

1.2 THE RIGHT CANDIDATE

LESSON OBJECTIVE
- talk about qualities that employers look for

1 LANGUAGE IN CONTEXT

A 1.04 **Look at the picture. Where are the people? What do you think their relationship is? What do you think they're talking about? Listen to their conversation to check your answers.**

B 1.04 **Listen again and read the script. Do you think she'll get the job? Why or why not?**

1.04 Audio script

A She was so nice. She'd be good with customers – **polite**, friendly, relaxed. She had a lot of **enthusiasm** too, really positive about working with us.

B And she seemed pretty **ambitious** too, you know? She wants to be **successful** in her job, and she's looking for a challenge.

A Yeah, and I really like it when candidates show **curiosity** about how things work here. It shows she's **confident**. I mean, she's not afraid to ask questions, to be **truthful** about what she *doesn't* know.

B No paid work **experience**, but she has other **qualifications**.

A Yeah, she's working on that community art project at the moment and really loving it. That shows **creativity**, too.

B Remember when she was talking about working with kids? She said, "I'm being really careful with how I use social media with them." That's great – it shows she's a **responsible** person.

A Totally! And she seemed to be pretty **independent**, too. Like, she doesn't need someone to tell her what to do all the time.

B Yeah. Well, I think we've found the right person for the job.

2 VOCABULARY: Describing key qualities

A 1.05 **Complete the chart with the bold words from the conversation. Listen and check.**

adjective	noun	adjective	noun	adjective	noun
ambitious	ambition	enthusiastic		qualified	
	confidence	experienced			responsibility
creative			independence		success
curious			politeness		truthfulness

B **Now go to page 141. Do the vocabulary exercises for 1.2.**

C PAIR WORK **Match four words from the chart with the definitions below. Then write short definitions for four others. Read them to another pair. Can they guess the word?**

1 belief in your own abilities
2 describing someone who doesn't lie
3 describing someone who can do things on their own
4 the education, training, and experience needed (pl)

D **Which qualities in the chart above do you think are most important for a new employee? A boss? A friend? Why?**

3 GRAMMAR: Dynamic and stative verbs

A **Circle all correct answers to complete the rules. Use the sentences in the grammar box to help you.**

1 Dynamic verbs describe …

a an action in progress. **b** an opinion. **c** a plan.
d a personal quality. **e** a preference.

2 Stative verbs describe …

a an action in progress. **b** an opinion. **c** a plan.
d a personal quality. **e** a preference.

3 … verbs usually are not used in the continuous form.

a Dynamic **b** Stative **c** Both dynamic and stative

4 Some verbs, such as *be* and *think*, …

a are only dynamic. **b** are only stative. **c** can be dynamic and stative.

Dynamic and stative verbs

Dynamic	She**'s working** on a community art project.
	She**'s thinking** of looking for a new job.
	I**'m being** really careful with how I use social media.
Stative	She **wants** to be successful in her job.
	I **think** she'd be good with customers.
	She**'s** a responsible person.

B **Now go to page 130. Look at the grammar chart and do the grammar exercise for 1.2.**

C PAIR WORK **Look at the verbs in the pairs of sentences. What's the difference in meaning?**

1 **a** I **love** chocolate cake!
b I**'m loving** this chocolate cake.

2 **a** She **studies** really hard for her exams.
b She**'s studying** really hard for her exams.

3 **a** I **think** swimming is a great sport.
b I**'m thinking** of going swimming.

INSIDER ENGLISH

Some stative verbs (*love, like, hate*) can also be dynamic to talk about enjoyment at the moment.

I'm loving it!

4 SPEAKING

A PAIR WORK **Think of job interview questions you could ask to find out if a job applicant has each of the qualities in the box. Then practice asking and answering the questions. What did you find out about your partner's key qualities?**

ambition
creativity
enthusiasm
independence
truthfulness

Do you prefer to work alone or on a big team?

1.3 WE GO WAY BACK

LESSON OBJECTIVE

- make and respond to introductions

1 FUNCTIONAL LANGUAGE

A PAIR WORK **Look at the picture. Where are these people? What is the relationship between the people? What are they saying to each other?**

B 1.06 **Read and listen to two conversations at the party. Which people know each other? Which people are meeting for the first time?**

1.06 Audio script

1	**Rosa**	Hi, **I don't think we've met before. You're new here, right?** I'm Rosa.
	Mike	Hi, Rosa. Nice to meet you. I'm Mike. And yes, I just started today.
	Rosa	So **this is your first day!** Welcome to the company! **Do you know anyone here?**
	Mike	Well, I've met a couple of people, but there are a lot of people I don't know yet.
	Rosa	Ok, **let me introduce you** to some people.
2	**Rosa**	Hey, Ricardo, do you know Mike?
	Ricardo	No, I don't. Hi, Mike. Nice to meet you!
	Mike	Hi, Ricardo. Great to meet you, too.
	Ricardo	Hey, **have you met Pedro?** He studied in Atlanta and then worked there for about six years. Pedro, come over here!
	Pedro	What's up? Hi, Mike! How are you settling in?
	Mike	Hey, Pedro. Great thanks.
	Rosa	**Do you two know each other?**
	Mike	Yeah, Pedro was the first person I met this morning.

C **Complete the chart with the bold expressions from the conversations.**

Meeting someone for the first time	Introducing someone to a coworker or friend
I don't think we've [1] ________ before.	Do you [3] ________ anyone here?
You're [2] ________ here, right?	Let me [4] ________ you to some people.
Is this your first day?	Have you [5] ________ Pedro?
	Do you two [6] ________ each other?

D 1.07 PAIR WORK **Complete the conversation with expressions from the chart, and check your accuracy. Listen and check. Then practice it with a partner.**

A Hi, I'm Dana. I don't think [1] ________________.
B No, we haven't. Nice to meet you, Dana, I'm Steve.
A Hi, Steve. You're [2] ________________, right?
B Yes, that's right. It's my [3] ________________.
A Hey, welcome! Let me [4] ________________
________________.

ACCURACY CHECK

Use *meet* for introductions. Use *know* for an ongoing relationship.

Nice to ~~know~~ you. ✗
Nice to meet you. ✓
Do you two know each other? ✓

2 REAL-WORLD STRATEGY

A 1.08 **Listen to two introductions. Do the people already know each other?**

RESPONDING TO AN INTRODUCTION

When someone is introducing you to another person, they usually start by asking, *Have you met / Do you know* [name]*?* You can respond with these expressions.

Yes, we met this morning! Nice to see you again.

Yeah, we go way back. How's it going?

I'm not sure, but hi, I'm …

No, I haven't / don't. Hi, I'm …

B 1.08 **Read the information in the box above. Listen again and complete the conversations.**

1 **A** Do you two know each other?
B Sure do!
C ______________________
A Really? I had no idea.

2 **A** Have you met Chris?
B ______________________
C Hi, Toni. Good to meet you.

C GROUP WORK **Work in groups of three. Student A asks Student B if they know Student C. Student B decides which answer to give. Students A and C react appropriately.**

3 PRONUNCIATION FOCUS: Saying the letter *y*

A 1.09 **Listen and repeat. Focus on the letter *y*.**

1 Hi **Y**olanda.
2 Have **y**ou met Ricardo **y**et?

B 1.10 **Listen. Who says the letter *y*? Write A or B.**

1 Yolanda ___	3 yet ___	5 yeah ___
2 you ___	4 year ___	6 yellow ___

C PAIR WORK **Say the words in exercise 3B to your partner. Does your partner say the letter *y* clearly?**

4 SPEAKING

A PAIR WORK **You are at a party together. Student B is a famous person (decide who together). Student A introduces Student B to the class with only a first name. The class greets Student B and asks questions until they figure out who he or she is.**

Hi, this is Maite.

Hi, Maite, nice to meet you. Your face looks familiar. Are you an actor?

1.4 FLIPPING YOUR JOB INTERVIEW

LESSON OBJECTIVE
- write a comment on a blog post

1 READING

A PREDICT **Look at the picture. What are the people waiting for? How are they feeling?**

B READ FOR GIST **Read the article from a job search site. Match each heading to the correct section in the article and write it there.**

Questions = Answers   The big day   A two-way street

Flipping your job interview

A ______

Finally! You've landed an interview for a great job. You've done your homework, prepared answers for all the usual questions, done your research on the company, its products, and its customers. There's nothing left to do but cross your fingers and hope. Or is there?

B ______

A job interview is not a one-way conversation. The company is looking for the right candidate, but you're also looking for something – the right job for you.

Come prepared with a few questions that show you are serious about the job. Think about how you want to develop your skills, your training interests, the types of projects you'd like to work on. You can also ask about the social side, if it's a fun place to work – though maybe not in so many words!

C ______

Your answers to their questions are important, but the questions you ask will also help you make a good impression. If you ask about training opportunities, they know you want to learn. If you ask about career paths, they know you have long-term goals. If you ask your interviewer about their own career, they know you are a person who respects their coworkers.

Flip the interview! Be confident and ask the questions that will help you decide if this is the job for you.

C **Read the article again. Choose the best summary.**

a The article recommends different ways to impress an interviewer.

b The article suggests a different way to prepare for a job interview.

c The article explains what happens after a job interview.

D INFER MEANING **Explain the meaning of the bold phrases.**

1 You've **landed an interview** for a great job.

2 You've **done your homework**, prepared answers for all the usual questions …

3 There's nothing left to do but **cross your fingers** and hope.

E GROUP WORK THINK CRITICALLY **Do you agree with the ideas in the article? Do you think this is a good approach in all job interview situations? Why or why not?**

I'm not sure this is good advice because …

I disagree. I think this is good advice because …

2 WRITING

A **Read the comments on the article. Which one is ...**

1. asking for more information? ____
2. disagreeing? ____
3. agreeing? ____

Comments

Share Like Comment

A 

I'm sorry, but I think you're being a bit unrealistic. In today's job market, not all jobs are going to be the perfect job. I think it could have a negative effect if you ask too many questions. And what if your questions tell the interviewer that you're NOT right for the job? You could hurt yourself rather than help yourself!

2 13 2

B 

Thank you for the really useful information. Can you help me with one thing? I'm not too clear on how best to phrase the questions you suggest. I don't want look like I'm interviewing them, but I do want to show them that I am a strong, focused, career-minded person. Your help would be great. Thanks!

1 4 5

C 

I'm a career counselor with an employment agency. I interview clients all day long and find possible jobs for them. Then they interview for the job with the company. The advice you give in this article is completely right. Companies love it when candidates have good questions and aren't afraid to ask them. It really shows them that you are serious about your career and the company.

4 20 8

B WRITING SKILL **Read the comments again. Find phrases used for the following purposes.**

1. to agree: ____
2. to disagree: ____
3. to show appreciation: ____

WRITE IT

C **Write your own comment in response to the article. Use appropriate phrases for agreeing, disagreeing, and/or showing appreciation. Write 50–75 words.**

D GROUP WORK **Share your comment with your group. Do you agree with each other's comments? Why or why not?**

REGISTER CHECK

In both formal and informal writing, use phrases like *a bit* and *a little* to soften a negative comment or opinion.

1.5 TIME TO SPEAK
Job interviews

LESSON OBJECTIVE
- practice a job interview

FIND IT

A **PREPARE** **Read the ad for a tour guide or use your phone to find another ad. What do you think are the main requirements for the job in each of the categories? Make notes.**

education	experience
personal qualities	skills

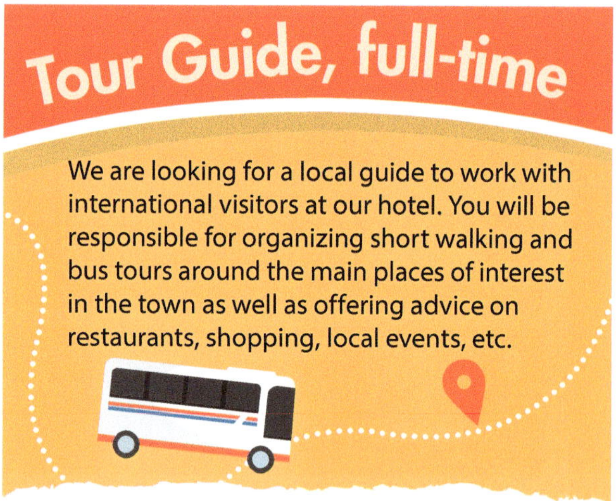

B **Work in two groups.**

Group A: You work for the employer. Decide on the questions to ask the candidates.

Group B: You have applied for the job. Prepare yourself for the interview (come up with any qualifications and experience you want) and think about questions you can ask about the job and the company.

C **PRESENT** **Each student from Group A interviews a candidate from Group B.**

Student A: Take notes on the answers given by Student B.

Student B: Make a note of any information you get about the job and the company.

D **AGREE** **Work again with your original group from exercise B.**

Group A: Report back on the various candidates and choose the best candidate.

Group B: Report back on the various companies and choose the best employer.

E **Share your decisions with the class and explain your choices.**

To check your progress, go to page 153.

USEFUL PHRASES

PREPARE

A college degree probably isn't necessary, but …

A tour guide needs to be friendly, organized, …

Previous experience would be …

PRESENT

Why do you want to be a … ?

Do you have any previous experience?

In the past, I have …

AGREE

I think … is the best candidate. She studied history, …

… would be a good employer because …

I wouldn't want to work for … because …

UNIT OBJECTIVES

- talk about trends
- talk about preparing food
- make, accept, and refuse offers in social situations
- write the results of a survey
- create a plan to improve a restaurant

THE FUTURE OF FOOD

2

START SPEAKING

A Look at the picture. What would you call this dish? What ingredients does it have? What ingredients does this type of food usually have? Would you like to try it? Why or why not?

B The dish is an example of a "fusion food": a mixture of different types of foods. What fusion foods do you know about? Have you tried any of them? Describe them. For ideas, watch Maryne's video.

REAL STUDENT

Do you know about this food?

2.1 MENU WITH A MISSION

LESSON OBJECTIVE
- talk about trends

1 LANGUAGE IN CONTEXT

A **Read the online article about chef Dan Barber. Which statement best summarizes Barber's ideas?**

a People shouldn't waste so much food.
b People should only cook and eat vegetables.

Would you order a "Dumpster Dive Vegetable Salad"? Would you eat food that other people throw away? Dan Barber is a respected chef, and he is offering his customers just that. For Barber, luxury ingredients are **a thing of the past**. His restaurants make the most of ingredients that are far from **fashionable.** Some would even call them trash. Barber doesn't care what food looks like, "if it tastes good, eat it!" So, if you prefer good flavor to good looks, you'll love his food.

Restaurants always offer a doggy bag if you want to take food home, but Barber takes it a step further and promotes "zero waste." And this isn't just a **fad**. The idea is **gaining popularity** in the restaurant world.

Barber's restaurants are among the **trendiest** in the U.S., which surprises me. Can his unusual dishes really be good? But I might agree to try something if a professional chef like Barber serves it – even those ugly carrots!

GLOSSARY

dumpster (*n*) large metal container into which people put waste

doggy bag (*n*) a small container to take home unfinished food

2 VOCABULARY: Describing trends

A 1.11 PAIR WORK **Look at the expressions in the box. Listen and say the words. Are they talking about an upward trend, a downward trend, or a description of something's popularity? Think of examples to support your answers.**

be a fad	be a thing of the past	be all the rage	be fashionable
be old-fashioned	be on the way out	be the latest thing	be the next big thing
be trendy	come back in style	gain interest	gain popularity
go out of style	lose interest	lose popularity	

A fad is something that is popular for a short time, so that's a description of popularity.

Yeah, fidget spinners are a recent fad.

B **Now go to page 142. Do the vocabulary exercises for 2.1.**

FIND IT

C GROUP WORK **Think of other trends and fashions. Complete the sentences so that they are true in your opinion and explain why. You can use your phone to find interesting images to support your opinion.**

1 For men, beards are definitely …
2 A trend I really like is …
3 … is definitely going out of style.
4 Some old-fashioned things are nice. I hope … come(s) back in style.

INSIDER ENGLISH

Use *be trending* to talk about a topic or issue that is very popular at the moment.

Gray hair for young women ***is trending*** *on social media.*

3 GRAMMAR: Real conditionals

A **Choose the correct option to complete the rules. Use the sentences in the grammar box to help you. (Remember that either clause can come first in a conditional sentence.)**

1 Use *if* + present, present to …
 a talk about future results. **b** tell someone what to do. **c** talk about things that are generally true.

2 Use *if* + present, *will / be going to / might* to …
 a talk about future results. **b** tell someone what to do. **c** talk about things that are generally true.

3 Use *if* + present, imperative to …
 a talk about future results. **b** tell someone what to do. **c** talk about things that are generally true.

Real conditionals

Restaurants offer a doggy bag if you want to take food home.
If you **prefer** good flavor to good looks, you**'ll** love his food.
I **might** agree to try something **if** Barber **serves** it.
If it **tastes** good, **eat** it!

B **Now go to page 130. Look at the grammar chart and do the grammar exercise for 2.1.**

C PAIR WORK **Rewrite the sentences as real conditionals. Then check your accuracy.**

1 Vegetarians don't eat meat.
 If you are a vegetarian, you don't eat meat.
2 You like Italian food, so it is possible that Tito's is a good restaurant for you to try.
3 Do you like fish? Yes? Then I think Japanese food is a great choice for you.
4 Here are some cookies. You have my permission to eat them.

✓ ACCURACY CHECK

Never use *will* or *might* in an *if* clause.

If I ~~won't/might not~~ eat, I'll be hungry. ✗
If I don't eat, I'll be hungry. ✓

D PAIR WORK **Complete the sentences about restaurants and eating out in your area. Discuss your ideas with your partner.**

1 If you want to try something new or different …
2 If you want really healthy food …
3 If you want to try a trendy restaurant downtown …

4 SPEAKING

A GROUP WORK **Which foods do you sometimes have to throw out? Why?**

I often throw out fruit because I buy too much and can't eat it before it goes bad.

B **Give each other advice about using that food. Then share your ideas with the class. Who has the best idea?**

If you have old fruit, make a smoothie!

2.2 FOOD YOU FERMENT

LESSON OBJECTIVE
- talk about preparing food

1 VOCABULARY: Preparing food

A 1.12 PAIR WORK **Listen and say the words. Then decide what type of food each item is: fish/seafood, vegetable, herb/spice, or fruit. Which foods do you like or dislike? Why?**

B 1.13 PAIR WORK **Look at the verbs for preparing food. Listen and say the words. Which foods can you prepare in this way?**

A ______

B ______

C ______

D ______

E ______

F ______

G ______

H ______

I ______

You should rinse fruits and vegetables before eating them.

C **Now go to page 142. Do the vocabulary exercises for 2.2.**

2 LANGUAGE IN CONTEXT

A 1.14 **Look at the pictures at the top of the next page. What dish do you think it is? Where do you think it comes from? Does it look easy or difficult to make? Listen to the podcast and check your answers.**

1.14 Audio script

Today we're going to prepare *kimchi*, a spicy cabbage recipe from Korea. Even if you don't like cabbage, after you hear this recipe, you'll want to try it. Let's begin!

First, **chop** a head of cabbage into small pieces, cover it with salt, and leave it in water. Let it stand for about two hours, then **rinse** the cabbage in cold water and drain it. **Stir** together the garlic, ginger, and sugar. Add in shrimp paste and a chili powder called *gochugaru*. Then add in the spring onions and radish. Use your hands to mix it all together with the cabbage – remember to wear gloves!

Finally, put the kimchi into a jar and leave it to ferment. You'll have to wait about five days until the kimchi is ready to eat. When the flavor is just right, transfer it to the fridge – that stops the fermentation process.

Kimchi will stay fresh in the fridge for up to three months. Your guests will be so impressed when they try it. You'll see!!

B 1.14 **Listen again. Put the images in the correct order and summarize each step of the recipe. Is this a dish that you would like to eat, or try to make?**

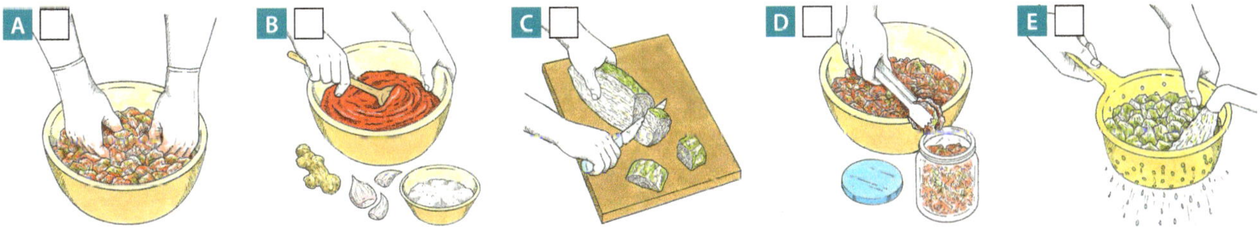

3 GRAMMAR: Clauses with *after, until, when*

A **Complete the rules. Use the sentences in the grammar box to help you.**

To talk about a sequence of events in the future …

1 use a time clause with *after, until, when* + **present** / **future** tense.

2 keep the main clause of the sentence in **present** / **future** tense.

Clauses with *after, until, when*

After you hear the recipe, you'll want to try it.

Your guests will be so impressed **when** they try it.

You'll have to wait about five days **until** the kimchi is ready to eat.

! **You can use many other time expressions with this structure: *as soon as, before, once* …**

*Your guests will love it **once** they try it!*

B **Write the verb in parentheses ( ) in the correct tense.**

1 After you __________ (bake) the cake, I __________ (come) over and decorate it with you.

2 Until I __________ (see) it for myself, I __________ (not believe) it.

3 Once she __________ (finish) school, she __________ (travel) in South America.

4 They __________ (join) us at the restaurant as soon as the concert __________ (be) over.

5 He __________ (give) you the recipe when he __________ (see) you next week.

C **Now go to page 131. Do the grammar exercise for 2.2.**

D PAIR WORK **Answer the questions so that they are true for you. Compare your answers with your partner.**

- What's the first thing you're going to do when you get home tonight?
- Is there anything you need to do before you go home today?

4 SPEAKING

A PAIR WORK **What are some typical dishes in your country or region? Are they easy or difficult to make?**

Gazpacho is a typical dish. It's delicious and not difficult to make.

FIND IT

B PAIR WORK **Describe a dish that you like and explain how to prepare it. You can find images on your phone to help you explain. For ideas, watch Maryne's video.**

REAL STUDENT

Would you like to try the dish Maryne described?

2.3 CAN I GET YOU A REFILL?

LESSON OBJECTIVE
- make, accept, and refuse offers in social situations

1 FUNCTIONAL LANGUAGE

A PAIR WORK 1.15 **Look at the photo. Discuss the questions. Read and listen to the conversation. Were you correct?**

1 What kind of food are the people having?
2 What other things do you think they will serve?
3 Is it a formal or an informal occasion?

1.15 Audio script

A **Can I get you** anything else to drink?
B Oh, yes. Can I have a soda, please?
A **Would you like** a regular one?
B Do you have sugarless ones?
A Sure, **here you go.** One diet soda.
B **Thanks, that's great.**
A No worries. **Anybody else want** a hotdog before I, um, burn them?
C Me, please!
A Coming right up! There's also dessert in the kitchen, you know, when you're ready for it. It's buffet style, so **help yourself**.
C **Awesome, I'll check it out** later. Great barbecue!
A Thanks. Oh, Grace, would you **care for a refill**?
D **No, I'm good. Thanks anyway.**
A **Can I offer you another** hotdog then?
D **That'd be wonderful.**
A You got it. Hey, there are plenty of hotdogs here. Anybody want seconds? Jason?
E **I better not.** I've already had thirds!

B **Complete the chart with the bold expressions from the conversation.**

Making offers	Accepting offers	Refusing offers
Can I get / offer you (something to drink)? 1 ______ you like / care for (a refill)? 2 ______ /There you go. Anybody else want (a hotdog)? 3 ______ yourself!	4 ______ , that's great. Awesome, I'll 5 ______ it out. That'd be wonderful.	No, I'm 6 ______ . No, but thanks anyway. I better not.

C 1.16 PAIR WORK **Complete the conversations with the expressions from the chart. Listen and check. Practice the conversations with a partner. Then change the offers and the responses. Use your own ideas.**

1 A 1 ______ I get you a refill?
B That'd be wonderful. I really need caffeine this morning!
A 2 ______ you go.
B Mm, thanks!

2 A Would you 3 ______ for more cake?
B No, I'm 4 ______ . I'm really full!
A Can I 5 ______ you more iced tea then?
B Yes! That'd be great!

2 REAL-WORLD STRATEGY

A 🔊 1.17 **Listen to part of the conversation again. What does the host say when people accept his offers?**

ACKNOWLEDGE AN ACCEPTANCE

When someone accepts your offer of food or drink, it's polite to acknowledge it.

You got it!

Coming right up! | *One sec.*

I'll be right back with that. | *Sure thing.*

B 🔊 1.18 **Read about acknowledging acceptance in the box above. Use the expressions there to complete the conversation below. Then listen and check.**

> ! *sec = second*

Attendant Hello. Can I get you something to drink, ma'am?

Customer Yes, hot tea, please.

Attendant 1 ____________________. Sugar?

Customer Yes, thanks. And could I have some milk for it, too?

Attendant 2 ____________________. I'll get some from the fridge. I'll be 3 ____________________.

C PAIR WORK **Student A: You are the flight attendant. Make two offers to the customer and acknowledge their responses. Student B: You are the customer. Accept one offer and reject the other. Change roles and do the conversation again.**

3 PRONUNCIATION FOCUS: Saying the vowel sounds /aɪ/, /i/, and /eɪ/

A 🔊 1.19 **Listen and repeat the three different vowel sounds.**

/aɪ/ like	/i/ please	/eɪ/ great
Would you **like** a regular one?	Can I have a soda, **please**?	That's **great**.

B 🔊 1.20 **Listen. Write A for words with /aɪ/. Write B for words with /i/. Write C for words with /eɪ/.**

1 Grace ___	**3** Jason ___	**5** caffeine ___
2 style ___	**4** refill ___	**6** iced tea ___

C 🔊 1.21 PAIR WORK **Listen to the conversations. Then practice with a partner.**

1 **A** Would you like a refill?
B Yes, please. That'd be great.

2 **A** Could I have another slice of cake?
B Coming right up!

4 SPEAKING

A PAIR WORK **Student A: You're hosting a few friends at home. Student B: You're a guest. Practice making and responding to offers involving food and drink. Then switch roles and do it again.**

Can I get you something other than water with your meal? A soda maybe?

No. I'm good with water. I'm watching my weight.

Are you sure? I have diet soda.

Oh, then yes, that'd be great.

2.4 COOL FOOD

LESSON OBJECTIVE
- write the results of a survey

1 LISTENING

A 1.22 LISTEN FOR GIST **Look at the pictures. What attitudes about food do you think they represent? Listen to a conversation between two friends and check your answers. Were you right?**

B 1.22 LISTEN FOR DETAILS **Listen again and answer the questions.**

1. What are Ricardo's objections to coconut water?
2. What reasons does Anna give for drinking it?
3. What does Ricardo say about gluten-free products?
4. Does Anna agree with him?

C PAIR WORK CRITICAL THINKING **Food packaging and labels provide information about the food we eat. Discuss the questions.**

- Do you read the information on food packaging? Do you think the information is important? Do you think it is accurate? Does it influence your food shopping decisions? Why or why not?
- How often do you try new foods or brands of food? How much do you think the packaging increases your curiosity about a new food item? Think of a time when you tried something just because you liked the packaging or label. What was it? Were you pleased or disappointed?
- What other information about food do you think is important to know? Should that information be on the packaging, too? Why or why not?

2 PRONUNCIATION: Listening for deleted /t/ sounds

A 1.23 **Listen to each sentence. Focus on the bold word. Do you hear the /t/ sound?**

		Yes	No
1	Do you **want** me to get you a coconut water?	☐	☐
2	Sure, I **trust** the experts …	☐	☐
3	I guess you've **got** a point …	☐	☐
4	The **latest** thing is eating gluten free …	☐	☐

B **Choose the correct word to complete the sentence.**

Final /t/ sounds are often deleted when they are followed by a *consonant / vowel.*

3 WRITING

A **As part of an economics course, some students conducted a survey about attitudes towards food. Read the results. Do the results surprise you? Why or why not?**

Changing food habits

Worldwide the food industry (including both growing and selling food) is estimated to be worth 4.8 trillion dollars every year. That makes it the world's largest industry. It also means that understanding people's attitudes about what they eat is very important. We recently conducted a survey of people's attitudes toward certain food trends.

Our survey shows that attitudes to health food trends are much more positive in Latin America than in the U.S. and Canada. In Latin America, a little over half of those we surveyed were willing to pay more for all natural foods. In the U.S. / Canada, the number was less than 25%. Similarly, 31% of people interviewed from Latin America said they would pay more for gluten-free products. But in the U.S. / Canada, 10% fewer people reported that they would pay more for gluten-free foods.

These trends can also be seen in food sales in both regions. In Latin America, sales of "healthy" foods grew 16% in a two-year period. In the U.S. / Canada, the growth in sales was less than 10%.

REGISTER CHECK

Using the passive voice can give your writing a more academic tone.

You can also see these trends in food sales in both regions. (informal, non-academic)

These trends can also be seen in food sales in both regions. (formal, academic)

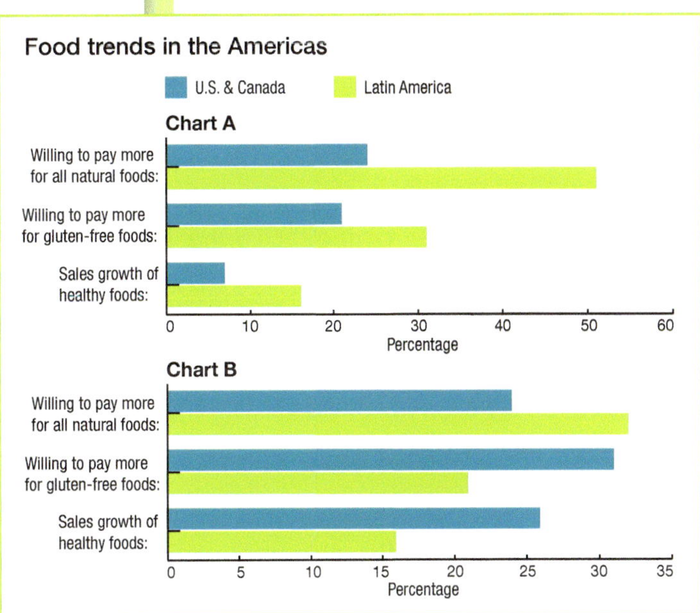

B **Look again at the survey results. Which chart matches the information?**

C WRITING SKILL **Complete the phrases used for giving results.**

1 Our survey ________________ that …
2 In Latin America, a little over half ________________ said …
3 31% ________________ from Latin America …
4 But in the U.S. / Canada, 10% fewer ________________ they …

D GROUP WORK **Work together to write 3–5 survey questions about some aspect of changing eating habits. Then conduct your survey individually.**

Our survey is about meal times. Question 1: What time did you eat breakfast when you were a child, and when do you eat breakfast now?

WRITE IT

E **Come back together and share results within your group. Work together to write the results of your survey. Write about 130 words. Make a chart to illustrate your results.**

Our survey shows that meal times … . As you can see in the chart, 25% of those we interviewed reported that they eat breakfast …

F **Share your group's survey topic and results with the class. Which group's results were particularly surprising or interesting to you?**

2.5 TIME TO SPEAK
Rescue the restaurant!

LESSON OBJECTIVE
- create a plan to improve a restaurant

A Look at the picture. Do you think the restaurant is successful? Why or why not?

B **RESEARCH** Divide into two groups, Group A and Group B. Group A: Read about Chow Mein Tacos on page 157. Group B: Read about Veggie Heaven on page 159. Identify the problems and make notes.

C **PREPARE** Divide each group into teams of three or four. As a team, think of possible solutions to the problems you identified in your restaurant. Then use your ideas to create an action plan for the restaurant owners. Some ideas to consider in your plan:

acoustics (sound quality and volume)
atmosphere (decoration, lighting, music)
client profile
ingredients
marketing
menu
premises
special offers

D **PRESENT** Present your team's plan to your group. Which ideas are the best or most original? Why? Combine the best ideas from all the teams into one action plan. Then present your restaurant, its main problems, and your action plan to the class.

E **AGREE** Which group has the better plan for improvement? Do you think it's possible to save either or both restaurants? Why or why not?

To check your progress, go to page 153.

USEFUL PHRASES

RESEARCH
To me, the biggest problem is …
They could solve this by …
If they only serve …, more people will …

PREPARE
To improve …, they could …
If they …, customers will …
They could try …

PRESENT
We suggest three main changes: …
If this restaurant wants to stay open, it'll have to …
After they redecorate, they'll need to …

UNIT OBJECTIVES

- discuss the relative importance of time and money
- discuss value and how we measure it
- apologize for damaging or losing someone else's property
- write a product review
- discuss ways to respond to a negative product review

WHAT'S IT WORTH?

3

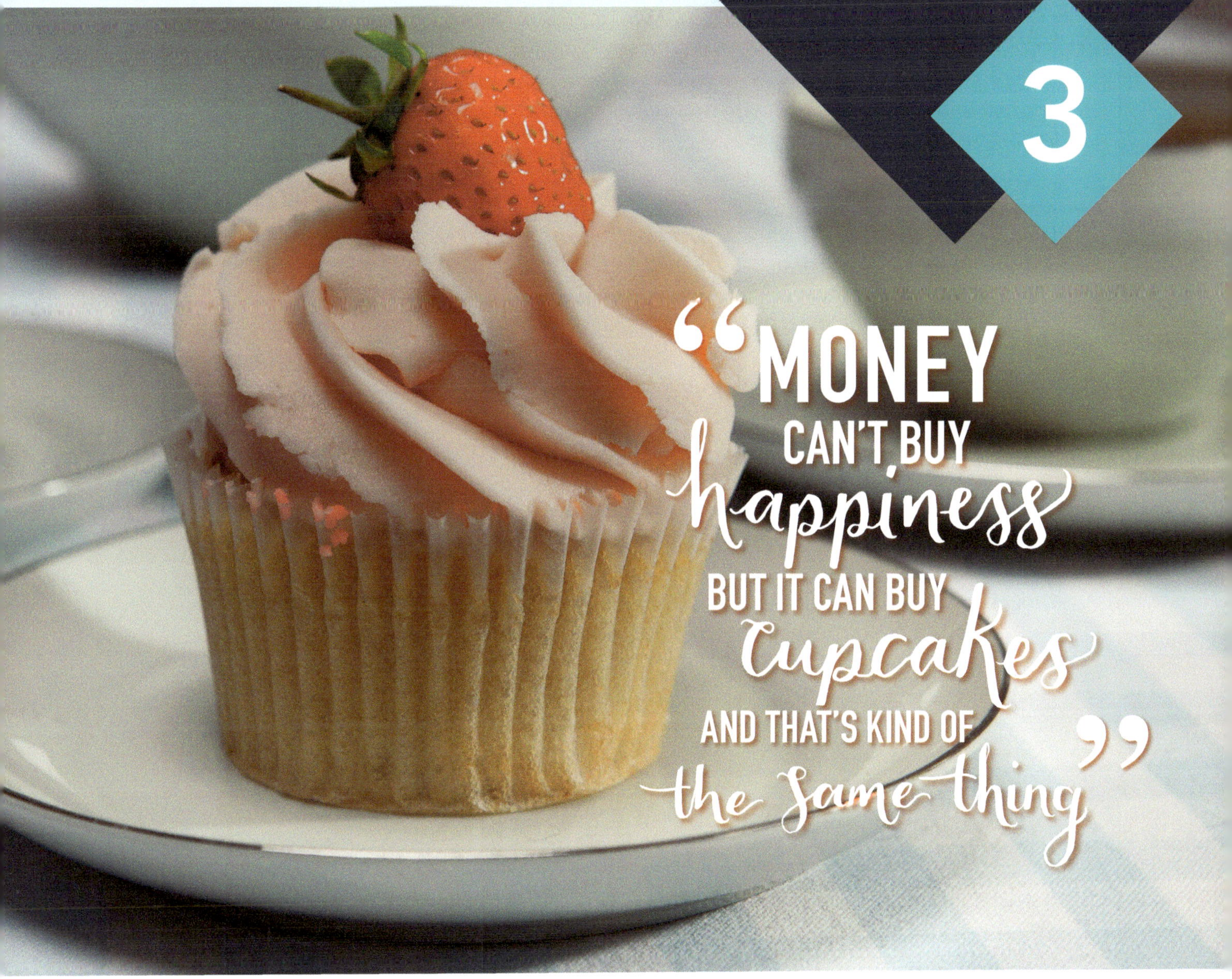

START SPEAKING

A **Look at the poster. Where would you expect to see it? Do you agree with the message? Why or why not?**

B **Write a list of five things money can't buy. Then write your own version of the message and share it with the class. For ideas, watch Andres's video. Whose version do you most agree with?**

Do you agree with Andres?

3.1 IS IT WORTH IT?

LESSON OBJECTIVE
- discuss the relative importance of time and money

1 LANGUAGE IN CONTEXT

A 1.24 **What is more important to you? Time or money? Why? Listen to a podcast interview with two young professionals. Which do they feel is more important? What are their reasons?**

1.24 Audio script

Host Time and money. Two things most people don't have enough of. With the [a] **cost of living** going up and long commutes, is it possible to find a good [b] **balance**? Sue Mendez hated the hour-long commute to work. Last fall, she took a new job in her neighborhood, but she also [c] **took a salary cut**.

Sue I was spending too much time on a bus. I'm glad I [d] **traded** my old job for my new [e] **lifestyle**. I had to move to a smaller apartment, but it [f] **was worth it**. I make enough money to get by, and I really [g] **value** all my free time!

Host Dirk Monroe, on the other hand, [h] **can't afford** a salary cut. He has a family and needs the money. He spends his hour-long commute listening to music.

Dirk I don't mind it. It's [i] **time well spent**. It's just long enough to help me relax after work. And I'm not too tired to play with the kids when I get home.

Host What about you, which do you value more? Money, to [j] **boost** your [k] **standard of living**, or time, to improve your [l] **quality of life**?

2 VOCABULARY: Talking about time and money

A 1.25 **Match the bold words and phrases in the podcast with the definitions below. Listen and check.**

1 exchange one thing for another (verb) _d_
2 a good use of time (phrase) ___
3 general level of happiness (phrase) ___
4 equal importance (noun and verb) ___
5 how much we have to pay for our basic needs (phrase) ___
6 make something bigger (verb) ___
7 ability to meet basic needs (phrase) ___
8 not have enough money to do or buy something (phrase) ___
9 the way you live (noun) ___
10 get less money for your work (phrase) ___
11 have a positive result (phrase) ___
12 feel the importance of (noun and verb) ___

B **Now go to page 143. Do the vocabulary exercises for 3.1.**

C PAIR WORK **What activities do you spend the most time on every week? Which ones do you think are time well spent? Which are a waste of time? Why?**

3 GRAMMAR: *too* and *enough*

A **Choose the correct words to complete the rules. Use the sentences in the grammar box to help you.**

Use (*not*) *too* and (*not*) *enough* with adjectives and nouns to say if a situation is acceptable or unacceptable.

1 *Too* and *not enough* tell us that something is **acceptable / unacceptable.**

2 *Not too* and *enough* tell us that something is **acceptable / unacceptable.**

3 Phrases with *too* and *enough* are often followed by ***to* + verb / verb.**

too* and *enough

Most people **don't** have **enough** time.
I was spending **too much** time on a bus.
My commute is just long **enough** to help me relax.
I'm **not too** tired to play with the kids when I get home.

B **Now go to page 131. Look at the grammar chart and do the grammar exercise for 3.1.**

C **Change the sentences in the grammar box to make statements that are true for you. Write four sentences. Check your accuracy.**

I just don't have enough time to go to the grocery store.

D PAIR WORK **Read your sentences to your partner. Are any of your sentences the same?**

ACCURACY CHECK

Remember, *enough* comes after an adjective but before a noun.

That's ~~enough good~~ for me. ✗
That's good enough for me. ✓
That's ~~pizza enough~~ for me! ✗
That's enough pizza for me! ✓

4 SPEAKING

A GROUP WORK **Discuss the questions.**

1 What do you think are the most important factors in having a good quality of life? Look at the ideas in the box to help you.

things to do in your free time	a group of close friends	a job you feel proud of
living near your family	access to education	a good salary
time to do the things you want to do		

2 Which do you think is the biggest problem for a good quality of life: time, money, or something different?

3.2 THE PRICE OF COFFEE

LESSON OBJECTIVE
- discuss value and how we measure it

1 LANGUAGE IN CONTEXT

A **How often do you go to cafés? What do you order to drink there? How much does it cost? Do you think it's a good price? Why or why not? Read the review of a coffee shop. What makes it different from other coffee shops?**

A coffee shop with a difference

I just treated myself to by far the best coffee I've ever had, and it was nowhere near as expensive as my usual coffee shop! There's nothing special about the café, though it is a little busier than other places. There's really just one thing that makes it different: You pay what you want.

Every café comes up with its own price to charge for a cup of coffee. It can be much cheaper than other places or a whole lot more expensive, depending on the café's own costs but also things people are willing to pay more for, like atmosphere. If there's a beautiful view, a café makes the most of it with big windows and raises the price a penny. If customers want to take advantage of the free Wi-fi, there's another penny. It all has an effect on the price.

This café, however, suggests a price for its coffee, but most people pay more. They know they can rely on the quality of the coffee, and they like that the café trusts them to pay a fair price for it. They feel they play an important role in the business. And when customers feel invested in your success, how can you lose?

B **Read the review again. Does the reviewer like the café? Do other customers like it? How do you know? Have you ever been to a café or restaurant where you can pay what you want?**

> **!** **A *penny* is a coin worth 1/100th of a U.S. dollar. It is often used to represent any small amount of money.**

2 VOCABULARY: Talking about prices and value

A 1.26 **Find the expressions in the text and complete them with the correct preposition. Listen and check.**

1 treat yourself ______
2 come up ______
3 charge ______
4 depend ______
5 make the most ______
6 take advantage ______
7 have an effect ______
8 suggest a price ______
9 rely ______
10 pay a fair price ______
11 play an important role ______
12 invest ______

B **Now go to page 143. Do the vocabulary exercises for 3.2.**

C PAIR WORK **Discuss the questions.**

1 Where do you go when you want to treat yourself to a special meal? Does that place charge a fair price for their meals? How much would you pay if you could come up with your own price?
2 Do you think it's a good idea for businesses to suggest a price rather than charge for things? Why or why not?

> *I like to treat myself to dessert at a little café near the station. They charge a lot for some things, but it's worth it!*

3 GRAMMAR: Modifying comparisons

A (Circle) the correct answer to complete the rules. Use the sentences in the grammar box to help you.

1 To show a small difference using comparative adjectives, use ***a little* or *a bit* / *a whole lot* or *much*.**
2 To show a big difference using comparative adjectives, use ***a little* or *a bit* / *a whole lot* or *much*.**
3 To show a small difference using an *as … as …* comparison, use ***nowhere near* / *almost* or *nearly*.**
4 To show a big difference using an *as … as …* comparison, use ***nowhere near* / *almost* or *nearly*.**
5 To show a big difference using superlative adjectives, use ***nowhere near* / *by far*.**

Modifying comparisons

I just treated myself to **by far the best** coffee I've ever had.
It was **nowhere near as expensive as** my usual coffee shop.
It's **a little busier** than other places.
The price can be **much cheaper** or **a whole lot more expensive**.

B **Now go to page 132. Look at the grammar chart and do the grammar exercise for 3.2.**

C PAIR WORK **Compare products and services using the adjectives in the boxes. Make at least three comparisons for each item.**

cheap expensive delicious

1 a burger from a fast-food restaurant / a burger from a local restaurant / a gourmet burger at a five-star restaurant

A burger from a fast-food place is much cheaper than a gourmet burger. A gourmet burger may be a whole lot more expensive, but it is by far the most delicious of the three.

cheap comfortable expensive fashionable

2 some sandals to wear on the beach / a pair of sneakers you bought at the mall / a pair of shoes you bought to go to a wedding

cheap exciting expensive long

3 a bus tour around your city / a train trip to your favorite city / a flight to another country

4 SPEAKING

FIND IT

A GROUP WORK **Look at the products in the box. Put them in order according to how much money you'd be willing to pay for each. Then compare your lists with another group and explain your ideas. You can look up examples on your phone to help support your answer.**

a birthday present
a new phone
a pair of sunglasses
a bottle of perfume/cologne
a pair of jeans

I don't really care about clothes, so I wouldn't spend more than $50 on a pair of jeans. I'd spend a lot more on a nice pair of sunglasses!

3.3 I'M SO SORRY!

LESSON OBJECTIVE
- apologize for damaging or losing someone else's property

1 FUNCTIONAL LANGUAGE

A **Look at the picture. What happened? How would you feel if this happened to you?**

B **1.27 Listen to Justin telling Kathy what happened. How does Kathy react? Why?**

1.27 Audio script

A **I'm really sorry**, but **I just did the dumbest thing.**
B What? What did you do?
A Well, you let me borrow your bike, remember?
B Yeah, I remember.
A Well, I left it outside a store, but only for, like, five minutes!
B Oh no, don't tell me somebody stole it!
A Well, not the whole bike … just the front tire.
B You mean you didn't lock the front tire?
A I know, Kathy, I know, **I can't believe I didn't lock it. I can't tell you how sorry I am!** I'll go out today and get you another one. I am so, so sorry.
B It's OK, Justin. It's not the end of the world. A new front tire shouldn't cost too much. How about I order one and let you know how much it is?
A Yes, yes, whatever you want. I'll pick it up from the bike store, too.
B OK, deal!

C **Complete the chart with the bold expressions from the conversation.**

Apologizing	Explaining what happened
I'm really sorry.	You'll never guess what I did.
I [1] ______ how sorry I am.	I just did the [2] ______ thing.
	I can't [3] ______ I (didn't lock it).

INSIDER ENGLISH

Use *"Oh no, don't tell me"* when you think someone is going to give you some bad news.

D **1.28 Complete the conversation with phrases from the chart. Listen and check.**

A I just [1] ______ thing! I'm so, so, so [2] ______.
B What did you do?
A I can't [3] ______ I did this, but I just spilled coffee all over your new white rug.
B You what?
A I can't tell you [4] ______ !

2 REAL-WORLD STRATEGY

A 1.29 **Listen to two more apologies. What are the people apologizing for?**

RESPOND TO AN APOLOGY

When you respond to an apology and you don't want the person to feel bad, you can use one of these phrases.

It's not the end of the world. *It's really no big deal.* *Don't beat yourself up about it.*

B 1.29 **Read the information in the box above and listen again. Which response does the second person use in each conversation?**

C 1.30 **Complete the conversation with an expression from the box. Listen and check.**

A Hey, where were you last night. We missed you.

B Missed me? Why? Oh no! I forgot about the study group! I can't believe it! It's even on my calendar! And I'm the only one with notes from the workshop! You needed those.

A Don't ______________________ . Just bring them tomorrow.

B I won't forget again. I swear!

3 PRONUNCIATION FOCUS: Saying /s/ at the beginning of a word

A 1.31 **Listen and repeat. Focus on the /s/ sounds.**

1 I can't tell you how sorry I am. 2 Don't tell me somebody stole it!

B 1.32 **Listen. Who says the /s/ sound clearly? Write A or B.**

1 sorry ___	**3** so ___	**5** stole ___
2 somebody ___	**4** spilled ___	**6** store ___

C PAIR WORK **Say the words in exercise 3B to your partner. Does your partner say the /s/ sound clearly?**

4 SPEAKING

A PAIR WORK **Think of a time when you apologized to someone. What did you do wrong? How did the other person react?**

B PAIR WORK **Act out the situation you described or one of the others below. Student A apologizes. Student B reacts to the apology and tries to make Student A not feel so bad. Then reverse roles: Student B apologizes, and Student A reacts.**

- You drank the last of the milk.
- You forgot to record something on TV.
- You deleted something important from someone's phone or computer.

3.4 BUYER BEWARE!

LESSON OBJECTIVE
- write a product review

1 READING

A ☐

B ☐

C ☐

A **Look at the three pictures. What problems might people have when they buy these things online? Read three stories about online shopping. Match them with the pictures. What were the problems each time? Which story has a happy ending?**

Posts | Related Posts | Search | Log in | Sign up

What is your best or worst online shopping story?

1 I saw a photo of a rug that was perfect for my room. The price was amazing, too – about a quarter of the price of other rugs. So, I bought it. When it came, I was a surprised. The box seemed really small for a rug. When I opened it, I saw why. It wasn't a rug at all – it was a mouse pad! I guess I got what I paid for! (Jensen, Texas)

2 I ordered a beautiful cake for my parents' anniversary – simple and elegant, just what I wanted. The website asked what I wanted written on the cake, and I wrote "nothing," because I wanted to do that myself. When it arrived, I opened the box and, you guessed it, **NOTHING** was written on top, in big black letters! I couldn't believe it! (Bella, Minnesota)

3 It was my grandfather's 75th birthday and I wanted to get him something special. When he was young, he wrote a book about fishing, but he lost his only copy in a fire years before. I tried to find another one at used bookstores and online book sites. One place claimed they could find it. They had no reviews, but I was desperate, so I took a chance. Three days later the book arrived! Grandpa was so happy. It's by far the best birthday present I've ever bought for anyone! (Harry, Chicago)

B READ FOR DETAILS **Read the stories again. Answer the questions.**

1 Why did Jensen want that particular rug?
2 What did Bella want to put on the cake?
3 Why was Harry unsure about the online bookstore?

C PAIR WORK THINK CRITICALLY **Discuss the questions.**

1 Who is to blame for Jensen's and Bella's shopping fails? The store owners? Jensen and Bella themselves? Why?
2 What could Jensen and Bella do differently next time, so they don't repeat their shopping fails?

INSIDER ENGLISH

"You get what you pay for."

People use this phrase when they think they bought something of high quality at a very low price, but in the end they were wrong. The quality is right for that price.

2 WRITING

A **Read the two product reviews. What products are they reviewing? How many stars do you think each reviewer will give their product?**

Product reviews

Reviews   Sign up   Log in   Basket

I was very disappointed with this product.

I bought the case for my summer vacation. I wanted to take photos when I was snorkeling. The case arrived on time and it looked good. I tested it without my phone and it seemed to be working fine.

In fact, it was great for the first 3 times underwater, then suddenly it filled with water while I was filming fish and completely ruined my new phone! It's a complete waste of money! By far my worst purchase ever! DO NOT BUY IT!

☆☆☆☆☆ Rate your purchase

I was really pleased with this product.

They're so comfortable to wear – much more comfortable than my last ones. I like the fact that they include different earpieces so you can find the best fit. And I love the little case – very convenient.

They have great sound quality and are really simple to take phone calls on. They also really block out background noise.

This is such a great set! They are small, portable with their own case, and very good at what they do! Great value for your money! I highly recommend them.

☆☆☆☆☆ Rate your purchase

B WRITING SKILL **Read the reviews again. Find phrases that ...**

1 describe the reviewers' feelings.
2 describe the positive features of the product.
3 describe the negative features of the product.
4 give a recommendation.

C PAIR WORK **Think of a product you have bought recently. Answer the questions and make notes.**

1 Where did you buy it? ______
2 When did you buy it? ______
3 Were you happy with it? Why or why not? ______
4 Would you recommend this product? Why or why not? ______

REGISTER CHECK

Writing a word or sentence in ALL CAPS can be used to express a very strong opinion or feeling. But be careful – it can also suggest an aggressive or angry tone.

WRITE IT

D **Write a short review for your product in about 100 words. Read the review to the class. Ask your classmates to guess how many stars you gave your purchase.**

3.5 TIME TO SPEAK
Damage control

LESSON OBJECTIVE

- discuss ways to respond to a negative product review

A **PREPARE** **With a partner, look at the picture. What problem are the people having? Did something like this ever happen to you?**

B **Read the reviews. What problems did each customer have? How do they feel about their purchases? How many stars do you think each customer will give in their product review?**

Worst. Vacation. Ever. This was my first vacation on a cruise ship – and my last! I expected a beautiful room with a view of the ocean. It was just the opposite – small, cramped, no window, and it smelled! The food was terrible, too. I can't believe I paid $4,000 for this trip. What a rip-off!

Like Comment ★★★★★

Great bike… if you can put it together. I got this bike for my son's birthday. I knew that I needed to put it together myself, but I didn't know it would be this hard! There's like 100 pieces and ONE page of instructions. It took me five hours to finish it, but now I'm afraid for him to ride it!

Like Comment ★★★★★

C **DECIDE** **Form a small group with another pair. Imagine you are the owners of the cruise ship or the do-it-yourself bicycle company. Come up with a plan of action. Discuss the actions in the box and think of others. What will you do? In what order? If the customer still isn't satisfied, what will you do next?**

apologize	offer a refund	offer a replacement

D **PRESENT** **Form a new group with three new partners. Take turns and present your original group's solution to the new group. Ask and answer questions and offer advice for improvement. Then return to your original group and compare notes. Revise your plan of action.**

E **AGREE** **Share your group's plan with the class. Discuss which one is best for each company and why. Do you think the customer in each case will be satisfied? Will they change their review? Why or why not?**

To check your progress, go to page 153.

USEFUL PHRASES

PREPARE

I had to put together a bookcase once, and it was …

I think the cruise ship passenger feels …

The parent didn't give more than … stars.

DECIDE

First, I think we should apologize to the passenger because …

We could offer a replacement for the bike, but …

PRESENT

We've decided to send them an email and apologize for …

Maybe call them instead of emailing. It's more personal.

REVIEW 1 (UNITS 1–3)

1 VOCABULARY

A **Put the words and phrases into the correct categories. Add three more to each category.**

a salary cut	ambitious	be a fad	be all the rage	boil
break a record	chop	confident	go out of fashion	curious
win a medal	mint	zucchini	gain interest	garlic
time well spent	truthful	enthusiastic	rise to a challenge	ginger
standard of living	rinse	cost of living	set a goal for yourself	stir

1 accomplishments ____________________
2 describing trends ____________________
3 food items ____________________
4 food preparation ____________________
5 personal qualities ____________________
6 time and money ____________________

2 GRAMMAR

A PAIR WORK **Complete the sentences with the correct form of the verbs in parentheses ( ). Then change the sentences so that they are true for you. Compare with a partner.**

1 I ____________ (think) of trying the Paleo diet. I ____________ (think) it's healthy and natural.
2 After I ____________ (finish) this course, I ____________ (start) my MBA. I ____________ (check) different schools for the past two months.
3 If I ____________ (save) enough money, I ____________ (go) to Thailand on my next vacation. I ____________ (always, want) to visit Bangkok.

B **Complete the paragraph with the words in the box.**

a little	a whole lot	by far	enough	too

I think *Pomodoro* is [1] ____________ the best Italian restaurant in town. It's [2] ____________ more expensive than the other Italian places around, but the atmosphere is [3] ____________ better. On weekends it can get [4] ____________ crowded, and you have to wait forever for a table. But the food is worth it. Too bad I don't have [5] ____________ money to eat there more often.

C PAIR WORK **What's your favorite restaurant in town? How does it compare to other restaurants?**

3 SPEAKING

A PAIR WORK **Talk to your partner about future goals. Ask and answer the questions.**

What is one of your goals for the near future?
What have you been doing to achieve that goal?
How will your life be different when you accomplish that objective?

B **Summarize what you learned about your partner.**

Ana wants to get a better job. She has been searching job sites, and she has applied for a few jobs. When she gets a better job, she'll move to her own apartment.

4 FUNCTIONAL LANGUAGE

A **Use the words and phrases to complete the conversations at a wedding reception.**

beat yourself up	care for	get you
how sorry	I'm good	know
that'd be great	introduce	
the dumbest	we've met	

1 **A** Hi, I don't think [1] ________ before. Are you friends with the bride or the groom?

B The bride, Stacy. We work for the same company. And you?

A Stacy is my second cousin. By the way, I'm Lucas. Nice to meet you.

B I'm Tricia. Do you [2] ________ anyone here?

A Just our relatives.

B Ok, let me [3] ________ you to a couple of people from the office.

A Thanks!

2 **A** Would you [4] ________ some more soda?

B No, thanks. [5] ________ .

A Can I [6] ________ a piece of the wedding cake?

B Yes, [7] ________ . Thanks.

3 **A** I'm really sorry, but I just did [8] ________ thing. I was parking my car and … I hit yours.

B Oh! Well, how bad is the damage?

A Just a scratch. Don't worry; I'll pay for the repairs. I can't tell you [9] ________ I am!

B That's all right. Don't [10] ________ about it.

5 SPEAKING

A PAIR WORK **Choose one of the situations below. Act it out in pairs.**

1 Introduce yourself to a new student and offer to introduce him/her to other classmates.

A Hi. I'm [name]. You're new here, right?

B Yes, it's my first day at this school. I'm [name], nice to meet you.

2 You're hosting some classmates at home. Offer them something to drink and eat.

A Can I get you anything to drink?

B Yes, please. Can I have …

3 You dropped your friends' belongings and the screen of her phone broke. Apologize and offer to have it fixed.

A I'm so sorry. You'll never guess what I did.

B What did you do?

B **Change roles and repeat the role play.**

UNIT OBJECTIVES
- speculate about a picture
- talk about viral stories
- exchange and discuss opinions
- write a response to a post about local businesses
- design an ad for a product

GOING GLOCAL

4

START SPEAKING

A **Look at the picture. Where do you think it was taken? How many different signs can you see? What do you think they are selling?**

B **How many different places do you see ads? How many ads do you think you see in one day? How many do you pay attention to? For ideas, watch Seung Geyong's video.**

REAL STUDENT

Is your experience like Seung Geyong's?

4.1 MORE THAN JUST A JERSEY

LESSON OBJECTIVE

- speculate about a picture

1 LANGUAGE IN CONTEXT

A **Look at the infographic. Do you recognize any of the team names? What sport do they represent? What type of information does the infographic give about the teams?**

Real Madrid
Annual revenue: €518 million
Ticket sales: €119 million
Broadcasting rights: €188 million
Sponsorships and merchandising: €211 million

Manchester United
Annual revenue: €424 milllion
Ticket sales: €127 million
Broadcasting rights: €119 million
Sponsorships and merchandising: €178 million

FC Barcelona
Annual revenue: €483 million
Ticket sales: €118 million
Broadcasting rights: €188 million
Sponsorships and merchandising: €177 million

Paris Saint-Germain
Annual revenue: €400 million
Ticket sales: €54 million
Broadcasting rights: €91 million
Sponsorships and merchandising: €255 million

B **Read part of an article on sports marketing. What is a major source of income for these soccer teams? Think of sports teams in your town or country. Do they make money in similar ways?**

Soccer is the world's highest earning sport. You might think that the money comes from ticket sales. But actually, a lot of it comes from sales of merchandise.

Take Real Madrid, for example. Business from its **sponsor** represents one-third of the team's total revenue. For the French team Paris Saint-Germain (PSG), sponsorship and **merchandising** represents over half. That could mean that PSG's **brand** is more valuable than the team itself!

All teams have corporate sponsorship deals, which usually means putting the sponsor's **logo** on the jersey. In the case of Real Madrid and PSG, the same sponsor appears on their jerseys – yes, the Emirates airline company sponsors both!

Sponsorship is everywhere in professional sports. These days if teams don't have sponsors on their jerseys, they can't be taken seriously. Even in the U.S., some NBA teams now have sponsors on their shirts, and TV **commercials** that **advertise** games are also **ads** for the sponsors' **products**.

Because sports team brands are so valuable, authentic jerseys are **status symbols** and **fashion statements**. Other branded products, from coffee mugs to mousepads, also bear the team's (and sponsor's) logo and/or **slogan**. All of this merchandising means fakes are everywhere, too. But if your Real Madrid jersey costs three times the price of one you see on the street, it must be the *Real* thing!

C **Read the article and the infographic again. Check (✓) the statements that are true. Correct the false ones.**

- [ ] 1 All soccer teams now get most of their revenue from merchandise sales.
- [ ] 2 It is possible for one company to sponsor two or more teams.
- [ ] 3 Sponsorship of NBA teams is a new trend.
- [ ] 4 The sponsor's name only appears on a team's jersey.

!

All the money a company takes in is its *revenue*. The money that is left after all expenses are paid is its *profit*. These are uncountable nouns.

***Revenue** is up this year, but **profit** is down because of higher costs.*

When a company has many sources of income, they can be countable.

***Revenues** from merchandising and ad sales are down, but **profits** from ticket sales and parking will balance that.*

2 VOCABULARY: Talking about advertising

FIND IT

A 1.33 **Listen and say the words. Find the words from the box in the article and try to figure out what they mean. You can use a dictionary or your phone to help you. Then discuss the questions.**

ad / advertisement	merchandising	advertise	brand
merchandise / products	status symbol	sponsor	logo
fashion statement	commercial	slogan	

What is the difference between …

1 a sponsor (*n*) and sponsor (*v*)?
2 merchandise and merchandising?
3 a brand, a logo, and a slogan?
4 advertise (*v*), an advertisement/ad, and a commercial?
5 a status symbol and a fashion statement?

B **Now go to page 144. Do the vocabulary exercises for 4.1.**

C PAIR WORK **Think of an ad that you really like and one that you really dislike. Why do you feel this way about them? Explain to your partner.**

> That commercial is terrible! The slogan is a little song, and it stays in my head for days!

3 GRAMMAR: Modals of speculation

A **Complete the rules. Use the sentences in the grammar box to help you.**

We can use *must, must not, may, might, can't,* and *could* to speculate.

1 When you're not sure that something is true, use ________________ , *could*, or *may*.
2 When you're sure that something is true, use ________________ .
3 When you're sure that something is not true, use ________________ and *must not*.

Modals of speculation

You **might** think that the money comes from ticket sales.
If it's three times the price, then it **must** be real.
If teams don't have sponsors, they **can't** be taken seriously.

ACCURACY CHECK

Don't use *can* for speculation.
They ~~can~~ be the best soccer team this season. ✗
They might be the best soccer team this season. ✓

B **Complete the sentences with an appropriate modal of speculation. Then check your accuracy.**

1 They ________________ be a very good soccer team. They haven't won a single game this season!
2 They ________________ be the best soccer team this year, but I'm not sure.
3 They ________________ be the best soccer team this year. They've won everything!

C **Now go to page 132. Look at the grammar chart and do the grammar exercise for 4.1.**

4 SPEAKING

A GROUP WORK **Look at the picture. Speculate about what is happening. Who makes the most interesting guess?**

> It can't be an actual game. It must be during practice.

> He might be teaching the dog to play soccer.

4.2 VIRAL STORIES

LESSON OBJECTIVE
- talk about viral stories

1 LANGUAGE IN CONTEXT

A 1.34 **Look at the picture. Do you know about this image? What do you think the story is about? Listen to the podcast and check your answers.**

1.34 Audio script

Today we're talking about viral stories and their impact. The internet is full of viral stories – stories that we see and share, and then others reshare, and reshare, etc. Surprisingly, viral stories are often not about **celebrities.** You don't have to be a famous **entertainer** or a cultural **icon** to go viral.

Take the story of Murtaza Ahmadi. Murtaza was an Afghani boy who made a copy of his **hero** Lionel Messi's jersey out of a plastic bag. Someone took a photo. It went viral and changed Murtaza's life. He got to travel to Qatar where his dreams came true and he met Messi.

Stories which warm our hearts are not the only ones that can go viral. Many are just silly or amusing. There are countless online **performers** that we only know thanks to YouTube. Many are people who don't even have any special talent.

There are people like Matt McAllister, who became famous for wearing 155 t-shirts at the same time! His video has had over 17.5 million views. It's not going to change the world, but it's something that might make us laugh. And sometimes, maybe that's enough.

B 1.34 **What categories do viral stories or videos usually fit in? Listen again and check.**

C PAIR WORK **What people can you think of who have become famous overnight and/or online? Do you think they deserve to be famous? Why or why not?**

2 VOCABULARY: Talking about people in the media

A

B

C

FIND IT

A 1.35 **Listen and say the words. Which words describe the people in the pictures? Look up any terms you don't know. You can use a dictionary or your phone to help you.**

1 audience *C*	5 DJ ___	9 icon ___
2 celebrity ___	6 entertainer ___	10 model ___
3 comedian ___	7 filmmaker ___	11 movie producer ___
4 designer ___	8 hero ___	12 performer ___

B **PAIR WORK** **Think of one person for each word.**

A celebrity can be anybody who is famous for something. For example, Stephen Hawking was a scientist, but he was definitely a celebrity.

C **Now go to page 144. Do the vocabulary exercise for 4.2.**

D **Complete the sentences so that they are true for you.**

1 A performer I really admire is …
2 My hero from childhood was …
3 An icon in my culture / country is …
4 A DJ I love to listen to is …
5 My favorite filmmaker is …
6 A well-known fashion designer here is …

3 GRAMMAR: Subject and object relative clauses

A **Look at the excerpt from the audio script. Then complete the rules.**

> The internet is full of viral stories – stories **that we see and share, and then others reshare, and reshare, etc.**
>
> Take the story of Murtaza Ahmadi. Murtaza was an Afghani boy **who made a copy of his hero Lionel Messi's jersey out of a plastic bag.** Someone took a photo. It went viral and changed Murtaza's life. He got to travel to Qatar **where his dreams came true.**

1 Relative clauses give extra information about ____________, things, or places.
2 A relative clause begins with a relative pronoun: *who*, *which*, ____________, or *where*.
3 In subject relative clauses, the relative pronoun is the subject of the clause and is always followed by a **noun or pronoun** / **verb**.
4 In object relative clauses, the relative pronoun is the object of the clause and is followed by a **noun or pronoun** / **verb**.

B **Now go to page 133. Look at the grammar chart and do the grammar exercise for 4.2.**

C **PAIR WORK** **Choose three items from exercise 2D. Ask your partner to tell you about them.**

Tell me about a performer who you really admire.

I really admire Carlos Vives. He's so talented. He can sing and he can act!

4 SPEAKING

Are your opinions similar to Alessandra's?

A **PAIR WORK** **Look at these sentences. Do you agree or disagree with them? Think of examples to support your opinion. For ideas, watch Alessandra's video.**

1 Most people who become famous on the internet have no real talent.
2 It's too easy to be a celebrity these days. In the past, you had to be really good!
3 It's great that we can all become stars. Anyone can be discovered – it's more democratic!
4 The media spend too much time talking about celebrity gossip. It's boring and unimportant.
5 I love all the news about celebrities. It's funny and distracts me from all the serious news in the world.

4.3 THAT'S A GOOD POINT, BUT ...

LESSON OBJECTIVE

- exchange and discuss opinions

1 FUNCTIONAL LANGUAGE

A 1.36 **Look at the picture. What are the two people doing? How does each person feel? Why do you think they feel that way? Read and listen to their conversation. Were you correct?**

1.36 Audio script

A Colombia is playing Uruguay this afternoon, want to watch it?

B Soccer? Well, not really. **As I see it**, soccer is just a bunch of guys running around for 90 minutes to score two, maybe three goals. To be honest, **I find it** really boring.

A **Now, just a second.** That's not fair at all. Even if the score is low, there's *a lot* happening. Sports are about strategy.

B OK, **that's a good point, but** 90 minutes? The strategy is that interesting?

A Yes, absolutely. And soccer is a cultural experience, too. **I really think** you'd enjoy that side of it at least.

B **It's not so much that** I'm not interested, **it's just that** I don't really understand the game. I just feel lost when I watch it.

A OK, **but the thing is,** you have to watch a sport to understand it. You like basketball now, but you didn't before we went to some games.

B **That's true, but** basketball was more familiar to me. With soccer, you're going to have to explain everything!

A I have to talk about soccer all afternoon? Hey, no problem.

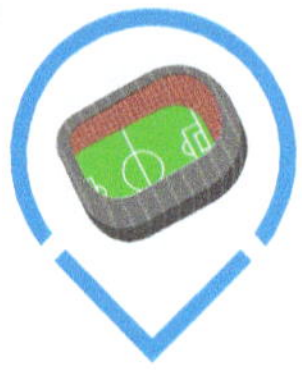

B **Complete the chart with the bold expressions from the conversation.**

Exchanging opinions	Discussing opinions
As I [1] ______ it, ...	Now, just a [5] ______ ....
I [2] ______ it /that (really boring).	That's a good [6] ______ , but ...
I [3] ______ think (you'd enjoy it).	But the [7] ______ is, ...
It's not so [4] ______ that ..., it's just that ...	That's [8] ______ , but ...

C 1.37 **Complete the conversations with expressions from the chart. Then listen and check.**

1 **A** Soccer is a multimillion dollar sport now, and money is destroying the game.
   B Now, [1] ______ – destroying the game? That's a bit strong.
   A Maybe, but I really [2] ______ it's true. It's all about money now.

2 **A** Advertising is such a creative industry these days, don't you think?
   B I guess, but I [3] ______ it kind of sad that so many talented people only ever do that.
   A Well, it's not [4] ______ their talent is wasted, it's just that they use it in a practical way.

D PAIR WORK **Practice the conversations above with a partner. Then have a new conversation about something you feel strongly about using the same expressions.**

I like smartwatches, but the thing is, I just don't like to wear jewelry.

2 REAL-WORLD STRATEGY

A 1.38 **Listen to two people talking about movies. What do they disagree about?**

MAKE OPINIONS MORE EMPHATIC

When we disagree strongly with someone, we often want to express an opinion more emphatically.

That's not true *at all.*

I couldn't disagree more.

You have it *all* wrong.

B 1.38 **Read the box above. Complete the conversation with expressions from the box. Listen and check.**

A Hey, do you want to go see that new superhero movie with me?

B A comic book movie? Uh, I'll pass. They're all so dumb.

A What? I [1] ______________________. The special effects are great, and they're really funny.

B Funny? Come on. They're written for 12-year-olds.

A That's [2] ______________________. Take *Deadpool*, for instance. That movie's very funny, and the jokes are definitely written for adults.

B If you say so. Personally, I'd much rather see a spy movie, like James Bond. They're exciting, but realistic.

A You've got to be kidding. Evil villains and spy gadgets? Now, that's silly.

B No, no. You [3] ______________________. That's the old ones. The new ones are really good.

C PAIR WORK **Student A: Give an opinion about a sports team, a movie, or an entertainer that you know. Student B: Disagree emphatically with A. Then switch roles and have a similar conversation.**

3 PRONUNCIATION FOCUS: Saying the vowel sounds /ɔ/ and /ɑ/

A 1.39 **Listen and repeat the two different vowel sounds.**

/ɔ/ **all** That's not fair at **all**. /ɑ/ **soccer** **Soc**cer is a cultural experience.

B 1.40 **Listen. Write A for words with /ɔ/. Write B for words with /ɑ/.**

1 **au**dience ___	3 m**o**del ___	5 sp**o**nsor ___
2 n**o**t ___	4 **aw**esome ___	6 c**au**ght ___

C 1.41 PAIR WORK **Listen to the conversations. Then practice with a partner.**

1 **A** Want to watch soccer this afternoon?
  B Sure. There's an **aw**esome game between England and Argentina.

2 **A** Why don't you like going to con**c**erts?
  B Being in a big **au**dience makes me nervous.

4 SPEAKING

A PAIR WORK **Choose <u>two</u> of the subjects to talk about. Practice giving opinions about the topic and responding to them, sometimes emphatically.**

an ad on TV right now   a global brand   a sports team (your choice)   a viral video

What do you think of that funny car ad with the big chicken? Kids really like it.

That's true, but kids don't buy cars. I really don't think it's a good ad.

4.4 BUILDING A BRAND

LESSON OBJECTIVE

- write a response to a post about local businesses

1 LISTENING

A PAIR WORK **Look at the sandals. Do you recognize this brand? Where is it from? Is it a local brand or a global brand?**

B 1.42 LISTEN FOR GIST **Listen to a report about the creation of the global brand, *Havaianas*. Check (✓) the ideas that are mentioned.**

- ☐ 1 origins of the brand
- ☐ 2 the advertising plan
- ☐ 3 international growth
- ☐ 4 problems in the business
- ☐ 5 how Havaianas are made

C 1.42 LISTEN FOR DETAILS **Listen to the report again. Choose the correct words to make true statements.**

1 *Everybody / Only some people* in Brazil wore Havaianas in the 1960s.
2 The company *only sells flip-flops / sells other items.*
3 Havaianas became a luxury item *in / outside of* Brazil.
4 The price of a pair of Havaianas in Brazil is *much less / much more* than in international markets.
5 The international success of this product is due to *the product itself / its marketing.*

INSIDER ENGLISH

Flip-flops get their name from the sound they make as you walk in them: *flip-flop, flip-flop*. There are a number of words in English that come from the sound something makes: *clap* your hands; a dog's *bark*.

FIND IT

D THINK CRITICALLY PAIR WORK **Havaianas were originally workers' shoes and are now a global fashion item. What other companies can you think of that started local and went global? Share the story with the class. You can use your phone to help you.**

Levi's jeans were for cowboys and farmers. In the 1960s, young people started wearing them too. Now people wear them almost anywhere.

2 PRONUNCIATION: Listening for topic organization

A 1.43 **Listen to extracts from the report. Write the words that receive the most stress.**

1 ______ / ______ ______

2 ______

3 ______

B **Choose the correct phrase to complete the sentence.**

Stress is often used to indicate the speaker is talking about *the same topic / a new topic*.

3 WRITING

A **Read the post on social media about the impact of global brands on local communities. What change does the writer describe? From whose point of view is this written?**

Posts | Related Posts | Search | Log in | Sign up

Recently, an international company opened a couple of convenience stores right on Main Street. There weren't any chain stores like this before, only small, family-run stores that sell local products. As a result, our town had a nice traditional feel.

These new stores are ugly, but they stay open late. Due to the large number of people who work the late shift at local factories, these stores are sometimes their only option for grocery shopping. Also, thanks to the fact that they're part of a large chain, they can offer a bigger range of products at lower prices than independent stores.

Consequently, a lot of the independent stores downtown are closing. They just can't compete. I think this is a real shame, as we are losing more than stores, we're losing an important part of the community.

Is the same thing happening where you are? Share examples from your community.

B **Read the post again. What reasons does the writer give for the new stores' success? Does he have a positive or negative opinion of the changes in his town?**

C WRITING SKILL **There are five expressions in the post that mark reasons and consequences. Find them and write them below based on similar meaning.**

1 because (of): ______ ______ ______

2 so: ______ ______

D PAIR WORK **Think of an example from your community. Consider the following questions:**

- Which new stores have appeared and which have disappeared?
- What are some reasons for the success of the new stores?
- How do the new stores affect local employment and/or local traditions?
- Is it, generally speaking, a change for the better or for the worse?

WRITE IT

E **Write a response to the post using your community as an example. Write 100–120 words. Include a description of the new business(es), the old business(es), and the reasons for and consequences of the change.**

F **Read your response to the class. Do your classmates agree with you? Why or why not?**

A big supermarket has opened in the downtown area. It sells food at cheaper prices and they have more choice. As a result, the little shops selling fruit and vegetables have closed. It's not good for the community at all.

4.5 TIME TO SPEAK
Design an ad

LESSON OBJECTIVE
- design an ad for a product

A **RESEARCH** **Read about advertising techniques. With a partner, think of types of products (toothpaste, running shoes, medicine, etc.) and discuss which techniques are typically used in their ads.**

Ads for high-end watches often have athletes in them. So that's an endorsement by a celebrity.

1 Endorsement: a respected expert or celebrity supports the product (for example, a movie star does commercials for a brand of shampoo, a famous soccer player puts his name on a new cologne for men)

2 Association of ideas: the product is connected to a particular idea (for example, cars = freedom)

3 "The camera never lies": the product looks visually attractive or appealing (for example, the perfect burger)

4 Technology: the product is (or uses) the latest and best technology (for example, the latest generation smartphone)

5 Guilt: the ad makes the customer feel bad for not having the product already (for example, a safer car seat for children)

B **DECIDE** **Work in small groups to design an ad for a product. Choose one of the products from the box or think of another one. Decide on the central idea or main image for your ad and also the technique(s) that would be best to sell your product. You can draw it or write a plan for it.**

car | cosmetics | food product | jewelry | sports equipment | TV show

Our product is jeans. We should use a DJ in a club where people are dancing. The technique might be association of ideas.

C **PRESENT** **Explain your group's idea to a student from another group. Ask for their feedback and take notes. Rejoin your group and share all the feedback. Work with your group to refine and improve your ad. Be sure your final ad includes the following:**

- a main image (or an idea for one)
- a slogan
- a short text to accompany the ad

D **AGREE** **Present your ads to the class and explain the technique(s) you chose to use. Watch the other presentations and decide which one is the most effective and most original. Explain your opinion.**

To check your progress, go to page 154.

USEFUL PHRASES

RESEARCH
The ad for … uses …
The people in the ad look like they …
Ads for … make me feel …

DECIDE
How about a food product?
Let's use the … technique.
We could use images of …

PRESENT
The central idea of our product is …
The advertising technique we plan to use is …

UNIT OBJECTIVES

- discuss different types of stories
- talk about plans and changes to plans in the past
- react to problems and disappointing news
- write a formal apology
- tell a story about a chance meeting

TRUE STORIES

5

START SPEAKING

A Look at the picture. What kind of story do you think she is telling? How do you know?

B When was the last time you heard a good story? What was it about? Who told it to you?

C Who is the best storyteller you know? What kind of stories do they tell?
For ideas, watch Maryne's video.

REAL STUDENT

Is Maryne's favorite storyteller similar to yours?

5.1 THAT'S ANOTHER STORY!

LESSON OBJECTIVES:
- discuss different types of stories

1 VOCABULARY: Describing stories

A 1.44 **Look at the different kinds of stories in the box. Listen and say the words. Which usually involve a happy ending? strong emotions? sad events?**

coming-of-age story	family saga	feel-good story	hard-luck story
horror story	human interest story	love story	mystery
personal tragedy	success story	tall tale	tearjerker

B **Now go to page 145. Do the vocabulary exercises for 5.1.**

C PAIR WORK **Think of three stories you've heard about recently on TV, in the news, or from a friend. Tell the main events and decide which story type(s) best describes each one.**

2 LANGUAGE IN CONTEXT

A **Read the introduction. What's the name of the company? What is a "pitch"? What services does the company offer? Read the whole page to check your answers.**

Sell your story!

Writers, are you tired of rejection letters? Maybe it isn't you. Maybe it's your pitch.
Let **PitchMasters** create a short, catchy pitch for your story that no publisher could resist.
Just tell us the plot, and get ready to be famous!

Comments

Crazy4wordz
My story is about a man and a woman who had secretly loved each other for years, but they'd never even spoken. Finally, the woman writes him a love letter. The next day he's in a terrible accident …

Sarahthewriter
I have the best idea for a story. It's about a woman who had written stories for years but hadn't had the courage to submit them. One day, her dad is cleaning out her old room and finds a story that she had written as a teenager. He sends it in, and it gets published! It sells millions! Basically, it's my story (I hope).

Starvingartist
My story will really scare you. It's a whodunit about a man who moves into a new house. But he doesn't know that the husband and wife who lived there before had died in the house. Pretty soon he starts hearing strange noises at night and …

B PAIR WORK **Read the plot summaries again. Which story types from exercise 1A best describe them?**

C PAIR WORK **Discuss the questions.**
- Which of the three story ideas do you think has the most interesting plot? Why?
- What kinds of stories do you generally enjoy? Why?
- Are there any kinds of stories you generally don't like? Why?

INSIDER ENGLISH

A *whodunit* is a type of mystery. *Whodunit* is a playful way to say "Who has done it?" (*who is guilty of the crime?*)

3 GRAMMAR: Past perfect

A **Choose the correct words to complete the rules. Use the sentences in the grammar box to help you.**

1 The past perfect is used to talk about things that happened **before** / **after** another event in the past.

2 When there are two completed events in the past, use the **simple past** / **past perfect** for the event that happened after the first event.

3 To form the past perfect, use ***had*** / ***would*** + past participle.

Past perfect

It's about a man and a woman who **had** secretly **loved** each other for years, but they**'d** never even **spoken**.
A woman **had written** stories for years but **hadn't had** the courage to submit them.

B **There are two actions in each sentence. Circle the action that happened first.**

1 We had been there an hour before he finally met with us.

2 When the game finally ended, our team had given up seven goals.

3 They had left by the time we arrived.

4 He was surprised that he had never seen that photo before.

C **Now go to page 133. Look at the grammar chart and do the grammar exercise for 5.1.**

D PAIR WORK **Complete the sentences so they are true for you. Use the past perfect. Read your sentences to a partner. Ask questions to find out more about your partner's stories.**

1 When I got home last night, ______ had already ______.

2 It was the first time I had ever ______. I loved it!

3 I had never ______ before, and I'm never going to do it again!

4 SPEAKING

FIND IT

A **Think of a person whose life would make an interesting book or movie. It can be someone you know or a celebrity or historical figure. Add background information using the past perfect. You can use your phone to look up details about the person.**

B GROUP WORK **Tell your stories to the group. Which of the stories did you find most interesting? Why?**

I think a story about Manuela Saenz would make a great movie. She had been married to an Englishman, but she left her husband in 1822 to fight with Simon Bolivar. She'd already been involved in the fight for independence for several years and …

5.2 LAST-MINUTE-ITIS

LESSON OBJECTIVE

- talk about plans and changes to plans in the past

1 LANGUAGE IN CONTEXT

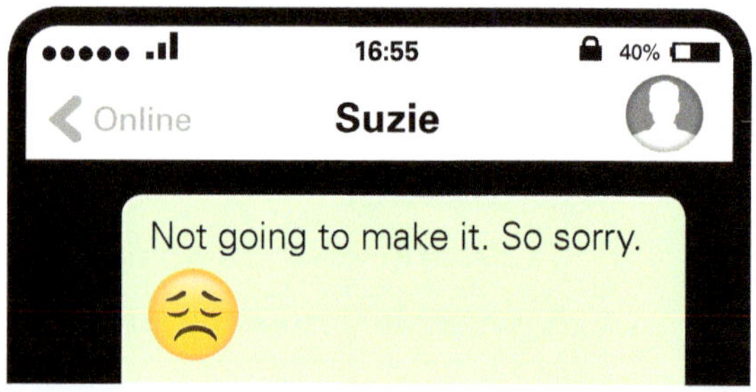

A 1.45 **Look at the text message. Do you often send or receive text messages like this? Listen to two friends discussing another friend, Suzie. What excuses does Suzie make? Do her friends believe her?**

1.45 Audio script

A What's up with Suzie lately? We were going to get together last night. I was really looking forward to it, but at the last minute, she texted that she was held up at work and to go ahead without her. I ended up just staying home.

B Last week, she really messed things up for me, too! I'd bought tickets to a concert. About an hour before we were supposed to meet, she texted, said she was sorry to let me down, but she couldn't go. She said her sister had split up with her boyfriend, and she had to hang out with her and try to cheer her up.

A No way! She's just making up excuses.

B I know! And it's always in a text.

A I'm about ready to give up on her!

INSIDER ENGLISH

We use the expressions *What's up with … ?* and *Something's up* to talk about problems.

2 VOCABULARY: Making and breaking plans

A 1.46 **Find the verb phrases in the conversation and complete them below. Then listen and check.**

1 be held ______
2 cheer ______
3 end ______
4 ______ together
5 give up ______
6 go ______
7 hang out ______
8 let someone ______
9 look ______ to
10 make ______
11 mess ______
12 split ______

B **Now go to page 145. Do the vocabulary exercises for 5.2.**

C GROUP WORK **Do the quiz. Which of you suffers most from last-minute-itis? How do you feel when people cancel or change plans at the last minute? Do you think it's rude? Why or why not?**

Do you suffer from last-minute-itis?

How many times did you do each of these things in the last week? Be honest!

- text a friend at the last minute to change plans
- cancel plans with friends because you didn't feel like going
- text that you were running late
- forget to show up for a meeting because you didn't put it in your phone.

3 GRAMMAR: *was/were going to; was/were supposed to*

A **Choose the correct words to complete the rules. Use the sentences in the grammar box to help you.**

1 The forms *was/were going to* and *was/were supposed to* describe an action that **was completed** / **was planned** in the past.

2 They are often used to say that a plan **happened** / **didn't happen**.

3 They are often followed by ***and*** / ***but*** and an explanation.

was/were going to; was/were supposed to

We **were going to** get together last night, but she was held up at work.

An hour before we **were supposed to** meet, she texted me to cancel.

B **Now go to page 134. Look at the grammar chart and do the grammar exercise for 5.2.**

C PAIR WORK **Read the two situations. What was the original plan? How do you know? Summarize using *was/were supposed to* or *was/were going to*. Check your accuracy.**

1 We were all packed and ready to leave, when it started to rain really heavily. There was no point in going. We didn't want to put up a tent in the rain!

2 We apologized to the people who had come to the meeting and took them for coffee. Then we set up a conference call and had the meeting over Skype.

ACCURACY CHECK

Remember not to drop the verb *be* in phrases with *going to* and *supposed to*.

The show ~~supposed~~ to start at 7:30. ✗

The show was supposed to start at 7:30. ✓

4 SPEAKING

A **Think about a time when your plans had to change for some reason. Use the questions below to help you. For ideas, watch Seung Geyong's video.**

- What were you going to do?
- What went wrong?
- What did you end up doing?

REAL STUDENT

Did something similar happen to you?

B PAIR WORK **Tell your partner what happened and listen to your partner's story. Ask follow-up questions to get more information.**

I was going to visit my cousin in Miami. I had bought the tickets and everything. But when I got to the airport, I realized that I had forgotten my passport at home …

5.3 THERE MUST BE A MISTAKE!

LESSON OBJECTIVE
- react to problems and disappointing news

1 FUNCTIONAL LANGUAGE

A 1.47 PAIR WORK **How would you describe the restaurant in the picture? Why would you choose to go to a place like this? Read and listen to the conversation between a customer and a restaurant host. What was supposed to happen? What's the problem?**

1.47 Audio script

A Hi there. Anderson, party of six, for 8 o'clock.
B I'm sorry, sir, but we don't have a reservation in that name.
A **I don't understand**, I made the reservation myself. **Can you check again, please?**
B Hmm, no, it isn't here.
A **There must be some kind of mistake.** I called last week. Is there a table for six we can have?
B I'm afraid there isn't, sir. We're fully booked.
A But **there must be something you can do.** We're supposed to celebrate my wife's birthday tonight. **I'd like to speak to the manager, please.**
B I'm afraid the manager isn't here at the moment, but let me check ... Ah! We have a table at 9. Would that be OK?
A Well, I guess it will have to be OK.
B I'm very sorry for the mistake. We'll give your table some appetizers as an apology.
A That would be nice. Thank you. **I'm glad it's settled.**

B **Complete the chart with the bold expressions from the conversation.**

! For reservations, a group of people is often called a *party*.

Reacting to a problem	Asking for a solution	Accepting a solution
I don't [1] ______ .	There must be [4] ______ you can do.	That'll work.
Would you mind taking another look?	I'd like to speak to the [5] ______ , please.	I'm glad it's / that's [6] ______ .
Can you [2] ______ again, please?	Is there someone else I could speak to about this, please?	
There must be some kind of [3] ______ .		

C 1.48 **Complete the conversation with expressions from the chart. Listen and check. Then practice it with a partner.**

A I'm sorry, sir, but I'm afraid you aren't going to be able to take this flight.
B What? I [1] ______ .
A The flight was over-booked. There aren't any seats available.
B There [2] ______ something you can do.
A Well, we can put you on the next flight. It leaves in two hours.
B Just two hours? Oh, OK, [3] ______ . I'll just be a little late for the meeting.

2 REAL-WORLD STRATEGY

A 1.49 **Listen to two conversations. What's the problem in each?**

ACCEPTING BAD NEWS

Sometimes there is nothing you can do about a bad situation or result, and you just have to accept it. Use these phrases to show you're disappointed, but you accept the situation.

That's not what I was hoping to hear, but what can you do?

Well, it is what it is.

Well, that's life.

That's too bad, but hey, …

B 1.50 **Read the information about accepting bad news. Use an appropriate expression to complete the conversations. Listen and check your answers.**

1 **A** I'm really sorry, ma'am, but there are no more tickets for tonight's show.
B Are you sure? What about tomorrow?
A I'm afraid there are no tickets left for tomorrow either.
B Oh, no. ________________ . Thanks anyway.

2 **A** Can I pick up my laptop later today?
B No, I'm sorry sir. It won't be ready until tomorrow.
A ________________ , but hey, I still have my phone!

C PAIR WORK **Practice the conversations with a partner.**

3 PRONUNCIATION FOCUS: Saying consonants at the end of a word

A 1.51 **Listen and repeat. Focus on the consonant sounds at the end of the words.**

1 Can you check again, please?

2 There must be some kind of mistake.

B 1.52 **Listen. Who pronounces the consonant sound at the end of the word clearly? Write A or B.**

1 check ____
2 mistake ____
3 celebrate ____
4 ticket ____
5 bad ____
6 glad ____

C PAIR WORK **Say the words in exercise 3B to your partner. Does your partner say the consonant sounds clearly?**

REGISTER CHECK

When something goes wrong at a business – even if the worker has made a big mistake, you should use a calm, polite tone and keep your language rather formal. Shouting or showing anger will make people less interested in helping you.

I'm sorry, sir, but I just rented out the last car.

I don't understand. I reserved a car for today online. May I speak with the manager, please?

4 SPEAKING

A PAIR WORK **Look at the list of disappointing situations. Choose one and act it out. One person gives bad news and the other reacts. Switch roles and act out another one, or think of a new situation.**

- You just missed your train. You ask the guard on the platform about the next train. There isn't one until tomorrow!
- You're buying a T-shirt for your sister for her birthday. They don't have her size in the shop. You can order one, but it won't arrive in time.
- You took your phone to be repaired. You go to pick it up. They tell you they can't fix it.

5.4 THE PERFECT APOLOGY?

LESSON OBJECTIVE

- write a formal apology

1 READING

A PAIR WORK **Look at the picture. What problems do you think this might cause for air travel? Read the article about an airline that made a big mistake. What was the mistake?**

THE PERFECT APOLOGY

In the winter of 2007, the U.S. was hit by a heavy snowstorm, which caused hundreds of flights to be canceled. At one airport, passengers who had already taken their seats on Jet Blue planes before their flight was canceled had to stay there, inside the plane but on the ground, for 11 hours. People were furious with Jet Blue. But Jet Blue's mistake is not what makes this story memorable.

The CEO quickly made a public corporate apology:

> Words cannot express how truly sorry we are for the anxiety, frustration, and inconvenience that you, your family, friends, and colleagues experienced … We know we failed last week … You deserved better—a lot better … and we let you down.

His apology was heartfelt. He admitted that Jet Blue had handled the situation poorly and recognized that a lot of people had suffered. He also offered every passenger compensation to make up for it, which cost his company more than $20 million. And he didn't stop there. He openly explained what had gone wrong and how the company was going to make sure it never happened again.

In short, he followed the three rules for a perfect apology: 1) say you're sorry; 2) promise it will never happen again; 3) do something to make up for it. These are rules that anyone can, and should, follow.

B INTERPRETING ATTITUDE **Read the article again. Why does the writer think the apology was so good? Underline the positive adjectives and adverbs he uses to show his opinion.**

C UNDERSTANDING MEANING FROM CONTEXT **Find words in the text with the following meanings:**

1 (*v*) experience pain or an unpleasant emotion ______

2 (*adj*) associated with business ______

3 (*n*) money you get when you have had a problem ______

4 (*phr v*) reduce the bad effect of something ______

D THINK CRITICALLY **Why did the CEO make a public apology? Is it usual for corporations to apologize when they make a mistake? Can you think of any recent examples? Is a public apology enough? Why or why not?**

2 WRITING

A **Read an excerpt from another famous corporate apology. In what way is it similar to the apology in the Jet Blue article? Does it follow the three rules for a good apology?**

To our customers,

At Apple, we strive to make world-class products that deliver the best experience possible to our customers. With the launch of our new Maps last week, we fell short on this commitment. We are extremely sorry for the frustration this has caused our customers and we are doing everything we can to make Maps better.

B **Read the apology again. What does "this commitment" refer to in the second sentence? Which of the phrases below could you use to replace "this commitment"?**

our agreement	our mistake
this goal	this promise to you

GLOSSARY

strive (*v*) try hard
deliver (*v*) give
launch (*n*) first release
fall short (*phrase*) not do as well as you should

C WRITING SKILL **Look at this short corporate apology. Use one of the phrases in the box above to avoid repetition in the second sentence.**

Last week our company accidentally released the personal data of some of our customers. We are deeply sorry for releasing the personal data for some of our customers.

FIND IT

D **Look at the situation below, or go online and find a similar situation that has been in the news recently. Answer the questions.**

A car company has discovered a dangerous mechanical problem and must tell their customers. They are offering to replace those cars with new ones.

- What's the problem?
- Who does it affect? In what way?

WRITE IT

E PAIR WORK **Write a public apology from the CEO of the car company. Write about 80 words. Remember to avoid repetition where possible.**

5.5 TIME TO SPEAK
A chance meeting

LESSON OBJECTIVE
- tell a story about a chance meeting

A **PREPARE** Look at the picture. What's happening? Where do you think they're going to meet? What are they going to do?

B Work in groups. Group A: Go to page 157. Group B: Go to page 159. Follow the instructions.

C **DISCUSS** Work with a partner from the other group. Tell each other your back stories. What do you think the two people said to each other on the phone? What do you think happens next? How does the story end?

D **PRESENT** Join another pair of students. Act out the story from the time they meet through your proposed ending. Ask and answer questions. How different are your two endings?

E Share your stories with the class. How many different endings are there? Look at the real end of the story on page 158. Did anyone get it right?

To check your progress, go to page 154.

USEFUL PHRASES

PREPARE
They are going to …
I think they're planning to …

DISCUSS
I think they're probably going to …
And then they might …
They definitely won't …

PRESENT
So this is what I know: …
She/He was supposed to …
But instead she/he …
From the woman's/man's point of view, …

UNIT OBJECTIVES

- discuss charities and volunteer work
- discuss acts of kindness in your community
- offer, refuse, and accept help with something
- write a report about a community project
- design an urban project for your community

COMMUNITY ACTION

6

START SPEAKING

A **Look at the picture of a volunteer organization. What do you think they're building? Who do you think they're building it for? Use your phone to learn more about this organization.**

B **Would you participate in a program like the one in the picture? Why or why not?**

C **Building homes for others is an "act of kindness." What other good deeds or acts of kindness can you do in your community? For ideas, watch Maryne's video.**

REAL STUDENT

Are your answers the same as Maryne's?

6.1 HELPING OUT

LESSON OBJECTIVE

- discuss charities and volunteer work

1 LANGUAGE IN CONTEXT

A 1.53 **Look at the logo. What do you think the organization does? Listen to the three people describe the organizations they are involved with. Which one matches the logo?**

SOCIAL BITE

1.53 Audio script

Hiro ______ "I **got involved with** this organization because I wanted to help people in my neighborhood. The Center is designed to **bring elderly people together** and keep them active and interested in life. I **volunteer** at the Center and I also visit people in their homes. You **get to know** them, and they really **connect with** you and trust you."

Sandra ______ "I **help out** at a shelter for stray animals that opened a few years ago. I **joined** last year, and I help **take care of** abandoned pets. Some people **donate** money to help us, but supplies are always needed, too. I love the work here because I'm making a difference."

Kemal ______ "Second chances aren't given out all the time, so I know I'm lucky. I was unemployed and homeless, but then I found the café. This place was set up to help people like me learn a practical skill. I serve food, but now I also **take part in** training sessions for new employees. This place changed my life, so I want to **pass on** things I've learned and help others."

GLOSSARY

shelter (*n*) a place that protects people or animals
stray (*adj*) living on the streets with no owner (for dogs and cats)

2 VOCABULARY: Discussing good works

A PAIR WORK 1.54 **Look at the bold words in the audio script. Match them with the correct definitions below. Listen and check.**

1 assist with something: *help out*
2 find that you have something in common with somebody: ______
3 learn more about someone: ______
4 look after someone or something: ______
5 share information with someone: ______
6 give money or other things to help an organization: ______
7 do something without receiving money: ______
8 participate in an activity: ______
9 become a member or work with an organization: ______ or ______
10 help people socialize: ______

B **Now go to page 146. Do the vocabulary exercises for 6.1.**

C PAIR WORK **Answer the questions.**

- What volunteer organization is special to you? When did you get involved with it?
- What group would you like to join someday? Why?

I'd like to get involved with Friends of the Earth, because I'm very worried about climate change.

3 GRAMMAR: Present and past passive

A **Look at the sentences in the grammar box. Underline the main action in each sentence. Do you know who or what did this action? Is it important to know?**

Present and past passive

The Center is designed to bring elderly people together.
Supplies are always needed at the shelter.
Second chances aren't given out all the time.
The café was set up to help people learn a skill.
My life was changed by this place.

B **Now go to page 134. Look at the grammar chart and do the grammar exercise for 6.1.**

C PAIR WORK **Complete the sentences with the correct passive form of the verbs in the box. Then check your accuracy. Some sentences have more than one correct answer.**

base	coordinate	donate	focus
found	organize	produce	support

ACCURACY CHECK

In passive sentences, the verb *to be* always agrees with the subject.

Our program ~~are~~ designed for elderly people. ✗
Our program is designed for elderly people. ✓

Friends of the Earth (FOE) is an international network of environmental organizations. It [1] ________________ in 1969 by Robert O. Anderson. Originally, it [2] ________________ in North America and Europe, but now it [3] ________________ on the developing world. One of their biggest campaigns against climate change was "The Big Ask." The project [4] ________________ by many celebrities, including musicians such as Paul McCartney. A song called "A Love Song to the Earth" [5] ________________, and all the profits [6] ________________ to FOE. Today, some activities [7] ________________ at the international level but a lot of different protests [8] ________________ by local FOE groups all over the world.

4 SPEAKING

A PAIR WORK **Look at the two logos. Do you know what organizations they stand for? What do you know about them?**

MEDECINS SANS FRONTIERES
DOCTORS WITHOUT BORDERS

WWF

FIND IT

B **Student A: Go to page 158. Student B: Go to page 160.** **Read about your organization and underline key information. You can also look up more information on your phone.**

C PAIR WORK **Complete the questions about your organization with the verbs in parentheses ( ). Then ask and answer the questions with your partner.**

1 When ________________ the organization ________________? (found)
2 Where ________________ it ________________? (base)
3 How ________________ it ________________? (fund)
4 What ________________ its work ________________? (focus on)

6.2 RANDOM ACTS OF KINDNESS

LESSON OBJECTIVE

- discuss acts of kindness in your community

1 LANGUAGE IN CONTEXT

A **When you borrow money and then return it, you "pay it back." But what do you think it means to "pay it forward"? Circle your answer. Then read the review to check your answer.**

a Be generous to everyone you meet and money will come to you someday.

b If someone is nice to you, then you should be nice to someone else next.

c When you don't owe anyone anything, you feel good about yourself.

BOOK REVIEWS Home News Reviews Account

Paying It Forward offers a stunning lesson on kindness

1 ______

In the book, *Paying It Forward: How one cup of coffee could change the world*, a university professor describes an experiment with **acts of kindness**. She tried to **lend a helping hand** to a stranger – offering her umbrella or giving someone coins for a parking meter. In return, she asked those people to do a nice thing for someone else.

2 ______

Her experiment showed that, for an act of kindness to be paid forward, it must be met with **gratitude**. But what happens if the person isn't **appreciative**? Your **thoughtful gesture** might not always be accepted with a **grateful** smile. Efforts to help can be interpreted as unwanted attention. You wanted to be **helpful**, but now you just feel bad!

3 ______

Even if someone **appreciates** your help, how much is too much? They say kindness is its own **reward**, but research shows that a kind act will not be carried out if it is too difficult or takes too much time. There is a point at which the effort becomes greater than the reward. Paying it forward isn't as simple as it sounds.

B **Read the review again. Write the headings in the correct places.**

There are limits A chain of favors Two sides to the story

2 VOCABULARY: Describing good deeds

A 1.55 **Complete the chart with the bold words and expressions from the review. Listen and check. Which word families refer to giving help and which to receiving help?**

verb	noun	adjective	expression
help	help	______	______
	______	______	show some gratitude
	______	kind	______
think	thought	thoughtful	______
______	appreciation	______	show your appreciation
	______	rewarding	… is its own reward

B **Now go to page 146. Do the vocabulary exercises for 6.2.**

C GROUP WORK **Discuss the questions.**

"Kindness is its own reward." What does that mean? Do you agree? How far are you willing to go to help others? Think of something that you are willing to do and something you are not willing to do. For ideas, watch Tayra's video.

Are your answers the same as Tayra's?

3 GRAMMAR: Passive with modals

A **Choose the correct words to complete the rules. Read the sentences in the grammar box to help you.**

1 To form the passive with a modal, use modal verb + *be* + **past / past participle**.

2 For something that is probable but not definite, use the modal ***can / might / must / will***.

3 For something that is one of many possibilities, use the modal ***can / might / must / will***.

4 For something that is definite or necessary, use the modal ***can / might / must / will***.

5 For something that is generally true in the situation, use the modal ***can / might / must / will***.

Passive with modals

An act of kindness **must be met** with gratitude.
Your gesture **might not** always **be accepted** with a smile.
Efforts to help **can be interpreted** as unwanted attention.
A kind act **will not be carried out** if it is too difficult.

B PAIR WORK **Complete the sentences with an appropriate modal verb. Sometimes more than one modal may be appropriate.**

1 If the program gets enough support, its goals __________ be achieved by the end of this year.

2 These rooms __________ be set up as a job center or a children's after-school program. We're not sure yet.

3 Unfortunately, these facilities __________ be adapted for the disabled because there is no place for an elevator.

4 Next winter, help __________ be provided to all families in need. You __________ donate used coats and blankets anytime.

C **Now go to page 135. Do the grammar exercise for 6.2.**

4 SPEAKING

A GROUP WORK **Do you agree or disagree with the statements? Why? Think of more statements to express your opinions on helping others.**

- Money should be given to charities not individuals.
- Food should be provided by local authorities for everybody who needs it.
- Our taxes should be spent on helping people in our local community.

I agree with the first statement because you never know what individuals are going to do with the money you give them.

6.3 IT'S ALL GOOD

LESSON OBJECTIVE

- offer, refuse, and accept help with something

1 FUNCTIONAL LANGUAGE

A 1.56 **Look at the picture. What is the person doing? Why is she doing it? Read and listen to the conversations. Which conversation matches the picture?**

> **INSIDER** ENGLISH
>
> **"*I insist*" is a polite way to show someone that you will not change your mind.**

1.56 Audio script

1 A Excuse me, **would you like to sit down?**
B Oh no, **I'm OK. Thanks anyway.**
A Please, I insist. I'm getting off at the next stop anyway.
B Well, OK. Thank you.
A No worries. Have a good day!
B You, too!

2 A You're getting really wet. **Let me share my umbrella** with you.
B Oh, **you don't have to do that.**
A I know, but it's pouring rain.
B Well, **OK then, thanks.**

3 A Well, hi there, neighbor.
B Hi, Mr. Samuels.
A **Let me give you a hand with that.**
B No, really, **I can manage.**
A Are you sure? Your hands look pretty full. Here, **let me do that.**
B Well, OK. **That's very nice of you.**
A There you go!
B **Thanks, I really appreciate it.**
A **Can I help you with** anything else?
B **Nope, it's all good.** Thanks again.

B **Complete the chart with the bold expressions from the conversations.**

Making offers	Refusing offers	Accepting offers
[1] ______ ______ like (to sit down)?	I'm OK. Thanks [4] ______ .	OK then, thanks.
[2] ______ ______ (share my umbrella with you).	You [5] ______ ______ to do that.	That's very [8] ______ / kind of you.
Let me give you a hand with that.	I can [6] ______ .	Thanks, I really [9] ______ it.
Can I [3] ______ you with (anything else)?	Nope, it's [7] ______ good.	

C PAIR WORK **Practice the conversations in exercise A, but change the expressions.**

Excuse me, would you like to share my umbrella?

That's very kind of you. Thank you!

2 REAL-WORLD STRATEGY

A 1.57 Listen to the conversations. What is the situation in each? What is the difference in the outcome?

IMPOSING ON SOMEBODY

Sometimes you have to make a request that others might not like. You can soften it by starting the request like this:

I'm sorry to have to ask, but is it OK if ... ? *I don't mean to be rude, but would you mind ... ?*

B 1.57 Read the information about imposing on someone and listen again. What expressions do the people use?

C PAIR WORK Student A: Change one of the conversations in exercise A so that you are imposing on someone, or create a new situation of your choice. Student B: Accept or reject the request. Swap roles and have another conversation.

I'm sorry to have to ask, but could you move over? It's difficult for me to sit in the middle with all these bags.

INSIDER ENGLISH

When someone in the back part of a line of people doesn't want to wait and moves to the front part of the line, they *cut the line* or *jump the line*.

3 PRONUNCIATION FOCUS: Saying /b/ or /v/ in the middle of a word

A 1.58 Listen to the words. Focus on the sound of the **bold** letters. Practice saying them.

/b/ um**b**rella /v/ con**v**ersation

B 1.59 Listen. Who says the **bold** letter correctly? Write A or B.

1 um**b**rella ___ 3 ha**v**e ___ 5 gi**v**e ___
2 con**v**ersation ___ 4 terri**b**le ___ 6 pro**b**lem ___

C PAIR WORK Say the words in exercise 3B to your partner. Does your partner say the /b/ and /v/ sounds clearly?

4 SPEAKING

A PAIR WORK Work with a partner. Choose one of the situations and act out a conversation. Then think of a situation of your own and act out that conversation.

1 A parent needs help going up some stairs with a stroller.
2 Somebody has dropped a lot of fruit and vegetables in the supermarket.
3 A person's car has broken down on the side of the road.

Hey, let me give you a hand with that.

Thanks! I really appreciate it.

6.4 PAINTING SAFER STREETS

LESSON OBJECTIVE
- write a report about a community project

1 LISTENING

A 1.60 LISTEN FOR GIST **Look at the picture of people painting a street. Why do you think they are doing this? Listen to the podcast to check your answers.**

Perhaps they are creating a pedestrian zone to give people a nice place to spend time.

B 1.60 LISTEN FOR DETAILS **Listen again. Answer the questions.**

1 What kind of people are involved in the intersection repair project?

2 Why do they paint the intersections in particular?

C 1.60 LISTEN FOR ATTITUDE **What is the attitude of each person who calls the show? What words do they use to describe the project? In what other ways can you detect their attitude?**

1 Eric has a positive/negative attitude about the project.
How do you know? ______

2 Isabel has a positive/negative attitude about the project.
How do you know? ______

3 Jeannette has a positive/negative attitude about the project.
How do you know? ______

D PAIR WORK THINK CRITICALLY **Discuss the questions.**

- Do you think public art is a good thing for communities and cities? Why or why not?
- Do you think there are other problems that are more important to address? What are some examples?

2 PRONUNCIATION: Listening for /j/ between words

A 1.61 **Listen to the extracts from the podcast. Listen for the /j/ sound between the underlined words.**

1 Today, we're going to Portland, Oregon, to hear about <u>the Intersection</u> Repair project.

2 And how was <u>the experience</u>?

3 Kids, <u>the unemployed</u>, <u>the elderly</u> – everyone just did whatever they could to help out.

B 1.62 **Listen. Underline the words you hear that are connected by a /j/ sound.**

1 We asked for Portlanders to call in and share their thoughts.

2 Me and my friends all worked on the project.

C **Choose the correct words to complete the statement.**

A /j/ sound is often used to connect two words when the first word *starts* / *ends* in an /i/ sound and the second word starts with a *consonant* / *vowel*.

3 WRITING

A **Look at the picture of another project. What do you think the idea behind it is? Read the report to check your answer.**

Vertical gardens cover the walls of art centers and apartment blocks in many cities around the world, but Mexico City is doing something more ambitious. Their "Verde Vertical" project is aimed at transforming hundreds of pillars that support overpasses into vertical gardens.

A spokesman from the company responsible for the gardens promises that pollution will be reduced and the cityscape will be improved: "We live in a very gray city, but as soon as we find a park, a green landscape, our mood changes. This is going to change people's routines."

When asked for comment, one driver said, "I drive to work every day on this road and there's a lot of traffic. It's stressful. Just seeing something green relaxes me, you know?"

However, a pedestrian disagreed: "A road is a road. They can disguise it with these plants, but it doesn't change anything."

The project aims to provide the city with an extra 40,000 meters of greenery to improve both air quality and the mood of the city's 20 million residents. The lives of those stuck in the city's traffic jams should be improved greatly – at least in theory!

GLOSSARY

overpass (*n*) a bridge that carries a road or railway over another road

B **Read the report again. What is the difference between this project and the Portland project (from exercise 1)? What do they have in common? Consider these points:**

- the people responsible for the project
- the people who benefit from the project
- the goals of the project

Which project do you prefer? Which one do you think is going to help the community more?

C WRITING SKILL **What opinions of other people are expressed in the report above? Find the phrases used to introduce these quotes and underline them.**

WRITE IT

D 1.60 **Listen again to the podcast from exercise 1. Write a short report (120–150 words) about the Portland project. Include a description of the project, how it was done, and positive and negative opinions from the callers. Be sure to introduce each quote**

6.5 TIME TO SPEAK
Your urban art project

LESSON OBJECTIVE
- design an urban project for your community

FIND IT

A **RESEARCH** **Look at the picture and read the description. Go online to find out more if you can. Then discuss the questions.**

- What do you think is especially interesting about this art project?
- How do you think it benefits the community and its people?
- How might this project inspire others?
- Is there anything similar (in appearance or inspiration) in your area? Describe it. Find pictures online if you can.

The Morrinho Art Project is a model of a *comunidade* (neighborhood) in Rio de Janeiro. It was created by 14-year-old resident Cirlan Souza de Oliveira to show pride in his community.

B **DECIDE** **Work in small groups. Think of a space in your town or city which could benefit from urban art. Discuss these points:**

1 The place: Decide on a place in your town or city that could benefit from a project.
2 The project: What are you going to create in this space?
3 The benefits to the community: What advantages will the project bring to the community? How will that happen?

The old city walls should be restored and volunteers from each of the city's neighborhoods can create a mural that explains something about their area – a visual history of the city.

C **DISCUSS** **Work with a student from a different group. Explain your projects to each other. Suggest improvements and possible changes to the projects. Make notes to show to your group.**

D **Return to your original group and compare notes. Make any changes necessary. Identify the main points of your project, give it a name, and prepare your presentation.**

E **PRESENT** **Present your project ideas to the class. Listen to all the presentations and decide on the most effective and the most original. Be prepared to support your opinion.**

To check your progress, go to page 154.

USEFUL PHRASES

DECIDE
We're going to focus on … (place)
We're going to create …
The project will help the area because …

DISCUSS
Our group decided to …
Your project could be improved by …
Have you thought about … ?

PRESENT
Our project is called …
We decided/ thought that …
We chose to … because …

REVIEW 2 (UNITS 4–6)

1 VOCABULARY

A **Which word or phrase doesn't belong in each set. Circle it. Then add it to the correct set.**

Advertising: logo DJ merchandising commercial fashion statement ______ ______ ______

Jobs in the media: comedian filmmaker designer entertainer volunteer ______ ______ ______

Story types: family saga personal tragedy feel-good story slogan success story ______ ______ ______

Plans with people: get together tall tale cheer somebody up give up on somebody hang out with ______ ______ ______

Community work: donate get involved with let someone down take part in help out ______ ______ ______

B **Think of two more words or phrases that you know for each category and add them above.**

2 GRAMMAR

A **Choose the correct words to complete the paragraph.**

I love everything about France. My husband, [1]*who / that* is a doctor, is from France, and that's [2]*why / where* we spent our honeymoon. Until then, I [3]*have / had* never been abroad. Last night we [4]*supposed / were supposed* to celebrate our wedding anniversary with friends at our favorite restaurant, the *French Hall*. The restaurant [5]*is located / locates* inside the Mondrian Hotel, which [6]*is / was* founded in 1752. It [7]*must / can* be the oldest hotel in town. However, we [8]*saw / had seen* an accident on the way, and we stopped to help. When we finally [9]*arrived / had arrived* at the restaurant, all our friends [10]*were / had* already left.

B PAIR WORK **Have you ever missed a celebration? What happened?**

C PAIR WORK **Complete the sentences with the modal verbs below. Use positive or negative forms as appropriate. Compare your sentences with a partner. Do you have similar views?**

can might must should will

1 School children ______ be allowed to work.
2 If everybody helps, poverty ______ be ended in less than 20 years.
3 Elderly people ______ be sent to special homes.

3 SPEAKING

A PAIR WORK **Talk to your partner about an experience you've had this year that you had never had before. Use the questions as a guide.**

- What was the experience?
- Why did you want to do it? Why hadn't you done it before?
- What was special about it? What have you learned or gained from it?

B **What have you learned about your partner? Tell the class.**

Juan had always wanted to join a community garden, and he finally did it. He's learned to take care of plants, and he's also connected with lots of people who …

4 FUNCTIONAL LANGUAGE

A **Complete the conversations that take place at a school with the words in the box.**

can manage	don't know	find
get it	let me	must be
really think	so much	what it is

1 **A** I [1] ______________ the new school TV commercial is fantastic.

B Yes, absolutely. And I [2] ______________ the slogan very strong: "Unlock your door to the future."

C I [3] ______________. It's not [4] ______________ that I don't like the slogan; it's just that I think it doesn't sound very modern.

2 **A** I'm sorry, but you're not in English 203. You're in English 205.

B I don't [5] ______________. I was supposed to be in English 203. There [6] ______________ some kind of mistake. Can you transfer me to 203?

A I don't think that's possible. That class is full. But I can put you on a waiting list.

B Well, OK. I guess it is [7] ______________.

3 **A** [8] ______________ give you a hand with those files. They look pretty heavy.

B No, really, I [9] ______________. But thanks anyway.

5 SPEAKING

A PAIR WORK **Choose one of the situations and act it out.**

1 A reporter has asked you and your friend about who you think the best soccer player today is. You disagree with each other.

A As I see it, (name of player) is the best soccer player this year.

B Sorry, I really don't agree …

2 You made a hotel reservation, but the receptionist can't find it. React and ask for a solution.

A I'm sorry, but we don't have a reservation in that name …

B There must be some kind of mistake …

3 You see an elderly person who is having problems putting something in their car. Offer to help.

A Can I help you with that?

B No, really, I can manage.

B **Change roles and repeat the role play.**

UNIT OBJECTIVES

- discuss the importance of messaging apps
- discuss written vs. spoken communication
- recount conversations, news, and stories
- write an email in a formal and informal register
- create and conduct a communication survey

CAN WE TALK?

7

START SPEAKING

A Look at the picture. What is the man doing? How do you think the other people feel?

B Is this a realistic situation? Why or why not? What does it say about the use of phones in our society?

C What other situations can you think of where you shouldn't use your phone? For ideas, watch Seung Geyong's video.

REAL STUDENT

Do you agree with Seung Geyong?

7.1 A COMMON LANGUAGE

LESSON OBJECTIVE
- discuss the importance of messaging apps

1 LANGUAGE IN CONTEXT

A PAIR WORK **Look at the picture and the title of the article. What are the people doing? Where are they? Read and check your answers.**

Smartphone lifeline

We use smartphone apps to **keep in touch with** family, **catch up with** friends, **congratulate** people on special events, **respond to** invitations, and even **gossip** about our favorite celebrities.

But for migrants who leave their families behind in search of a better life, messaging apps provide the best (sometimes the only) way to **inform their families of** their progress. Many migrants have limited resources, but their relatives **persuade** them to buy a device. Refugee camps now provide charging stations. Greenpeace recently **reported** that use of their stations had increased greatly.

Some recent immigrants to the U.S. **commented** that WhatsApp had eased their sense of isolation. One new arrival **explained** that the app allowed him to **contact** his family: "I tell them about things I wouldn't have **mentioned** in a once-a-week phone call, and they can **reply to** me at once. You feel they are really close."

For most of us, smartphone apps make daily life easier and more fun, and we even **criticize** people for using them too much. For migrants, however, messaging apps are an absolute lifeline.

GLOSSARY
lifeline (*n*) something that you depend on

B **Choose the correct phrase to complete the statements.**

1 For migrants, a messaging app is often *a fun way / the only way* to communicate with family.
2 Charities now provide *charging stations / messaging apps* to help refugees stay in touch with family.

2 VOCABULARY: Describing communication

A 2.02 **Categorize the words in the box according to similar meaning. Listen and check.**

catch up with	comment	congratulate	contact
explain	gossip	inform of	reply to

A respond to, ____________
B mention, report, ____________, ____________, ____________
C keep in touch with, ____________, ____________
D criticize, persuade, ____________, ____________

B **Now go to page 147. Do the vocabulary exercises for 7.1.**

C PAIR WORK **Answer the questions.**

- How do you keep in touch with people who live far away?
- When was the last time that you congratulated a friend on something? What was it?
- When did you persuade somebody to do something? What was it?

3 GRAMMAR: Reported statements

A **Choose the best options to complete the rules. Use the sentences in the grammar box to help you.**

1 To report a present tense statement, use the **present** / **past**.
2 To report a past tense statement, use the **past** / **past perfect**.
3 To report a present perfect statement, use the **past** / **past perfect**.
4 To report instructions and suggestions, use the **present** / **past** + pronoun + (*not*) *to* + verb.

Reported statements

One new arrival explained that the app **allowed** him to contact his family.
Some immigrants commented that WhatsApp **had eased** their sense of isolation.
Greenpeace recently reported that use of their stations **had increased** greatly.
Their families **persuaded** them to buy a smartphone.

B **Now go to page 135. Look at the grammar chart and do the grammar exercise for 7.1.**

C PAIR WORK **Take turns making statements that are true for you. Report your partner's statements.**

1 live with family
"I live with my family." Manny explained that he lived with his family.
2 know how to drive
3 visit Spain
4 see ocean
5 try app / not like it

D PAIR WORK **Think of things that you have heard about this week. How did you hear about them? Use reporting verbs to explain the news to your partner.**

My brother mentioned that he had won a prize at school. We congratulated him.

The media reported that unemployment is lower this quarter.

! **We usually change the tense of the verb when making reported statements, but when talking about facts, habits, or ongoing actions it is OK to keep the original tense.**
*"I'm **going to** buy a new phone."*
*She said she **is going to** buy a new phone.*

4 SPEAKING

A PAIR WORK **How do you use messaging apps like WhatsApp? Check (✓) the statements that describe you. Then compare answers with a partner.**

- ☐ I use messaging apps for practical purposes only.
- ☐ I use them for all kinds of communication.
- ☐ I use them for work.
- ☐ If I really miss somebody, I prefer to call them.
- ☐ I don't use them. Having contact with people far away makes me miss them more.
- ☐ I only use written text. I don't like to leave voice messages.
- ☐ I use messaging apps to call people. Texting is too slow.

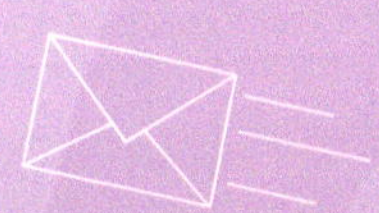

B GROUP WORK **Join another pair of students. Report your answers to the other pair. What similarities and differences did you find?**

Bernard said that he used WhatsApp for everything, for work and pleasure.

Celia stated that she only uses it for meeting friends.

7.2 TO TEXT OR NOT TO TEXT

LESSON OBJECTIVE

- discuss written vs. spoken communication

1 LANGUAGE IN CONTEXT

A 2.03 **Read and listen to the first part of an interview about a research study on communication. What questions were people asked?**

2.03 Audio script

Host	On today's podcast, we look at some research on digital technology and how it is affecting how we communicate. We have here Professor Dorothy Zárraga from Brown University. Dr. Zárraga, tell us about your research.
Dr Zárraga	Well, we interviewed people from different age groups to see if different generations communicate differently.
Host	And what types of questions did you ask?
Dr Zárraga	We asked some questions about how they preferred to communicate. For example, we asked if they preferred to text or speak face to face. And we also asked them why they had that preference. We asked who they thought it was appropriate to text. Oh, and we also asked them when they thought it was inappropriate to text. Finally, we asked if they had social media accounts and how often they posted to them.
Host	Well, it all sounds very interesting. Let's talk about your findings.

B 2.04 **Now listen to the full interview and check (✓) the statements that are true.**

- ☐ 1 Millennials prefer digital communication, except at work.
- ☐ 2 Older people felt that text messages are professional enough for work.
- ☐ 3 All age groups reported using text messages to communicate with other family members at home.

2 VOCABULARY: Communicating online

FIND IT

A 2.05 **Listen and say the words and phrases in the box. Which things can you identify in the picture? You can use your phone or a dictionary to help you.**

clickbait	geo-tag	hashtag
lifecaster	lurker	meme
newsfeed	podcaster	profile
status update	tag	timeline
trending topic		

B **Now go to page 147. Do the vocabulary exercises for 7.2.**

C PAIR WORK **Answer the questions.**

- What do you usually click on when you're looking at social media (photos, memes, trending topics)?
- What clickbait do you enjoy (animal videos, "Ten best" lists, celebrity gossip, personality quizzes, etc.)? What are some possible consequences of looking at clickbait?

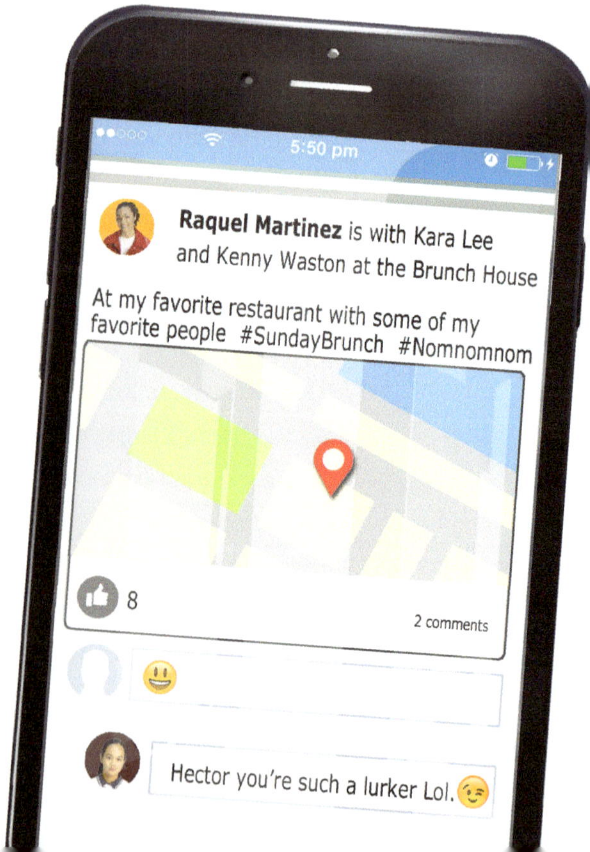

3 GRAMMAR: Reported questions

A **Choose the correct words to complete the rules. Use the sentences in the grammar box to help you.**

1. To report a question, **use** / **do not use** a question mark at the end of the sentence.
2. In a reported question, the subject comes **before** / **after** the verb. **Use** / **Do not use** the auxiliary *do/does* or *did*.
3. To report a *yes/no* question or a question about specific preferences, use ***that*** / ***if***.
4. As with reported statements, verbs in reported questions change to the **present** / **past**.

Reported questions

Question		Reported question
"Do you prefer to communicate by text or face to face?"	→	We asked them if they preferred to communicate by text or face to face.
"Who do you think it is appropriate to text?"	→	We asked them who they thought it was appropriate to text.
"How often do you post to social media?"	→	We asked them how often they posted to social media.

B **Now go to page 136. Do the grammar exercise for 7.2.**

C PAIR WORK **Think of some questions that you were asked recently. Report them and your answers to your partner. Check your accuracy.**

A friend asked me if I wanted to go to the movies tonight. I said yes.

A guy asked me where the tourist information office was. I didn't know!

✓ **ACCURACY** CHECK

When reporting questions, remember to use the word order of an affirmative sentence.

She asked what ~~did I do?~~ ✗
She asked me what I did. ✓

4 SPEAKING

A PAIR WORK **Look at the questions. Choose two or three to ask and answer.**

- Do you prefer to contact your coworkers by email, text message, or phone? Why? What about good friends or family?
- Who do you text most frequently? How often do you see that person face to face?
- Do you ever contact people via a social media message board? Why do you (or would you) use that kind of communication?

B PAIR WORK **Report the questions you were asked and the answers you gave to a different partner.**

Maria asked me if I preferred to contact coworkers by email, text, or phone. I said that I liked to call people. It's much quicker.

7.3 AND I'M LIKE …

LESSON OBJECTIVE

- recount conversations, news, and stories

1 FUNCTIONAL LANGUAGE

A 2.06 **Look at the photos. What do you think the story behind them is? Read and listen to the conversations. Which conversation are the photos about? What do the stories have in common?**

2.06 Audio script

1 A **I heard that** David missed Andrew's wedding because he lost his phone. **Apparently,** he had all the info in there!

B That's not what I heard. **Someone told me** that he "accidentally" overslept.

A What? Who told you that?

B Lauren. She asked him if he was upset about missing the wedding, and **he was like**, "Of course!" But **she was like**, "You don't look upset." Well, **turns out**, he was mad at Andrew and just didn't want to go.

2 A **You'll never believe what happened to** Marta! She was in a meeting at work, and **what happened was,** she fell asleep, right there in front of her boss!

B You're kidding!

A **The funny thing was**, she had been up all night preparing for that meeting!

B What did her boss do?

A At first he looked angry, but **in the end**, he laughed about it. Now it's a big joke around the office.

B Really? I'm not sure that's any better!

B **Complete the chart with the bold expressions from the conversations.**

Recounting a conversation or story
I [1] ______________ that (David missed the wedding).
Apparently, …
Someone [2] ______________ me that …
He was [3] ______________, "(Of course.)"
Well, turns out, …
You'll never [4] ______________ / guess what happened to …
What [5] ______________ was, …
The funny / strange [6] ______________ was, …
In the [7] ______________, (he laughed about it).

C 2.07 **Complete the conversation using expressions from the chart. Listen and check. Then practice the conversation with a partner. Change some of the key information and do it again.**

A Barbara didn't come to work yesterday. She said she was sick.

B What? I sat with her on the bus. She wasn't sick.

A I know! Well, [1] ______________ ______________, she had an interview for another job.

B I thought so! She was wearing a very nice suit, and I'm [2] ______________, "You must have a job interview!" But she denied it.

A The [3] ______________ ______________ was, the person who interviewed her called me to ask if she was a good employee! [4] ______________, Barbara wrote *me* down as a reference.

B Ha! I guess her secret isn't a secret anymore!

2 REAL-WORLD STRATEGY

GETTING BACK ON TRACK

Sometimes you get interrupted or go off the topic when you're telling a story. You can use these expressions to get back on track.

As I was saying …

Where was I? Oh yeah, …

What was I saying?

I lost my train of thought!

A 2.08 **Read the box about getting a conversation back on track. Then listen to another conversation. How does the listener interrupt? What does the speaker say to get them back on track?**

B PAIR WORK **Student A: Tell one of the stories from exercise 1A. Deal with any interruptions from Student B. Student B: Interrupt Student A's story two times. Student A: Get the conversation back on track. Switch roles and tell the other story.**

3 PRONUNCIATION FOCUS: Saying /s/ or /z/ at the end of a word

A 2.09 **Listen and repeat. Focus on the sound of the bold letters.**

/s/ course /z/ was

B 2.10 **Listen. Write A for words with /s/. Write B for words with /z/.**

1 boss ___ 3 bus ___ 5 office ___

2 as ___ 4 turns ___ 6 lose ___

C PAIR WORK **Say the words in exercise 3B to your partner. Does your partner say the /s/ and /z/ sounds clearly?**

4 SPEAKING

A **Work in pairs. Student A: Go to page 158. Student B: Go to page 160. Read each story and act out a conversation for each one. Add details as you go.**

You'll never guess what happened! Gabrielle won first prize out of 20 candidates in the painting contest at school.

I know! And the funny thing is, she was the youngest one!

7.4 THE EMOJI CODE

LESSON OBJECTIVE

- write an email in a formal and informal register

1 READING

A PAIR WORK **Look at the pictures. In what contexts do you think the emoji and hashtag were used? In what situations do people generally use emojis, hashtags, and abbreviations (e.g. LOL)?**

The #Paris might be to promote tourism.

B READ FOR MAIN IDEAS **Read the article from a student website and take notes. What is Dr. Patel's main argument? What is Prof. Yilmaz's main argument?**

IT'S A #WORLD

We all know that languages grow and change over time, new words are added to the dictionary, and old ones are removed. But what do we do with things like emojis and hashtags? They help us communicate, but are they language? We asked two professors for their opinions.

Arundhati Patel, professor of linguistics, says yes. Emojis are language because when you send a 😃 or a 😫, your message is immediately clear. Modern communication symbols are like body language – they help you express yourself.

Daniel Yilmaz, professor of English, disagrees. "There is a reason that the English language has more than 100,000 words in common use," he said. Real communication is complicated.

Symbols reduce our thoughts to simple personal opinions: #IhateMondays, 😣. Language, on the other hand, expresses deeper thoughts and complex ideas.

"But most of our daily communication needs are simple," Dr. Patel pointed out, "so why not satisfy them simply?" Prof. Yilmaz believes this "simplicity" is actually laziness. On most smartphones, for example, emoji menus come up automatically, so people take the easy road.

Dr. Patel and Prof. Yilmaz agree on one thing: hashtags are not language, they are politics. They unite people around ideas and attitudes.

So the debate continues. Do these modern communication symbols belong in the dictionary or not? Do we really have to decide? 😕

C IDENTIFY OPINIONS **Read the article again and answer the questions.**

1 Why does Dr. Patel think modern communication symbols are the same as language? What comparison does he make?

2 Why does Prof. Yilmaz claim emojis are not language? What does he think of emoji menus on smartphones?

3 What do the two professors agree on? What is their shared opinion?

FIND IT

D THINK CRITICALLY PAIR WORK **Do you think symbols help people communicate better? Why or why not? You can use your phone to find examples to support your opinion. For ideas, watch Alessandra's video.**

REAL STUDENT

Do you agree with Alessandra?

2 WRITING

A **Look at the two emails. In what context would you read each one? How do you know? What is the difference between them?**

Email A

Reply Forward

To: Patrick
From: Melanie
Subject: Final figures

Hi Patrick,

How's things? Strange day at the office. Very boring meeting! – 😴 then big meal 🍔. But can meet 2:30ish?? Have to be at the docs at 4 😷

Ok with you??? Let me know when you get a sec.

Speak soon!

😘

Melanie

Email B

Reply Forward

To: Patrick
From: Melanie
Subject: Final figures

Dear Patrick,

I'm writing to see if we can find a time to meet later today. We need to go over the final figures together. I have a meeting all morning, and I'm meeting a client for lunch. I can meet around 2:30, but I'll need to leave at 4 for a doctor's appointment.

Does that time suit you? If not, could you suggest another time?

Looking forward to speaking with you,

Melanie

B WRITING SKILL **Identify the elements of informal register in email A and formal register in email B. How do the emojis change the register?**

C **Find the formal equivalents in email B for these informal phrases in email A.**

Informal	**Formal**
Very boring meeting!	*I have a meeting all morning.*
OK with you???	
Speak soon!	

D GROUP WORK **Think of other information that you could include in email B (formal). Check the elements that would be appropriate. Which of them would be appropriate for an informal email, too?**

- **a** Gossip ☐
- **b** Your health ☐
- **c** Changes at work ☐
- **d** Scheduling meetings ☐
- **e** Free time – weekend plans ☐
- **f** Question about a work problem ☐

WRITE IT

E **Write two short emails – one formal message to a coworker and one informal message to a friend. In both messages, update the person on what you have been doing at work or in your free time and include plans to meet. Be sure to use different registers in the two messages. Write a maximum of 100 words in each email.**

F PAIR WORK **Read your emails. Identify different elements of formal and informal register. Are the appropriate words and phrases used in each message?**

7.5

TIME TO SPEAK
Online Communication Survey

LESSON OBJECTIVE

- create and conduct a communication survey

A **PREPARE** Look at the pictures. How are these people using their smartphones? What are some other ways to use a smartphone? How many of the uses are related to communicating with someone?

B **DISCUSS** With a partner, read the survey about online communication and add some questions of your own. Then answer all of the questions and take notes on your answers.

1 How many social media accounts do you have? What do you use each one for?
2 How many text messages do you write every day? Who to?
3 How many calls do you make every day? Who to?
4 How do you keep up with the news? Which source do you use most? Why?
5 ______
6 ______
7 ______

C **PRESENT** Report your results to the class and listen to the other results. Then, with your partner, draw conclusions about the full results of the survey.

D **AGREE** Share your conclusions with the class. Did everyone reach the same or similar conclusions? Discuss the points you disagree on.

To check your progress, go to page 155.

USEFUL PHRASES

PREPARE
To me, these images mean …
I think they represent …

DISCUSS
I think we should ask about …
So, which social media sites … ?
My favorite news source is … because …

PRESENT
The results of this survey clearly show …
From this survey, we can conclude …
The results don't give us enough information on …

8 LIFESTYLES

UNIT OBJECTIVES:

- talk about different work lifestyles
- talk about wishes and regrets
- talking through options to reach a decision
- write a comment about a podcast
- plan and discuss a digital detox weekend for your class

START SPEAKING

A **Look at the people in the picture. What words would you use to describe them? What do you think their lifestyle is like?**

B **Think about your work life (current or future). Will your job determine what kind of lifestyle you have, or will you choose a job that matches the lifestyle you want? For ideas, watch Maryne's video.**

REAL STUDENT

Are your answers the same as Maryne's?

8.1 THE PERFECT JOB?

LESSON OBJECTIVE
- talk about different working lifestyles

1 LANGUAGE IN CONTEXT

A **Look at the picture and its caption in the post below. What job is the ad for? Read the full post. Is the writer interested in applying for the job? Why or why not?**

If you saw this job ad on your timeline, would you click to find out more? I did, along with 300,000 other people!

The island of Maatsuyker in Tasmania is looking for two temporary caretakers to live on the island for six months each. No television or internet access. The work is not very stressful, as the lighthouse runs automatically. The caretaker's job is basically to report on data from the weather station, so it's not a tough job. It rains a lot, but the views and the wildlife are amazing. Everybody who visits falls in love with the island.

Island seeks lighthouse caretaker for six months.
Click here to apply!

What was your first reaction? Would you enjoy being cut off from the rest of the world for six months? Does that sound like your dream job?

I'm not so sure I could do it! Maybe if I was single and didn't have kids I might do it. But with a family, I need a permanent job – preferably one that's high-paying! What about you? If you were free to do it, would you apply for this job?

FIND IT

B PAIR WORK **Do you think you could do the job described in the ad? Why or why not? You can use your phones to find out more about the island before you answer.**

2 VOCABULARY: Describing jobs

FIND IT

A 2.11 **Listen and say the words in the box. Which ones are in the post? Do they have a positive or negative meaning? What about the other words? Look them up in a dictionary or on your phone if needed.**

challenging	desk job	dream job	freelance	full-time
government job	high-paying	main job	part-time	permanent
second job	stressful	temporary	tiring	tough

B **Which words in the box are useful to give a factual description of a job? Underline them. Which words express an opinion? Circle them.**

C **Now go to page 148. Do the vocabulary exercises for 8.1.**

D PAIR WORK **Describe the jobs in the box using the descriptions in exercise A.**

babysitter	doctor	firefighter
lifeguard	fashion designer	sales assistant

Well, being a babysitter is probably a part-time job, and it isn't very high-paying, but it is very challenging.

3 GRAMMAR: Present unreal conditionals

A **Read the sentences in the grammar box. Then complete the rules.**

Present unreal conditionals

If you **saw** this ad on your timeline, **would** you **click** to find out more?

If you **were** free to do it, **would** you **apply** for this job?

If I **was** single and **didn't have** kids and **wanted** to write a book or something, I **might do** it.

REGISTER CHECK

In formal language, use *were* for all subjects, including 1st and 3rd person.

If I were selected, I would devote myself to it.

In informal language, you can use *was* for 1st and 3rd person subjects.

If I / she was feeling better, I / she would go.

1 The sentences refer to **a real** / **an imagined** situation.

2 Look at the **bold** verbs. The verb form that follows *if* is **simple present** / **simple past**. It **refers** / **doesn't refer** to a past situation.

B **Now go to page 136. Look at the grammar chart and do the grammar exercise for 8.1.**

C PAIR WORK **Complete the questions with the correct form of the verb in parentheses ( ). Ask and answer the questions with your partner.**

1 If you ________ ________ (can do) any job in the world, what job ________ you ________ (choose)? Why?

2 ________ you ________ (consider) doing a job you loved if you ________ (not be) paid well? Why or why not?

3 What ________ you ________ (do) with your free time if you ________ ________ ________ (not have to) work?

4 SPEAKING

A **Read about two more jobs. How are they similar to the lighthouse caretaker job?**

Resort caretaker: In the summer we work with the tourists, but in the winter, it's just my wife and me. It snows a lot and the mountains are beautiful. There's a lot of work to do maintaining all the buildings, but there's plenty of free time, too. And the wildlife is fantastic! Last winter we had bears come to visit us. That was awesome!

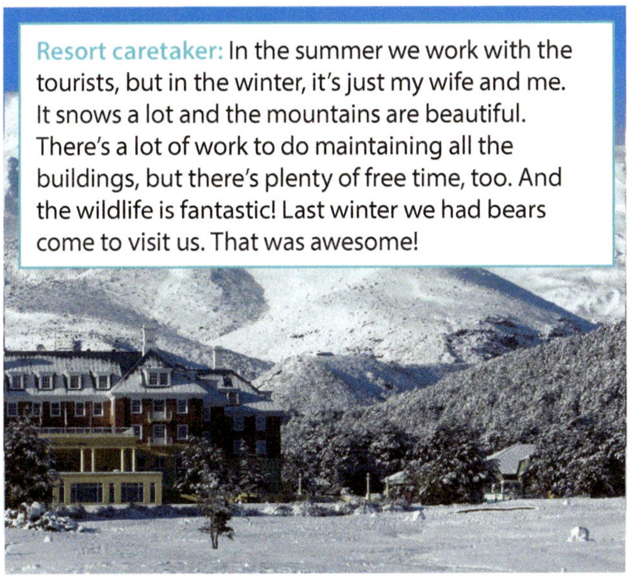

Drone pilot: I'm working with a team to help study seabirds. Using drones, I get amazing pictures of the birds in their nests with their babies. The scientists who run the project come about once a month, but mostly we have the island to ourselves. Our housing and food are pretty basic, but I'm learning a lot, and getting college credit!

B PAIR WORK **If you had to choose one of the three jobs in this lesson, which one would you choose? Why? What do you think daily life would be like?**

If I was the resort caretaker, I'd have a lot of free time to do all kinds of snow sports.

If a drone pilot was a high-paying job, I'd pick that one.

8.2 FINDING A BALANCE

LESSON OBJECTIVE
- talk about wishes and regrets

1 LANGUAGE IN CONTEXT

A 2.12 **Listen to a psychologist discussing the problem of finding the right work/life balance. What solution does she suggest?**

B 2.12 **Listen again and read the script. Find at least three examples of things we associate with work and three things we associate with free time.**

2.12 Audio script

Have you ever said, "I wish I didn't have to work such long hours?" Whether you're an executive with one meeting after another, a full-time student attending **lectures** and **seminars**, or a parent who works the late **shift**, the problem is always the same – How can I have a life with such a **busy schedule**?

I hear it all the time: I wish I had more time for **family life**, I wish I hadn't promised to work this weekend, I wish I could take some **time off**, I wish I had more **me time**! There are hundreds of articles out there about how to balance work and life, but we need to stop seeing work and life as two opposing forces that we have to balance. We need to think about how to *combine* them.

Take this example: a client of mine now schedules **downtime** into his working day. He takes a short walk, has a relaxing lunch with a friend, or goes home a little early to spend time with the kids. Then, after they're asleep, he sits down and writes that report he needs for tomorrow.

Making your job and your life work together is a great way to enjoy them both.

C PAIR WORK **Do you think it's a good idea to combine your work or school life with your social life? Why or why not?**

2 VOCABULARY: Talking about work/life balance

FIND IT

A 2.13 PAIR WORK **Listen and say the words and phrases in the box. Discuss where they should go in the Venn diagram. You can use your phone or a dictionary to help you.**

always connected	assignments	busy schedule	chilling out	commitments
downtime	family life	lectures	me time	office hours
seminars	shift	social life	time off	9-to-5

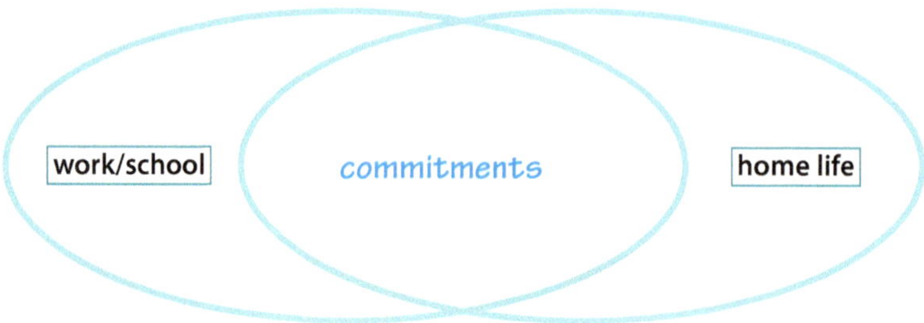

Commitments: I guess that could be work, school, or home life. Let's put it in the middle.

B **Now go to page 148. Do the vocabulary exercises for 8.2.**

C GROUP WORK **Do you feel you have a busy schedule? Do you get enough downtime? Is your downtime also "me time"?**

3 GRAMMAR: *I wish*

A **Choose the correct words to complete the rules. Use the sentences in the grammar box to help you.**

1 *"I wish"* sentences express that you want things to **stay the same / be different**.

2 The main verb of the sentence **stays in the same tense / changes tense**. The modal *"can"* **stays the same / changes to** ***could***.

3 Affirmative statements **change to negative / stay affirmative**.

4 Negative statements **change to affirmative / stay negative.**

I wish

I **have to** work long hours.	→	I wish I **didn't have to** work such long hours.
I **don't have** much free time.	→	I wish I **had** more free time.
I **can't take** any time off next week.	→	I wish I **could take** some time off next week.
I **promised** to work this weekend.	→	I wish I **hadn't promised** to work this weekend.

B **Now go to page 137. Look at the grammar chart and do the grammar exercise for 8.2.**

C PAIR WORK **Complete the wishes so that they are true for you. Review them with a partner and check your accuracy.**

1 I wish I knew ______

2 I wish I could ______

3 I wish I wasn't/weren't ______

4 I wish I didn't have to ______

5 I wish I hadn't ______

6 I wish I had ______

ACCURACY CHECK

Don't confuse *wish* and *hope*. Use *hope* to talk about something you want to happen in the future.

I hope you'll be there on Saturday.

Use *wish* to talk about a situation you can't change.

I wish you could come on Saturday, but I know you have to work.

4 SPEAKING

A PAIR WORK **Look at the list of wishes. Which do you think are the most common? Why?**

I wish I had gone to a different college.
I wish I had studied harder in high school.
I wish I could play a musical instrument.
I wish I could get a different job.
I wish I could travel more.
I wish I was younger.
I wish I was older.

B PAIR WORK **Think of three more common wishes. Who might have them? Compare your ideas with other students. For ideas, watch Seung Geyong's video.**

REAL STUDENT

Are any of your wishes the same as Seung Geyong's?

8.3 I WOULDN'T DO THAT!

LESSON OBJECTIVE:
- talking through options to reach a decision

1 FUNCTIONAL LANGUAGE

A 2.14 **Laura has a meeting on Saturday morning but she doesn't want to go. Listen to Laura and her mother discussing Laura's options. What do you think Laura decides to do?**

2.14 Audio script

A Great! My boss just scheduled a meeting for Saturday. It's going to take so long to get there and get back, you know, with the weekend train schedule.

B Too bad, Laura. **Is there any way you can** get out of it?

A Well, I guess I could stay at a hotel Friday night, but that's expensive.

B Well, it's a possibility, but it isn't ideal. **Have you tried talking** to your boss? **If I were in your shoes,** I'd explain the situation and offer an alternative. I mean, **it can't hurt,** right?

A I guess I could, but what alternative?

B Well, **you might want to** suggest meeting up on Monday morning to catch up, or **maybe you could** offer to attend remotely instead? **I'd try that if I were you.**

A Yeah, I guess I could ask him if I could attend by phone or Skype.

B **It wouldn't hurt** to ask. I mean, **you've got nothing to lose.**

B **Complete the chart with the bold expressions from the conversation.**

Talking through options
Is there any [1] ______ you can (get out of it)?
Have you [2] ______ (talking to him)?
If I were in your [3] ______, I'd (explain the situation).
You might [4] ______ to (suggest meeting on Monday).
Maybe you [5] ______ (offer to attend remotely).
Encouraging actions
It can't [6] ______.
I'd (try that) if I [7] ______ you.
It wouldn't [8] ______ (to ask).
You've got nothing to [9] ______.

INSIDER ENGLISH

You can use *I guess* to consider suggestions.

I guess I could.

I guess it wouldn't hurt.

C 2.15 PAIR WORK **Complete the conversation with phrases from the chart. Listen and check your answers. Then practice the conversation.**

A I really don't want to go out to dinner tonight. I'm so tired, but I promised Ellen.

B [1] ______ suggesting another time?

A Yes, but she's leaving for school tomorrow. I'd really like to see her before she goes.

B Well, you might [2] ______ ask her to meet up earlier. Or maybe you [3] ______ invite her over to your place instead? I'd try that [4] ______ I were you.

A Yeah, that's a great idea. I'll text her now. Thanks!

2 REAL-WORLD STRATEGY

A 2.16 **Listen to two short conversations. What's the situation in each?**

OFFERING A WARNING

Sometimes you want to encourage someone *not* to do something.

You don't want to do that!
I wouldn't do that if I were you.
You might not want to do that.
I'd avoid that if I were you.

B 2.16 **Read the information about warnings in the box and then listen again. What warning is offered in each conversation? What advice is given?**

C PAIR WORK **Read each statement and discuss why it's a bad idea. What warning would you give? What would you suggest instead?**

1 "I need to cancel a meeting with my boss for this morning. I think I'm going to tell him I'm sick."
2 "I really don't want to go to Dale's birthday party tonight. I think I just won't go."
3 "I really should study tonight. I did really bad on the last test. But I think I'll go to Ben's party instead.

3 PRONUNCIATION FOCUS: Saying the vowel sounds /ɜ/ and /u/

A 2.17 **Listen and repeat the two different vowel sounds.**

/ɜ/ hurt It wouldn't hurt to ask. /u/ lose You have nothing to lose.

B 2.18 **Listen. Write A for words with /ɜ/. Write B for words with /u/.**

1 schedule ___	3 you ___	5 birthday ___
2 alternative ___	4 school ___	6 few ___

C 2.19 PAIR WORK **Listen to the conversations. Then practice with a partner.**

1 A What are **you** doing for your b**ir**thday?
B Not much. I have to go to sch**oo**l.

2 A This r**oo**m is a little small. Should we ask for a nicer one?
B It can't h**ur**t to ask. We've got nothing to l**o**se.

4 SPEAKING

A **Choose one of the topics and think of a situation where someone might have many options to consider. Make notes about different options and the kind of advice you could offer.**

family health money relationships studies work

Health: someone wants to get in shape
Advice: start swimming, running, bicycling; do yoga, zumba; take an exercise class

B PAIR WORK **Use your notes to act out the situation. Decide who is going to ask for advice and who is going to give it. Try to include a warning as well. Then switch roles.**

8.4 DIGITAL DETOX

LESSON OBJECTIVE

- write a comment about a podcast

1 LISTENING

A PAIR WORK **Look at the pictures. What are the main differences between the two situations? Which one do you think shows a more positive use of mobile technology? Why?**

B 2.20 LISTEN FOR ATTITUDE **Listen to an extract from a podcast about mobile technology. What is a "digital detox"? How do the two speakers, Tim and Kayla, feel about the idea? Would you ever consider a digital detox?**

C 2.20 PAIR WORK **Read the extracts. Who do you think said each one? Write *T* (Tim) or *K* (Kayla). How do you know? Listen again to check your answers.**

1 I love my phone too much! ____
2 I would never do that, not for a million dollars! ____
3 You don't always have to share everything. ____
4 What's wrong with sharing? ____
5 It's so important that we know what's going on in the world. ____
6 I could be doing something better. ____
7 I am very happy with my 24/7, always connected life. ____

INSIDER ENGLISH

The phrase *not for a million dollars* is often used to show strong dislike for an idea.

I'd never give up my phone – not for a million dollars!

D CRITICAL THINKING **Who do you agree with more? Do you think people need to learn how to control their use of digital devices? Do you think a digital detox is the best way? Can you think of other ways?**

2 PRONUNCIATION: Listening for emphasis

A 2.21 **Listen to the extracts from the podcast. Focus on how the speaker says the bold words.**

1 A digital detox, me? Are you kidding? No way, I love my phone **way** too much.
2 I'm glad you stepped up, Tim, because I would **never** do that!
3 We did it in this cabin out in the forest, and it was **really** quiet and relaxing.

B **Choose the correct words to complete the sentence.**

When a speaker wants to add emphasis to an idea, they often say the word *higher* / *stronger* and *shorter* / *longer.*

3 WRITING

A **Read the two comments that were left on the podcast. Which one was written by the podcast host and which one by a listener? How do you know?**

Comments

Sign out Account

1 I really enjoyed listening to this week's podcast. Good for you, Tim, trying a digital detox! It's something I've thought about. If I had the time, I'd do it. There was one thing in particular that interested me in your conversation, when you were talking about sharing photos. It made me think of how I use social media to keep in touch with friends and family that I don't get to see that often. I don't think I'd be as good at keeping in touch if I didn't have social media. Do you think social media might actually help us have better social relationships? And, as Kayla said, it is important to keep up with what is going on in the world. Looking forward to hearing your opinion!

Share Like Comment

2 Hi there. Thanks for leaving your comment. That's a really interesting question, and I'm really not sure how to answer it. You point out that social media makes it easier to keep in contact with friends and family. Personally, I think face-to-face contact with people is always better, and nothing beats spending time with someone. But if they live in another city or country or something, then I guess maybe smartphones and social media do help a lot. I wonder what other people have to say about that!

Share Like Comment

B WRITING SKILL **Look at the two comments again. <u>Underline</u> the phrases that reference another person's statement or opinion.**

C PAIR WORK **Read the comments again. Do you think smartphones help us have better social relationships? Why or why not?**

WRITE IT

D **Write a response to the two comments. Remember to 1) refer back to both the question and the answer, 2) make a positive reference to the podcast, and 3) invite other opinions on the topic.**

8.5

TIME TO SPEAK
Planning a digital detox

LESSON OBJECTIVE
- plan and discuss a digital detox weekend for your class

A **DISCUSS** **As a class, discuss this question: If you had to live without your phone for a week, how would that affect your day-to-day life? Think of all the things you usually do with your phone. What would you miss the most?**

B **You and a partner are going to arrange a digital detox weekend for your class. Think of the answers your classmates gave. Who do you think would suffer the most from the detox? Why?**

C **A TV company is going to sponsor your weekend and make a documentary about the experience. Think about these things:**

- Where could you hold the detox? Think of places in or near your city.
- What facilities would you need? Think of alternatives to digital devices, for example, a gym or a library.
- What activities would you like to offer? How could you help people when they're missing their phones? Think of a variety of different activities for both daytime and evening hours.

There are some big houses by the beach. We'd need lots of bedrooms but just one kitchen. A gym would be great, and if we had a library, people could still read, just not on their tablets. Our experience is going to be filmed, so we should have some conflicts too, for drama, like some sports activities.

D **DECIDE** **Create a plan for the weekend. Include this information:**

- what time the program starts on Friday and ends on Sunday
- morning, afternoon, and evening activity choices for the full three days

E **PRESENT** **Present your program to the class. Answer any questions from the audience.**

F **AGREE** **Which pair of students has planned the best program? Why do you think so?**

To check your progress, go to page 155.

USEFUL PHRASES

DISCUSS
If I had to …, I think I'd …
I'd really miss …
If we held the detox [place], then people might …

DECIDE
I think we should / could …
Why don't we … ?
What about … ?

PRESENT
We decided / thought that …
We chose to …
We want to / We'd like to …

UNIT OBJECTIVES

- talk about rules and regulations in your everyday life
- discuss rules and regulations in the past
- make generalizations
- write a letter of complaint
- discuss improvements to your town

YES, YOU CAN!

9

START SPEAKING

A **Look at the signs. What does the original sign mean? Describe how it was changed. Do you think this is funny? Why or why not?**

B **Think of another way the sign could be altered and draw it. Compare your design with the rest of the class. Who has the best one?**

C **What interesting graffiti or street art can you see in or around your neighborhood? For ideas, watch Seung Geyong's video.**

REAL STUDENT

Have you ever seen something similar?

9.1 READING THE SIGNS

LESSON OBJECTIVE
- talk about rules and regulations in your everyday life

1 LANGUAGE IN CONTEXT

A 2.22 PAIR WORK **Look at the signs. What do you think they mean? Listen to two people discussing some of the signs. Check (✓) the ones they mention. Were you right about their meanings?**

A ☐ B ☐ C ☐ D ☐ E ☐ F ☐ G ☐ H ☐ I ☐

2.22 Audio script

Bart So many signs everywhere! *No parking, No skateboards, No entry* …

Luisi There's one saying you aren't supposed to bring your pets inside. And there, you *are* allowed to bring your guide dog inside.

Bart And look there! You're required to wear a hard hat on the **construction site**.

Luisi That makes sense, but I've noticed some strange ones recently. Outside the **arts center** one said you aren't allowed to wear a hoodie inside! I think it's so someone can't hide their face – the security cameras should be able to see you clearly.

Bart Oh, I get it. I saw a cool sign at **city hall**, just outside the **courthouse**. It's a pair of hands and a speech bubble. It means that you may request a sign language interpreter if you need one.

Luisi Hey, that *is* cool! Oh! I saw a really strange one on the **boardwalk** – it was a wheelchair underwater!

Bart A wheelchair underwater? I don't get it.

Luisi It means there's no access for wheelchairs. Like, it's not physically possible for wheelchairs to get to the beach.

Bart Oh. That's a shame.

2 VOCABULARY: Talking about places

FIND IT

A 2.23 PAIR WORK **Listen and say the words in the box. Look up the ones you don't know on your phone or in a dictionary. Which sign(s) from exercise 1A would you expect to see in each place?**

arts center	boardwalk	city hall	consulate
construction site	courthouse	highway rest stop	laboratory
playground	public space	residential area	toll plaza

INSIDER ENGLISH

I get it **or** ***I don't get it*** **means that you do or don't understand something.**

What? I don't get it.

B **Now go to page 149. Do the vocabulary exercises for 9.1.**

C PAIR WORK **What other signs do you see around you every day? Where do you see them? Do people generally obey these signs? Are there any signs that people sometimes ignore?**

There are "no cell phones" signs in the movie theater. I wish more people obeyed them!

3 GRAMMAR: Prohibition, permission, obligation (present)

Prohibition, permission, obligation (present)

Prohibition	You **may not** skateboard here.
	You **aren't allowed to** wear a hoodie.
	You **aren't supposed to** bring your pets inside.
Permission	You **are allowed to** bring in your guide dog.
	You **may** request an interpreter.
Obligation	The cameras **should** be able to see you.
	You**'re required to** wear a hard hat.
	You**'re supposed to** ring the bell for service.

A **Read the sentences in the grammar box. Then circle all the correct answers to complete the rules.**

1 Prohibition can also be expressed with …

a *can't* **b** *must not* **c** *won't*

2 Permission can also be expressed with …

a *want to* **b** *would like to* **c** *can*

3 Obligation or necessity can also be expressed with …

a *(don't) need to* **b** *(don't) have to* **c** *shouldn't*

B **Now go to page 137. Look at the grammar chart and do the grammar exercise for 9.1.**

C GROUP WORK **Choose one of the places in the box or another place that everyone knows. Think of at least five rules for that place. Use different structures from the grammar box in your rules.**

airport terminal campground hospital school theater

D **Read your rules to the class. Can anyone guess which place it is?**

4 SPEAKING

A GROUP WORK **Discuss the questions.**

- What rules and regulations do you have to follow at work or school? In your house or apartment?
- Which rules would you like to change or get rid of completely? Why?
- What new rules would you like to introduce? Why?

B GROUP WORK **Choose two of the rules you'd like to introduce (from the previous exercise) and draw a sign to illustrate them. Show them to the class. Can they guess what your rules are?**

My new rule is "no one is allowed to chew gum in the study area."

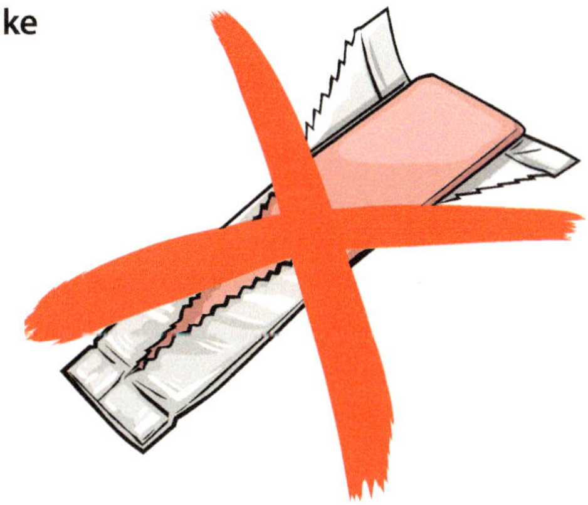

9.2 RULES OF THE ROAD

LESSON OBJECTIVE
- discuss rules and regulations in the past

1 LANGUAGE IN CONTEXT

A **Look at the pictures. What can you see in each one? What traffic rules are represented? Imagine driving in a city where there were no traffic rules. What would happen?**

B **Read this article about William Eno. What's the connection with the pictures above?**

STOP and GO

Before cars were invented, horse-drawn carriages were allowed to circulate freely. There were no signs to **control** traffic and no speed **limits**. As cars started to appear on the streets, rules that would **permit** traffic to flow safely were desperately needed.

In 1903, William Eno published "Rules for Driving" – the first official traffic code. Drivers had to drive on the right, they were supposed to show other drivers when they wanted to turn, and they were **prohibited** from parking on the left. His greatest innovations were the traffic circle and one-way streets, which **obliged** all traffic to travel in the same direction. He also helped introduce crosswalks to protect pedestrians. At the same time, new laws **required** vehicles to be **registered** and have license plates and also **banned** drivers under sixteen, though drivers did not have to take a driving test until 1934.

The most curious thing about Eno, the father of road safety, was that he never learned to drive a car!

GLOSSARY
license plate (*n*) a sign on a car that shows its registration number

C **Read the article again. Check (✓) the statements that you can infer from the text. Find information in the text to support your answers and underline it.**

- ☐ **1** Before cars, there were very few problems with traffic in big cities like New York.
- ☐ **2** There was no traffic code before cars.
- ☐ **3** Eno's "Rules for Driving" included more than just rules for drivers.
- ☐ **4** Eno was not physically able to drive a car.

2 VOCABULARY: Talking about rules

A 2.24 **Complete the chart. What idea do the words express? Write *M* (must), *A* (allowed), *N* (not allowed), or *R* (rules apply). Listen and check.**

verb	noun	meaning
	ban	
control		R
limit		
	obligation	

verb	noun	meaning
	permission	
	prohibition	
register		
	requirement	

B **Now go to page 149. Do the vocabulary exercises for 9.2.**

C GROUP WORK **What are three problems caused by traffic where you live? Suggest solutions for each of the problems. For ideas, watch Nicolle's video.**

REAL STUDENT

Do you agree with Nicolle?

3 GRAMMAR: Prohibition, permission, obligation (past)

A **Complete the sets. Use the sentences in the grammar box to help you. Then decide which set each example sentence belongs to: *A*, *B*, or *C*.**

A To express prohibition in the past: *couldn't*, ________

B To express permission in the past: *could*, ________

C To express obligation in the past: *had to*, ________

Prohibition, permission, obligation (past)

Carriages **were allowed to** circulate freely before 1903.	B
Eno's rules said that drivers **had to** drive on the right.	
They **were not allowed to** stop in the middle of the street.	
Pedestrians **were required to** cross at the crosswalk.	

B **Now go to page 138. Look at the grammar chart and do the grammar exercise for 9.2.**

C GROUP WORK **Write three rules from your childhood. Use three different structures from the grammar box, and check your accuracy. Read your rules to the group. Whose parents were the strictest?**

ACCURACY CHECK

Prohibition and permission are usually expressed in the passive because the person / authority responsible for the law is known and doesn't need to be named.

City regulations allow cars to park here. (correct, but authority is known)

Cars are allowed to park here.

4 SPEAKING

A GROUP WORK **Read the laws. Three of them were real laws in the past. Which is the fake law? Why do you think people passed the real laws?**

1 You couldn't drink soda on Sunday.

2 All men were required to grow beards.

3 Female school teachers were not allowed to get married.

4 Only people who weighed more than 100 pounds (45 kilograms) could vote in elections.

FIND IT

B **Do you know any old laws from your country? Go online and find out if they are still laws. Find some strange laws from other countries, too.**

9.3 TO TIP OR NOT TO TIP?

LESSON OBJECTIVE
- make generalizations

1 FUNCTIONAL LANGUAGE

A 2.25 PAIR WORK **Look at the picture. Where is the person? How much money do you think they're giving? Listen to Charlie and Júlia talking about tipping in the U.S. Is it similar in your country?**

2.25 Audio script

A I'll pick up the check if you leave the tip, Júlia.

B OK, thanks, Charlie. But how much should I leave?

A Well, **generally speaking** we leave 15–20%.

B Really? That much? In Brazil, people don't **tend to** tip nearly as much as that. Oh! Should I tip in cafés as well, and fast food places?

A If there's no table service, we **generally** don't tip, but there may be a jar on the counter for you to drop some coins into if you want.

B I've seen that in Brazil, too. What about taxi drivers? Are you required to tip them?

A Required? No, not really, but, **on average**, people tip 5–10% of the fare.

B Ten percent! Wow, all these tips must get expensive!

A Well, you know, **on the whole,** service jobs don't pay well, so people in the service industry really rely on tips to make a living.

B **Complete the chart with the bold expressions from the conversation.**

Making generalizations

Generally [1] ________________, (we leave 15–20%).
People don't [2] ________________ to (tip so much).
We [3] ________________ (don't tip in fast food places).
On [4] ________________, (people tip 5–10%).
On the [5] ________________, (service jobs don't pay well).

! **Use *on average* with a number or quantity.**
On average, *people tip drivers 5–10% of the fare.*

C **Complete the generalizations using a phrase from the chart. Are they true in your country?**

1 ________________ speaking, we don't really give that many tips.
2 People ________________ to tip more in nicer restaurants.
3 ________________, service industry workers don't depend on tips.
4 People ________________ don't tip taxi drivers unless it's a long journey.
5 ________________, people tip around 10% in restaurants.

2 REAL-WORLD STRATEGY

A 2.26 **Listen to Júlia and Charlie discussing two other cultural differences. What are they?**

CONTRASTING INFORMATION

When you want to contrast cultural information, you can use several different expressions.

We don't tip nearly as much as that.
Really? We don't do that where I come from.
We don't do it that way in my country.
We do things differently back home.
We handle tipping differently where I come from.
That's not how we do / say it in (Portuguese).

B 2.26 **Read the information on contrasting information in the box and listen again. What phrase does Júlia use to contrast their customs each time?**

C PAIR WORK **Look at these common customs in the U.S. Are they the same in your country?**

1. The waiter refills your coffee cup at no extra charge.
2. The national anthem (national song) is played before every professional sporting event or game.
3. On an escalator, people stand on the right side and walk on the left side.

3 PRONUNCIATION FOCUS: Saying /d/ at the beginning of a word

A 2.27 **Listen and repeat. Focus on the /d/ sounds.**

1 We generally **d**on't tip. 2 We **d**o things **d**ifferently.

B 2.28 **Listen. Who says the /d/ sound? Write A or B.**

1 drop ___	3 depend ___	5 difficult ___
2 different ___	4 do ___	6 deep ___

C PAIR WORK **Say the words in exercise 3B to your partner. Does your partner say the /d/ sound clearly?**

4 SPEAKING

A **Think about a time when you visited a new town or country. In what ways were things different there?**

B PAIR WORK **Tell your partner about your impressions. React to your partner's impressions with surprise when appropriate.**

On the whole, people wear more colorful clothes than we wear back home.

9.4 THE STORY OF THE RAMP

LESSON OBJECTIVE
- write a letter of complaint

1 READING

A READ FOR GIST **Look at the picture in the article. What is the red structure? In what ways is it useful? Read the article to check your answers. Then choose the best title for the article. Why is it the best?**

a Ed Roberts and the independent living movement
b A short history of wheelchair ramps
c Student life at the University of California

Ed Roberts was the first student with significant disabilities to be allowed to attend The University of California at Berkeley. It was the 1960s, and there was no access for wheelchairs on campus. Roberts and other disability activists fought for access and even built their own ramps in the middle of the night so that wheelchair users could enter university buildings independently.

Thanks to the work of Roberts and other disability activists, the first Center for Independent Living was founded in Berkeley in 1972. It offered support for disabled students, and was staffed by people with disabilities who had personal experience of fighting for equal access. There are now more than 400 centers around the United States.

Over the next 20 years, the independent living movement grew in number and strength. In 1990, the Americans with Disabilities Act was passed. This law requires all businesses and institutions to provide access to wheelchairs, which opened up a world of new opportunities. After Robert's death in 1995, a nonprofit organization called the Ed Roberts Campus was founded in his memory. The Campus facilities provide community meeting rooms, offices for non-profit organizations, and many other community focused services. One of its most recognizable features is the famous red ramp.

There are still battles to be won, however. Wheelchair users are still fighting for their right to equal access. A ramp may seem like a very simple thing, but it's a powerful tool in supporting independent living.

B PAIR WORK RECALL KEY INFORMATION **Before you read the article again, look at the numbers and dates in the box. Can you remember what they referred to? Check your answers in the article.**

1960s 1972 400 1990 1995

C GROUP WORK THINK CRITICALLY **Think about public spaces where you live. Can wheelchairs access them easily? Is access required by law? Who do you think should pay for providing wheelchair access in shops: the business, the local authorities, charities or someone else? Why?**

2 WRITING

A **Read this message that a customer left for a restaurant owner on their website. What was the problem? What does the customer want to do? Why?**

Your message:

Last week I visited your restaurant. It was the first time I'd visited, and I was excited about going. I use a wheelchair, so building access is always a worry and going anywhere new means doing some research first. But things looked good. Fortunately, your website showed a ramp leading up into your entrance so I was confident I could get in.

And, in fact, I got up the ramp and entered the front door without any trouble. Disappointingly, inside there's a step down to the dining room. It's just one step, but it may as well have been a wall. Embarrassingly, I had to ask your staff for help, and soon all eyes in the restaurant were on me. Happily, from then on everything was wonderful. We enjoyed a delicious meal and great service.

I imagine you're aware that there's a law that requires your business to provide access to wheelchair users. I represent an association that helps businesses make simple changes so that they meet the requirements of the law. I'd be happy to meet you at your restaurant to go over some ways to make your business more accessible to people like me.

I look forward to your reply.

Send

REGISTER CHECK

When writing to a business or a person about a problem, you can end with *"I look forward to your reply"* to show that you expect action to be taken.

B WRITING SKILL **Read the message again. What was the writer happy with at the restaurant? What was he not happy about? Underline four adverbs that communicate the writer's attitude.**

C **Which adverbs from the box below can replace the adverbs you underlined in the message. More than one answer may be possible.**

amazingly luckily sadly surprisingly unfortunately unluckily

WRITE IT

D **Think of a time when you were unhappy with a product or service, and write your own message to register a complaint in about 100 words. Use some of the words from exercises B and C to show your attitude.**

E PAIR WORK **Read each other's messages. What do you think the receiver will do – ignore it, apologize, or try to make it right? Why?**

9.5 TIME TO SPEAK
Making a difference

LESSON OBJECTIVE
- discuss improvements to your town

A **DISCUSS** Look at the pictures. What problems are the different people facing? What types of problems might they face where you live? Think of access to buildings, facilities in public spaces, etc.

B Work in pairs or small groups. Look at the groups of people below and think of other groups with common interests and issues. Discuss the things they might want to do (use public transportation, access public spaces, go shopping, etc.) and think of three problems they might face in your neighborhood.

- families with young children
- wheelchair users
- dog owners

C Choose a group to focus on. Discuss possible solutions to the three problems you identified. What laws or rules could be introduced to help them? What facilities could be offered? What other solutions might there be?

D **PRESENT** Present to the class both the problems you identified for the group of people you selected and your solutions to those problems.

E **AGREE** Vote on the most ambitious, the most practical, and the most imaginative solutions.

To check your progress, go to page 155.

USEFUL PHRASES

DISCUSS

They might have problems getting …
They may not be able to …
They may not be allowed to ….
Local businesses could …
Local authorities should …
It'd be a good idea to …
If there were enough space, they could …

PRESENT

We discussed …
We decided that …
We suggest that …

REVIEW 3 (UNITS 7–9)

1 VOCABULARY

A **Complete the chart with the words and phrases below. Then write a category for each group.**

arts center	ban	boardwalk	congratulate	criticize
downtime	high-paying	lectures	oblige	persuade
playground	prohibit	shift	temporary	time off

______	______	______	______	______
gossip	part-time	assignments	city hall	permit
comment	9-to-5	busy schedule	courthouse	require
______	______	______	______	______
______	______	______	______	______
______	______	______	______	______

B **Think of at least two more words or phrases for each group.**

2 GRAMMAR

A **Choose the correct words to complete the conversation.**

A I'm so tired. I wish I [1]*can / could* go away for the weekend.

B Why don't you? What about your brother's place? If my brother [2]*has / had* a cabin in the mountains, [3]*I'd go / I went* there every weekend.

A I thought of that. I asked my brother if he [4]*invited / had invited* anyone for the weekend.

B What did he say?

A He said he [5]*wasn't / hadn't* sure, and then he mentioned that his wife [6]*invites / had invited* her parents over.

B Too bad. Hey, why don't we go camping at South River Park?

A Now, that's an idea. Do you know if dogs [7]*allowed / are allowed* in the park?

B Not anymore. Sorry, but Buddy [8]*may not / couldn't* come along.

B PAIR WORK **What is something you wish you could do this coming weekend? Why can't you do it? What could you do instead?**

3 SPEAKING

A PAIR WORK **Discuss the questions.**

- What are young people allowed to do now that you weren't allowed to do when you were younger? Are you happy about this change?
- What are you required to do at work or school that you think you shouldn't have to do? Why?

Young people are generally allowed to stay out later than I was. I don't think it's a good change because it can be dangerous to be out late at night.

At school, we're required to sign the attendance list at the beginning of each class. I think we should choose which classes we want to attend.

4 FUNCTIONAL LANGUAGE

A **Complete the conversation with the words and phrases below.**

apparently	going to believe	It wouldn't hurt
kidding	you tried	wouldn't

A You're not [1] ________________ what Pedro did last night. He arrived over an hour late to Gina's dinner party. And he didn't even apologize.

B No way! Are you [2] ________________ ?

A [3] ________________ , he thinks it's OK because no one said anything about it last night, but I think I'm going to say something to him today.

B I [4] ________________ do that if I were you.

A Why not? Don't you think it was rude?

B Sure. But it was Gina's party. It's really her place to talk to him if she was upset about it. Have [5] ________________ talking to her about it?

A No, but you know how she is, she wouldn't say anything even if she was upset.

B Maybe, but people generally don't like it when other people speak for them without their permission. [6] ________________ to at least talk to her about it first.

5 SPEAKING

A PAIR WORK **Choose one of the situations below. Act it out in pairs.**

1 Think of a difficult conversation you've had with a friend, a relative, or a coworker. Give details of what you said, and how the other person reacted.

A A while ago I had a very tough conversation with a close friend who was always borrowing money but never paid me back.

B Oh really? And what did you say to your friend?

2 You have been through a stressful personal experience. You want to convince your boss to let you take some time off. Get advice from your partner.

A I'm so stressed out. I really need to take some time off, but we're so busy at the office right now.

B Have you tried talking to your boss? You might want to …

B **Change roles and repeat the role play.**

UNIT OBJECTIVES

- speculate about events in the past
- talk about alternatives and possibilities
- keep your listener engaged
- write comments about things you can and can't live without
- share the story of an influential discovery or invention

WHAT IF ... ?

10

START SPEAKING

A **What picture did these people want to take? How do you think the people feel about this photo? How would you feel?**

B **This is an example of "photobombing." Have you ever photobombed someone's picture, or has someone photobombed yours? Was it an accident or a joke?**

C **Have you ever taken a picture of something that went wrong in a funny or interesting way? For ideas, watch Andres's video.**

Did something similar happen to you?

10.1 ACCIDENTAL DISCOVERIES

LESSON OBJECTIVE
- speculate about events in the past

1 LANGUAGE IN CONTEXT

A **Look at the pictures in the article. How are these two things connected? Read the article and check your answers.**

TOP 10 ACCIDENTAL DISCOVERIES

Author Mark Twain said, "*Accident* is the name of the greatest of all inventions." Scientists carry out all kinds of **research** and face many **challenges** to make great **discoveries** and **breakthroughs**, but sometimes it is pure chance that provides the **solution**.

1 The Microwave Oven

In 1940, engineer Percy Lebaron Spencer was walking past an active magnetron in his lab when he noticed that the candy bar in his pocket had melted. Spencer was not the first to notice this **phenomenon**, but he decided to investigate it. If the candy hadn't melted, he wouldn't have made the **connection**, and we wouldn't have the microwave oven!

2 The Terracotta Army

The famous Terracotta Army was buried in Xian, China, about 2300 years ago. It was discovered by chance in 1974. If farmers hadn't needed to dig a well for water, they wouldn't have found the army. By studying the army, we have gained **knowledge** about ancient Chinese society. It has provided enormous **insight** into how Chinese emperors lived.

Read on to learn about #3 on the list →

FIND IT

B PAIR WORK **Which discovery do you think is more important? Why? What other accidental discoveries do you think are on the top 10 list? Use your phone to find other possibilities.**

2 VOCABULARY: Talking about discoveries

A 2.29 **Match the collocations to the correct definitions. Read the article again to help you. Then listen and check.**

1 find out something important *a*
2 prepare to do something that is new and difficult ___
3 find out something important after working a long time ___
4 get more information or understanding about something ___
5 study something formally ___
6 give the answer to a problem ___
7 join things together ___
8 give new understanding about something ___
9 see something that is happening and understand that it is important ___

a make a discovery
b make a breakthrough
c face a challenge
d make a connection
e provide insight
f gain knowledge
g notice a phenomenon
h carry out research
i provide a solution

B **Now go to page 150. Do the vocabulary exercises for 10.1.**

C PAIR WORK **Write sentences about issues that affect society today using the vocabulary and collocations above. Discuss the sentences with your classmates.**

They have made breakthroughs in AIDS research, but they haven't found a cure yet.

3 GRAMMAR: Past unreal conditionals

A **Read the sentences in the grammar box, and then choose the correct option to complete the rules.**

> **Past unreal conditionals**
>
> If the candy **hadn't melted**, he **wouldn't have made** the connection.
>
> If farmers **hadn't needed** to dig a well, they **wouldn't have found** the army.

1 The sentences are about events from **the present** / **the past**.

2 The sentences are about actions that **really happened** / **didn't happen**.

3 The verb form in the *if* clause is **simple past** / **past perfect**. The main clause uses *would* (*not*) + *have* + **simple past** / **past participle**.

B **Now go to page 138. Look at the grammar chart and do the grammar exercise for 10.1.**

C PAIR WORK **Complete the statements with the correct form of the verb in parentheses ( ). Do you know who or what the sentences refer to? (Answers at the bottom of the page.)**

1 If he ____________ (not sit) under an apple tree, he ____________ (not discover) gravity.

2 If Frank Epperson ____________ (not leave) his soda outside one cold night, the wooden stirring stick ____________ (not freeze) in the cup, and we might not have these sweet summer treats today.

3 If Alexander Fleming ____________ (not add) bacteria to the petri dish, he ____________ (not invent) this life-saving drug.

4 If George Crum ____________ (not slice) his potatoes extra thin, he ____________ (not create) this popular snack.

5 Sylvan Goldman ____________ (never think of) this helpful grocery store item if his office chair ____________ (not be) on wheels.

4 SPEAKING

A PAIR WORK **Think about three things that you did earlier this week. Tell your partner and together imagine what would have happened if you hadn't done those things.**

I left my house late, and I hit a terrible traffic jam on the way to class. If I'd left my apartment an hour earlier, I wouldn't have hit that traffic jam.

B GROUP WORK **Do the same thing in groups. Add to the chain of events to create stories. How long can you keep a logical chain of events going?**

If my friend hadn't moved to Berlin, I might not have gone to Germany for vacation. I probably would have gone to Australia instead.

If you had gone to Australia, what cities would you have visited?

1 Isaac Newton 2 Popsicles 3 penicillin 4 potato chips 5 the shopping cart

10.2 BIG MISTAKE!

LESSON OBJECTIVE
- talk about alternatives and possibilities

1 LANGUAGE IN CONTEXT

A 2.30 **Look at the pictures on this page. What do you think happened in each one? Listen to the podcast and check your answers.**

2.30 Audio script

People **get things wrong** all the time, but some **mistakes** are bigger than others. At the 2016 Oscars ceremony, *La La Land* was wrongly declared Best Picture. The acceptance speeches had already begun when the **error** was discovered. The host had to **make it right** quickly. He apologized for the **mix-up** and announced the real winner, *Moonlight*.

Who was to **blame**? Some said the presenters should have checked the envelopes more carefully, but could it have been a simple **misunderstanding**? In the end, they discovered it was the **fault** of a backstage worker who gave the presenters the wrong envelope. He was tweeting! If he had paid attention, he could have **fixed the problem** in time, and the **confusion** never would have happened!

Other **blunders** live forever. In a 1986 World Cup match between England and Argentina, Diego Maradona scored the winning goal – with his hand! The referee should not have allowed the goal. If he had **corrected his mistake**, England might have won the World Cup. This **epic fail** became known as "the hand of God" goal!

2 VOCABULARY: Discussing right and wrong

A 2.31 PAIR WORK **Look at the bold words in the script. Make a chart like the one below and write them into the correct category. Listen and check.**

Right / good behavior	Wrong / bad behavior
make something right	*get something wrong*

B **Now go to page 150. Do the vocabulary exercises for 10.2.**

C PAIR WORK **When was the last time you or someone you know made a big mistake? What was the mistake? Was it big enough to be called an epic fail? For ideas, watch Nicolle's video.**

Was your mistake as bad as Nicolle's? Was it worse?

3 GRAMMAR: Modals of past probability

A **Read the sentences in the grammar box. Then choose the correct option to complete the rules.**

> **Modals of past probability**
>
> He **could have fixed** the problem.
> The referee **should not have allowed** the goal.
> England **might have won** the World Cup.

1 Use *could* and *might* to **criticize / suggest alternatives to** events from the past.
2 Use *should* to **criticize / suggest alternatives to** events from the past.
3 After the modal, use *have* + **past tense / past participle.**

B **Now go to page 139. Look at the grammar chart and do the grammar exercise for 10.2.**

C PAIR WORK **Have you ever regretted something you've said or done?**

1 Who was involved (a family member, a friend, a coworker, a stranger)?
2 What did you do or not do?
3 What could or should you have done differently?
4 Does your partner agree about what you could or should have done?

> I shouldn't have posted this one photo of my friend on social media. If I had asked her permission first, she might have said yes. But I didn't, and now she's mad at me.

4 SPEAKING

FIND IT

A GROUP WORK **Look at the pictures. What should the people have done differently? Share ideas about what might have happened and check your accuracy. You can find other pictures on your phone or online to speculate about.**

> In A, they shouldn't have put the plate of cookies so close to the edge of the table.

> That might not have helped. The dog could have just jumped on the table.

> ✓ **ACCURACY CHECK**
>
> **When talking about the past, the modal verb *can* always changes to *could* in the affirmative.**
>
> *She ~~can~~ have gone to the store.* ✗
> *She could have gone to the store.* ✓

A

B

C

10.3 YOU'LL NEVER GUESS!

LESSON OBJECTIVE

- keep your listener engaged

1 FUNCTIONAL LANGUAGE

A 2.32 **Look at the pictures. What mistake might a customer make about these two places? Listen to part of a conversation to check your answer.**

2.32 Audio script

A … **But that's not all!** We finally got to the hotel about midnight. We went to the check-in desk, but the clerk didn't have our reservation. **Wouldn't you know it?** I had booked the wrong hotel!

B Oh, no! How did you manage that?

A **You won't believe this, but** there are two hotels called The Miramar in that town – one in the city center, which I thought I had booked, and one about 20 kilometers away.

B So, what happened then?

A Well, **you can imagine.** We had to call another taxi, put all the bags back into the other car, and go to the other hotel. But **you know what?** It turned out the location was beautiful. That hotel was simpler than the one downtown, but the staff was really friendly, and, **are you ready for this?**

B What?

A They upgraded us to a bigger room! **Isn't that amazing?** I guess they felt sorry for us. Anyway, it was all so nice, we decided to go there again next summer!

B **Complete the chart with the bold expressions from the conversation.**

Keeping your listener engaged
But that's not [1] ______ !
[2] ______ you know it?
You won't [3] ______ this, but …
You can [4] ______ !
You [5] ______ what?
Are you [6] ______ for this?
Isn't that [7] ______ ?

INSIDER ENGLISH

In conversation, *anyway* is commonly used as a way to change the subject, return to an earlier subject, or get to the most interesting point.

C 2.33 **Complete the conversation with expressions from the chart. Listen and check.**

A OK, [1] ______ ? I had a job interview last week, for a web designer job, but the questions they asked me were all about sales.

B Sales? Why were they asking you about sales?

A Well, after like 20 minutes, I was wondering that myself, so I asked them. And, [2] ______ ? I was in the wrong interview.

B No! That's so funny! You must have been so embarrassed!

A Oh, totally! But they were embarrassed, too. But [3] ______ . I got it. I got the job! [4] ______ ? I got the *wrong* job!

2 REAL-WORLD STRATEGY

A 2.34 **Listen to two short conversations. What's the situation in each story?**

SHOWING INTEREST IN A STORY

You can show interest in what someone is saying by interjecting some of these expressions:

Don't tell me you … !

Let me guess – you … !

That's (so) funny / strange / great / crazy / awful / sweet!

You must be joking. / You can't be serious.

B 2.34 **Read the information about showing interest in a story, and then listen again. How does the listener express interest in each story?**

C PAIR WORK **Do a role play. Student A: Think of a common mistake that someone might make and create a story about it. Student B: Show that you are interested in the story. Switch roles and do it again.**

3 PRONUNCIATION FOCUS: Saying long and short vowel sounds

A 2.35 **Listen and repeat. Focus on the bold vowel sounds.**

Short vowel sounds	add	bed	dim	sock	cub
Long vowel sounds	aid	bead	dime	soak	cube

B 2.36 **Listen and repeat. Focus on the bold letters. Write L for a long vowel sound or S for a short vowel sound.**

1 ho tel ___
2 ki lom et er ___
3 de ci ded ___
4 res er va tion ___
5 bags ___
6 a ma zing ___

C **Look at the words in exercise B again. When a syllable ends in a vowel sound, is that vowel sound usually long or short?**

4 SPEAKING

A **Think of a true story from your life or a friend's life that people might find difficult to believe. Use the topics in the box to help you.**

family health sports money vacations work

B PAIR WORK **Tell the story to your partner. Show interest and/or surprise when you listen to your partner's story.**

I found a wallet in the street with $100 in it. I turned it into the police.

That's so nice! I think I might have kept it.

Well, you won't believe this, but the owner gave me a reward – $100!

10.4 I CAN'T LIVE WITHOUT IT!

LESSON OBJECTIVE

- write comments about things you can and can't live without

1 LISTENING

A PAIR WORK **Look at the pictures. Which do you think gives a more realistic view of cars and driving today? Why?**

B 2.37 LISTEN FOR DETAILS **Listen to part of a podcast about the car and other inventions. Answer the questions.**

1 What three bad inventions are mentioned at the beginning?
2 What does Renato compare the car to? According to him, what is the difference?
3 What does Paula like about cars?
4 What other three inventions are mentioned?
5 Which one do they finally agree about?

C 2.38 PAIR WORK LISTEN FOR TONE **Read and listen to the extracts. Circle the tone that correctly describes the speaker's attitude.**

1 It's part of my life.	positive	negative
2 Life would be better without them.	positive	negative
3 No one needs a machine for that.	aggressive	defensive
4 Are you sure about that?	aggressive	defensive

D THINK CRITICALLY **Who do you agree with more, Renato or Paula? Of the four inventions discussed, which do you consider the best and worst? Why?**

2 PRONUNCIATION: Listening for weak words

A 2.39 **Listen to extracts from the podcast. Focus on the bold words. How is the sound different from the written words?**

1 … could anyone have imagined how much we **would** depend on them one day?
2 Just think for a moment what life **would** be like without them.

B **Choose the correct option to complete the statement.**

Would is often weak when the word before it ends in a *consonant* / *vowel* sound.

3 WRITING

A **Read the comment that was left on the podcast's website that expresses opinions about other inventions. How does the writer say we should judge whether an invention is good or bad?**

INVENTIONS PODCAST

Sign up Log in

COMMENTS

I enjoyed yesterday's show about the best and worst inventions. Both your guests had interesting points, but I think I agree more with Renato. He seemed more interested in an invention's impact on the planet and on society, whereas Paula seemed more interested in whether an invention made her life easier.

Personally, I think the worst inventions are the ones that harm the planet or society, even if they also happen to be really convenient. Cars definitely fit that category. Similarly, I would say that Styrofoam is a terrible invention.

Good inventions, by contrast, are ones that improve society or help the planet even if they create a little more work for us. Subways and other forms of public transportation are good examples. Sure, they might not always be as convenient as driving your own car, but they're way better for the environment.

5 20 9

REGISTER CHECK

Start a statement with "*Personally,*" to show that it is your own opinion and that you understand other people may hold other opinions. It is a way of softening your statement.

B WRITING SKILL **Look again at the comment. Find the words that are used to show similarity and underline them. Find the words that are used to show contrast and circle them.**

C PAIR WORK **What inventions or discoveries could you not live without? Which ones do you wish didn't exist? What makes an invention good or bad in your view?**

WRITE IT

D **Write a comment similar to the one above expressing your opinion. Write about two things you couldn't live without and two things that you wish didn't exist. Use the phrases for similarities and contrasts from exercise B.**

E GROUP WORK **Share your comment with your classmates. How many people agree with you? How many disagree?**

10.5

TIME TO SPEAK
TURNING POINTS

LESSON OBJECTIVE

- share the story of an influential discovery or invention

A **DISCUSS** In a group, look at the pictures. What early inventions or discoveries do they show? Which was invented or discovered first? Which was last? Put them in order.

FIND IT

B Think about the modern discoveries and inventions below. How did each change human history? Think of two more big discoveries or inventions. You can use your phone to help you.

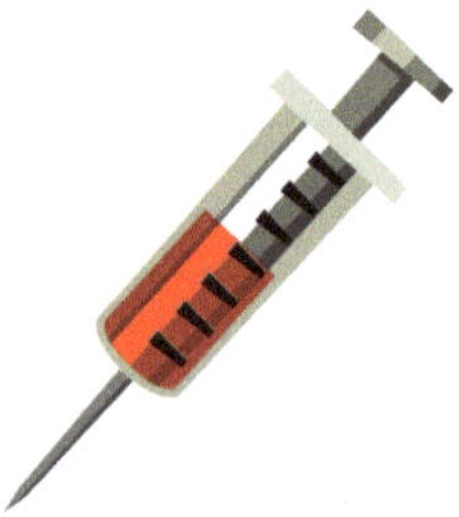

C **DECIDE** Choose the invention or discovery that you agree has had the greatest impact on human history. Is it still important today? What would life be like without it (or if it had never been discovered or invented)? Think of at least five differences, both positive and negative.

D **PRESENT** Share your ideas with the class. One of you summarizes your discovery or invention, and the others each describe one way it changed human history.

E **AGREE** As a class, discuss the ideas presented. Which invention or discovery do you all think has had the greatest effect on human history? Is that effect mostly positive or mostly negative? Why do you think so?

To check your progress, go to page 156.

USEFUL PHRASES

DISCUSS

The invention of … was a turning point because …

…. changed history by …

DECIDE

I think the most important invention was …

If … hadn't been discovered, we wouldn't …

AGREE

I think group A's invention was the most important because…

… was a more important discovery than … because

UNIT OBJECTIVES

- discuss college life
- discuss scientific facts
- discuss alternatives and give recommendations
- write a comment presenting an argument
- present a proposal to solve a problem

CONTRASTS

11

START SPEAKING

A **Look at the picture. Where do you think the two men are? What's the difference between them?**

B **Where and when do you wear formal clothes? Does the way you dress ever affect the way you feel or act?**

C **Do you think it's true that people judge others by their appearance? Is that fair? Why or why not? For ideas, watch Nicolle's video.**

REAL STUDENT

Do you agree with Nicolle?

11.1 STUDENT STORIES

LESSON OBJECTIVE
- discuss college life

1 LANGUAGE IN CONTEXT

A **What aspects of student life are shown in the brochure? Which are more academic and which are more social? Read about two students' experiences. Which aspects do they enjoy most?**

Lee, film studies **major**

"I'm an **undergraduate,** in my third year now, but I'll never forget getting my acceptance letter. It was a dream come true! The program is great, the **professors** are awesome, and the **campus** is beautiful. But what I like most about college is the extracurricular activities. There are so many student clubs and **associations** to get involved with. I'm president of the film **society** this year. I've learned so much about dealing with people and managing events. If you stop to think about it, that's an education all by itself. Of course, I have to remember to study, too!"

"There are excellent professors on the **faculty,** and the **facilities** are absolutely amazing! I still remember seeing the labs for the first time. I spend whole days there – I even forget to eat! I feel so lucky. But when I was a **freshman** I didn't appreciate things. I got too involved in campus life and my **grades** started to drop. So I stopped doing all that. The next **semester** I moved out of the **dorm** and got serious. I mean, your **degree** is the reason you're here, so that has to come first."

Allie, biomedical engineering major

GLOSSARY

extracurricular (*adj*) not part of academic study

2 VOCABULARY: Talking about college education

A 2.40 **Look at the bold words in the text. Write them in the correct categories. Then listen and check.**

People: ________, ________, ________, ________

Places and buildings: ________, ________, ________

Academic life: ________, ________, ________, ________

Organizations: ________, ________

B **Now go to page 151. Do the vocabulary exercises for 11.1.**

C PAIR WORK **Discuss the questions.**

1. What is (or would be) the best and worst thing about being a freshman? Is it better to live in a dorm or an apartment as a freshman? As a sophomore, junior, or senior? Why?
2. What's the coolest major you can think of (oceanography, nuclear physics, musical theater, etc.)? Why do you think it's cool? Is it something you'd like to study?

> **!** **Generally speaking, undergraduates earn a bachelor's degree in four years: freshman (1st year), sophomore (2nd year), junior (3rd year), senior (last year(s)). These terms are nouns (people) or adjectives.**
>
> *He's a sophomore now, but he's going to study in Spain his junior year.*
>
> **Postgraduates earn a master's degree then a doctorate. There are no divisions by year.**
>
> *He's getting his master's in economics.*

3 GRAMMAR: Gerund and infinitive after *forget, remember, stop*

A **Choose the correct answer to complete the rules. Use the sentences in the grammar box to help you.**

1 When *forget, remember,* and *stop* are followed by a gerund (*-ing*),…
   a a definite action is finished. **b** an action is general and indefinite.

2 When *forget, remember,* and *stop* are followed by an infinitive (*to* + verb),…
   a a definite action is finished. **b** an action is general and indefinite.

Gerund and infinitive after *forget, remember, stop*

I'll never **forget** getting my acceptance letter.
I **remember** seeing them for the first time.
I **stopped** doing all that.

Sometimes I even **forget** to eat!
I have to **remember** to study, too!
If you **stop** to think about it, that's an education all by itself.

B PAIR WORK **Discuss the differences in meaning in the sentence pairs. Say each sentence another way to make sure the meaning is clear.**

1 **a** I'll never forget meeting with my advisor for the first time.
   b I can't forget to meet with my advisor tomorrow!

2 **a** I remember putting my keys in my bag, but now I can't find them.
   b I have to remember to put the key in the mailbox before I leave.

3 **a** I stopped buying groceries at that store. It's so dirty.
   b I stopped to buy groceries on the way home.

C **Now go to page 139. Do the grammar exercise for 11.1.**

D GROUP WORK **Complete these sentences so that they are true for you. Read your sentences to the group. Are any of your answers the same?**

1 After I get home tonight, I have to remember to …
2 Tomorrow, I can't forget to … or I'll be in trouble!
3 In the new year, I promise I'm going to stop …

4 SPEAKING

A **Choose one of the topics from the box. Think about the things you remember or something you'll never forget. For ideas, watch Tayra's video.**

first day at school/on campus
last day at school/on campus
taking up a new sport or hobby
giving up a sport or hobby

REAL STUDENT

Is your answer similar to Tayra's?

B PAIR WORK **Tell your partner about the topic you chose. Ask your partner questions about their experience to add details.**

C GROUP WORK **Tell your partner's story to other students.**

11.2 FOLK REMEDIES

LESSON OBJECTIVE

- discuss scientific facts

1 LANGUAGE IN CONTEXT

A 2.41 **A folk remedy is a medical treatment from long ago. Look at the pictures. What folk remedies might be connected to these foods? Listen to part of a podcast discussing folk remedies. Were you right?**

2.41 Audio script

Host So, Dr. Wendt, are folk remedies usually based on **scientific** fact or are they just snake oil? For example, do carrots really help you see better at night?

Dr. Wendt Not all folk remedies are backed up by real **science**, but that one is. Our **research** shows that the vitamin A in carrots can sharpen night vision. It's been **scientifically proven.**

Host Great. So, is it also true that honey calms a cough and lets you sleep at night? I'd say yes to that one. I swear by it!

Dr. Wendt You're right! It's true. **Medical researchers** have tested this, and there is **proof** that honey can be as effective as most cough **medicines.**

Host So, my tea with honey is **medically approved**! That's good to know. OK, here's one from a listener: Does eating cheese before bed cause nightmares?

Dr. Wendt I'm afraid there is no scientific **basis** to support the idea that cheese makes people have bad dreams. But a heavy meal, with or without cheese, may disturb your sleep or make you remember your dreams more clearly.

B 2.41 **Listen again and read. What does science say about each of the folk remedies?**

INSIDER ENGLISH

We use the term *snake oil* to dismissively refer to something that does not give the positive results that it promises. The term originally referred to fake medicines, but it's now used for any product that does not deliver the benefits it claims.

2 VOCABULARY: Talking about science

A 2.42 **Look at the bold words in the audio script and complete the chart. One word can be used twice. Listen and check.**

abstract noun	verb	person	adjective	compound adjective
______		scientist	______	______
______	research	______		research-based
______	prove		proven	______
base/______	base		based (on facts)	science-based
______			medical	______

B **Now go to page 151. Do the vocabulary exercises for 11.2.**

C **Read some questions sent in by listeners of the full podcast. Do you know the answers? How could researchers test these ideas? If you can, use your phone to do some real research!**

FIND IT

1 You said that people with red hair feel more pain. Is that a medical fact or an assumption based on reports from red-headed people?

2 Has research proven that it is better to wear dark-colored clothes in very hot, sunny places? It seems like light colors would be better.

3 I've read that some people (like taxi drivers, for example) are naturally better at navigation. Is there any scientific basis for that claim?

3 GRAMMAR: Causative verbs *help, let, make*

A **Choose the correct option to complete the rules. Use the sentences in the grammar box to help you.**

1 The verbs *help*, *let*, and *make* are used to talk about the effect caused by **something or someone else** / **our own actions**.

2 Causative verbs are always used with another verb in the ***to*** **+ verb** / **verb without** ***to*** form.

3 The object (*me, you, him, people*, etc.) goes **between** / **after** the two verbs.

Causative verbs *help, let, make*

Carrots **help you see** better at night.

Honey calms a cough and **lets you sleep** at night.

Cheese **doesn't make people have** nightmares.

ACCURACY CHECK

Use the base form of the verb, NOT the *to* + verb form, after *help*, *let*, and *make*.

Carrots help you ~~to see~~ better at night. ✗

Carrots help you see better at night. ✓

B **Now go to page 139. Do the grammar exercise for 11.2.**

C PAIR WORK **Use the words to form questions. Check your accuracy. Then discuss the questions with your partner. Think of at least three answers for each one.**

1 What / study / stay awake / you / can help / for a test ?

____

2 sometimes / sleep / not let / What problems / you ?

____

3 feel / makes / you / more relaxed / What / if stressed ?

____

4 SPEAKING

A GROUP WORK **Read the statements. Do people in your culture have the same beliefs? Which do you think might be based on real science? Why?**

- Eating bread crusts will make your hair curl.
- Eating oily fish helps you study better.
- If you go outside with wet hair, you'll catch a cold.
- Counting sheep helps you fall asleep.
- A full moon makes people go a little crazy.

B **What other folk remedies or beliefs do you know about? Do you think they might be based on science? You can use your phone to find out more.**

FIND IT

11.3 CAN YOU SUGGEST AN ALTERNATIVE?

LESSON OBJECTIVE
- discuss alternatives and give recommendations

1 FUNCTIONAL LANGUAGE

A **Look at the pictures of different kinds of mosquito repellent. Which ones have you tried? Can you think of others? Which ones do you think are the most effective? Why?**

B 2.43 **Listen to a conversation between a pharmacist and a customer. Which repellent does the pharmacist recommend? What does the customer choose?**

2.43 Audio script

A Hi, I'm looking for a good mosquito repellent.

B Ah, yes. This one is scientifically proven to last at least eight hours. And this one's always worked well for me.

A Maybe not a spray. I don't think they're very healthy. **Can you suggest an alternative?** Do you have anything more natural?

B Well, **another option would be** these patches. They're 100% natural. Here, smell this. Can you smell the citronella?

A Yes. **That looks like a good alternative.** Do you put the patches on your skin?

B No, you put them on your clothes, or, for example, on the bed at night.

A No, **I'm looking for something different.** I mean, something you can actually wear.

B Well, we have these wristbands. **They're a good alternative.** They're 100% natural and should be effective for up to 12 hours. But **I don't think they're a great choice** for nighttime. I mean, you shouldn't wear them while you sleep.

A I see, so I could wear the wristband during the day and maybe use the patches at night. **That could work.**

B Yes, that's probably your best option.

C **Complete the chart with the bold expressions from the conversation.**

Asking for options	Suggesting alternatives
Do you have anything else?	You could also try …
1 ______ ?	3 ______ (these patches).
2 ______ .	4 ______ .
Discussing disadvantages	**Responding to suggestions**
It might not be the best option.	I like that option.
5 ______ (for nighttime).	6 ______ .
	7 ______ .

D PAIR WORK **Discuss the possible alternatives in these situations. Use the expressions in the chart.**

1 You want to go out for dinner, but you don't want to spend too much money.
2 You want to take up a new sport, but you don't have much free time.

We could try the food court at the mall. There's a good salad bar there.

But it's so crowded there. I don't think …

2 REAL-WORLD STRATEGY

GIVING A PERSONAL RECOMMENDATION

Use these expressions when you want to give a personal recommendation.

This one's always worked well for me.

If I were you, I'd choose/pick/go with …

I've always had luck with …

A 2.44 PAIR WORK **Read the information in the box about giving a personal recommendation. Then listen to two short conversations. What are they talking about? Which expressions from the box do they use?**

1 Topic: ______________________

Expression: ______________________

2 Topic: ______________________

Expression: ______________________

B PAIR WORK **Think of a time when you gave a personal recommendation to someone. What was it for? What was your recommendation? What were your reasons for it?**

REGISTER CHECK

When giving advice, avoid using imperative statements. Use "*I* statements" to show that you respect the other person's perspective and don't want to force your opinion on them.

~~*Buy this one. It's the best.*~~

I've always had good luck with this one.

3 PRONUNCIATION FOCUS: Stressing long words

A 2.45 **Listen and repeat. How many syllables are in each word?**

1 scientifically ___

2 alternatives ___

3 disadvantages ___

4 situation ___

5 recommendation ___

B 2.45 **Listen again. Which syllable is stressed? Circle it.**

C PAIR WORK **Practice saying the words in exercise 3A with a partner. Does your partner stress the correct syllable?**

4 SPEAKING

A **Look at the pictures of laptop bags and prepare to perform a role play. Prepare for both roles by yourself (not with a partner).**

Customer: You want to buy a bag for your laptop. You're not sure which to buy. Think about your needs and your style. Prepare some questions for the sales clerk.

Sales clerk: Think of some good points about each of the bags. Think about which bag you would recommend to different people in different situations or with different needs.

B PAIR WORK **Do the role play two times, once as the customer and once as the sales clerk. Then do a new role play using your story from exercise 2B or a new idea. You can be in a store or talking with a coworker or friend.**

11.4 DRIVERLESS CARS? NO WAY!

LESSON OBJECTIVE
- write a comment presenting an argument

1 READING

A **Look at the picture. Do you think it shows a positive view of technology? Why or why not?**

B INFERRING ATTITUDE **Read the opinion piece on the role of technology in our lives. Which sentence best describes the writer's attitude?**

a Technology is ruining our lives, so we should reject it in favor of real experiences.

b Technology will reduce our ability to experience life's pleasures if we're not careful.

c Technological developments are good only if they make life easier.

Embrace the technical revolution? Not me!

Dishwashers, cell phones, the internet – all great inventions that make life easier, more comfortable, and more fun. But when technology goes too far, it automates experiences and takes the enjoyment out of life.

Take driverless cars. Or in my case, don't take them! I love driving my car. I love to feel the wheels respond to my touch. I love to drive long hours on empty roads, with my hand hanging out the window, feeling the wind between my fingers. I don't want the car to drive me, and half the American population are with me on this.

Another example of unwanted technology takeover is robot waiters. Do you really want your meal served by a machine? I can see it might appeal to children, but where's the human touch – the shared smile, the pleasant banter, the thoughtful attention? Robot waiters are becoming more and more popular in Asia, and the trend is surely going to spread.

In the world of entertainment, people once worried that live streaming would kill live events. Statistics show, however, that more and more people are attending live concerts and music festivals all around the world. The urge to share an experience, to feel the buzz of thousands of other people, is stronger than the lazy comforts of technological shortcuts.

Technology can, no doubt, make life a lot easier in many ways, but we need to make sure it isn't robbing us of the real pleasures that make life worth living.

GLOSSARY

embrace (*v*) accept with enthusiasm
automate (*v*) use machines to do something
banter (*n*) light, funny conversation
buzz (*n*) excitement

C IDENTIFYING ARGUMENTS **Read the opinion piece again. What are the writer's arguments against the following examples of technology?**

Driverless cars

Robot waiters

Streaming live events

D THINK CRITICALLY **Do you agree with the writer? Why or why not? Do you think she may be exaggerating? Why or why not? What are some other examples of technology that's "gone too far" in your opinion? Why do you think so?**

2 WRITING

A **Read a comment that was posted in response to the opinion piece. Does the writer generally agree or disagree with the original piece? Do you agree with the writer's arguments? Why or why not?**

Embrace the technical revolution? Yes, please!

First of all I'd like to say that, as much as I love technology, I think there are times when we need to get back to basics. Live music is so much better when you're there in person, and I may be old-fashioned, but I much prefer a paperback to an e-reader. But those are just my preferences, and I totally respect the fact that others may not agree with me.

Where I strongly disagree with the article is on the point of driverless cars. Research suggests that the use of driverless cars would help the flow of traffic, and **more importantly**, it could reduce the number of accidents significantly. **It's also important to remember that** driverless cars don't speed, they don't run red lights, and they aren't impatient. **Additionally,** they will help elderly people and the disabled travel independently. **And finally,** they're optional. If you really want to drive yourself, no one's going to stop you.

B PAIR WORK WRITING SKILL Look at the **bold** phrases in the text. Which are used for each purpose?

1 to begin an argument: ______

2 to add a new argument: ______

3 to conclude: ______

C PAIR WORK **Think of three arguments for and three arguments against robot waiters. Which arguments do you think are the most convincing? Why?**

WRITE IT

D **Follow the steps to write your own comment in response to the opinion piece.**

1 Choose a title:

Robot waiters? Yes, please! *Robot waiters? No way!*

2 Choose the three points (for or against) you want to include from exercise C.

3 Read the opinion piece and the comment above again. Choose the transition phrases that work best for your points.

4 Write your comment. Write about 150 words.

E GROUP WORK **Read all the comments. Make a note of any particularly convincing arguments. Then vote on whether you think robot waiters are generally a positive or negative innovation. Share your ideas with the class.**

11.5 TIME TO SPEAK
MEDIATION

LESSON OBJECTIVE
- present a proposal to solve a problem

A **Look at the picture. Where do you think this tree is? What problems might the tree cause for the people who use this area?**

B **PREPARE** **The tree has grown too big, and the people in the building are going to hold a meeting to decide what to do about it. Divide into three groups to prepare for the meeting.**

Group A: You like having a tree here, so you want to replace this tree with a smaller one. Think about arguments for having a tree near the building.

Group B: You think this area could be used for more useful purposes, like extra parking space. Think about arguments for other ways to use this space.

Group C: You are the mediators. You will listen to both sides and try to help them reach a compromise. Discuss possible arguments and suggestions you could make to keep both sides happy.

C **DISCUSS** **Now make new groups of three, with one student from each group. Students from Group A and Group B put forward their arguments, and the Group C student mediates and tries to help the others come to an agreement.**

D **PRESENT** **The Group C students report back on the discussions to the class. Listen to all the solutions. Who has the best solution? Take a class vote to decide.**

To check your progress, go to page 156.

USEFUL PHRASES

PREPARE

One argument for keeping/removing the tree is …

Another good argument might be …

As an alternative, we could …

DISCUSS

We think it's really important to …

We need to consider …

Would you consider … ?

PRESENT

The main arguments for/against keeping it were …

In the end, we decided to …

We couldn't come to an agreement because …

UNIT OBJECTIVES

- describe a special photo and the story behind it
- discuss childhood memories
- recall and share past experiences
- write a summary and response about keeping pets
- recall and discuss a national moment

LOOKING BACK

12

START SPEAKING

A Look at the picture for 15 seconds, then cover it. Make a detailed list of things in the picture.

B Compare your list with other classmates. How many things did they remember that you didn't? What things are in the picture but not on anyone's list? Why do you think some things were more memorable than others?

C Do you have a good memory for names, dates, or faces? How easily do you remember facts, stories, or appointments? For ideas, watch Andres's video.

How does your memory compare with Andres's?

12.1 PHOTO STORIES

LESSON OBJECTIVE
- describe a special photo and the story behind it

1 LANGUAGE IN CONTEXT

A **Look at the pictures and read the stories about them. Match the people to the pictures. What does the picture represent for them?**

Gary, Trenton, New Jersey, U.S.A.

What I remember most about my childhood is my pet dog, Milo. Here, I'm 10 and in our back yard with him. I loved that **fresh** smell of grass. I can almost feel his **smooth** fur and **damp** breath now. (Sometimes it was pretty **stinky**, but I didn't care.) The thing I love about this photo is that it brings back all those **bright** summer days.

Sonia, San Miguel de Allende, Mexico

The air in my grandma's house was **scented** with spices. She baked all kinds of **flavorful** cakes decorated with **colorful** icing. The thing I liked most was licking the **tasty** icing off my fingers. She called me her "helper"! What I love about this photo is that it helps me remember our special relationship.

Alex, Kingston, Jamaica

What I miss most about my grandpa are the hours we spent listening to music. This picture represents that for me. I remember his record cabinet had a **musty** smell, but I liked it. His hands were big and **rough**, but he handled those records so gently. He'd sing along with a **deep**, **melodic** voice. My voice sounded so **high-pitched** next to his!

A ______

B ______

C ______

B PAIR WORK **Which of the senses – touch, smell, taste, sound, sight – do the people mention? What do they talk about exactly?**

Sonia talks about the smell of spices in the air.

2 VOCABULARY: Talking about the senses

A 2.46 **Look at the bold adjectives in the stories. Write which sense they describe. Listen and check. Which ones usually describe a positive sensation? A negative sensation? Neither?**

Smell: ______, ______, ______, ______

Sound: ______, ______, ______

Touch: ______, ______, ______

Taste: ______, ______

Sight: ______, ______

B **Now go to page 152. Do the vocabulary exercises for 12.1.**

C PAIR WORK **Describe some of the things that you have experienced today using sense adjectives.**

I opened the curtain and the light was really bright… I hate mornings!

3 GRAMMAR: Adding emphasis

A **Choose the correct option to complete the rules. Use the sentences in the grammar box to help you. Can you find two more examples in the text?**

1 To give emphasis and focus to an idea, you can use the phrase "*What I* + verb" OR "*The thing I* + verb" at the **end** / **beginning** of the sentence.

2 The thing you want to emphasize comes at the **end** / **beginning** of the sentence.

3 Use the verb ***be*** / ***have*** to link the two parts of the sentence together.

Adding emphasis

What I remember most about my childhood **is** my pet dog, Milo.

The thing I liked most **was** licking the tasty icing off my fingers.

B **Now go to page 140. Look at the grammar chart and do the grammar exercise for 12.1.**

C PAIR WORK **Rewrite the sentences and add emphasis.**

1 I really liked the sunroof in my family's old car.

The thing I really liked about my family's old car was the sunroof.

2 As a child I loved mangoes more than anything!

3 I miss cooking with my grandma most of all.

4 From my childhood I remember riding on trains most clearly.

5 As a teenager I really loved skateboarding.

D PAIR WORK **Are the sentences in exercise C true for you? If not, change them to make them true.**

I didn't like mangoes. The thing I loved as a child was ice cream!

4 SPEAKING

FIND IT

A PAIR WORK **Find a photo on your phone or other device that you could post to an online forum. Describe the story behind it. Use sense adjectives to describe how you felt in the photo.**

I was at the beach on vacation. What I remember about that moment was the salty smell of the sea and the fresh wind in my face.

B GROUP WORK **Share your photos and stories with the rest of the group. Which ones involve the most senses?**

12.2 DID THAT REALLY HAPPEN?

LESSON OBJECTIVE

- discuss childhood memories

1 LANGUAGE IN CONTEXT

A 2.47 **The title of this podcast is "Did it really happen?" What do you think it's about? Listen and check your answer.**

2.47 Audio script

Has something ever **brought back** a **vivid** memory, but later you find out it never actually happened? Most people feel sure about the accuracy of their own memories of their own life. I know I do, but how trustworthy are our **early** memories really? Listen to David's story:

> *"In 2nd grade, a new student, Nolan, arrived at my boarding school. We became friends, and he came home with me for winter break once because his family lived far away. I have a very **clear** memory of all this when I **look back on** it. Even today, the smell of burning wood **reminds me of** winter breaks spent sitting in front of the fire, especially the one with Nolan.*
>
> *Forty years later I met Nolan again. He didn't **recognize** me at first or remember much about that time. He had a **vague** memory of me, but he was positive that he had never stayed with my family. I was shocked!"*

Our **long-term** memory can play tricks on us. Psychiatrist Rochelle Rivas explains:

> *"The more often you **recall** a specific memory, the more distorted it becomes. It's like making a copy of a copy of a copy. That's why this only happens with **distant** or **childhood** memories, not with **short-term** or **recent** ones."*

Do you have a false memory? If so, send us an email and tell us about it.

B 2.47 **Listen again and read along. Choose the correct words to complete the sentences.**

1 Nolan and David *stayed friends / lost contact.*

2 Nolan and David recall their time together *the same way / differently.*

3 Dr. Rivas compares recalling distant memories to *recalling short-term ones / making copies of copies.*

C PAIR WORK **Do you have a memory that other people say happened differently? Is there any way to find out who's right? Do you think people sometimes distort memories on purpose? Why or why not?**

2 VOCABULARY: Describing memories

A 2.48 **Listen and say the words in the box. Categorize the words into adjectives and verbs. Which adjectives are opposites of each other? What verb is a synonym for all the verbs here?**

bring back	childhood	clear	distant
early	long-term	look back on	recall
recent	recognize	remind of	short-term
vague	vivid		

! ***remember*** vs. ***remind of***

*"I **remember** you." but "You **remind me of** my cousin. You are similar in many ways."*

B **Now go to page 152. Do the vocabulary exercises for 12.2.**

3 GRAMMAR: Substitution and referencing

A **Choose the best option to complete the rules. Use the sentences in the grammar box to help you.**

1. To avoid repeating **an uncountable / a countable** noun, we can use *one / ones.*
2. To avoid repeating a verb or verb phrase, we can use the auxiliary verb for that tense. For example, in the present tense, we use ***so / do***.
3. To avoid repeating a question, we can use ***so / do***.
4. To reference a noun or noun phrase, we can use *it/them* for **specific things / whole ideas** and *this/that* for **specific things / whole ideas.**

Substitution

That reminds me of winter breaks, especially the **one** with Nolan.

Most people feel sure about the accuracy of their memories. I know I **do.**

Do you have a false memory? If **so**, send us an email.

Referencing

When you recall a memory often, **it** becomes distorted.

When you recall a memory often, it becomes distorted. That's why **this** only happens with distant memories.

B **Now go to page 140. Do the grammar exercise for 12.2.**

C PAIR WORK **Read the conversation. Change the underlined words to substitutions or referents. Then check your accuracy.**

A Do you have a favorite childhood memory? If [1]you have a favorite childhood memory, tell me about [2]your favorite childhood memory.

B No, I [3]don't have a favorite childhood memory. But did I tell you about the time I met Harrison Ford?

A No, you never told me about [4]the time you met Harrison Ford! I love to hear celebrity-sighting stories.

B I know! I [5]love to hear celebrity-sighting stories, too! And I really like telling [6]celebrity-sighting stories.

ACCURACY CHECK

When substituting with *one/ones*, make sure the pronoun agrees with what it is substituting.

It happens with childhood memories, not recent ~~one~~. ✗

It happens with childhood memories, not recent ones. ✓

4 SPEAKING

A **Look at the pictures. Do you remember these things? If so, what kinds of childhood memories do they bring back for you?**

B PAIR WORK **Discuss the questions.**

1. What kinds of things do you look back on most fondly (with nice feelings) – school days, family events, sports events, etc.?
2. Think about a time when you met an old friend. Did you recognize each other? What did you talk about? Did you remember events from your past the same way or differently?
3. Think about a nice early memory. Is it possible that someone told you about it and that you don't really remember it at all?

12.3 THAT RINGS A BELL

LESSON OBJECTIVE

- recall and share past experiences

1 FUNCTIONAL LANGUAGE

A 2.49 **Look at the picture of old friends sharing memories. Listen to their conversation. Why is Rebecca frustrated with Peter?**

2.49 Audio script

A That reminds me of the White Mountains. **Do you remember that time** we got lost there, Peter? It was getting really dark, and we didn't know which way to go. Remember? It was about five years ago …

B We got lost?

A **Don't tell me you don't remember.**

B I remember us hiking in the White Mountains, but **I don't recall getting lost.** But you know how my memory is. And **that whole period's a bit vague** anyway. I've kind of blocked things out around then.

A But it was, like, really scary.

B Yeah, I just don't … What happened exactly?

A We got lost! And then your flashlight didn't work, and I totally panicked …

B The flashlight – yeah, **that rings a bell.** Yeah, **it's all coming back to me now.** Just after that we found the path again, right?

A Right!

B And it turned out that we were, like, only a hundred meters from the campground!

B **Complete the chart with the bold expressions from the conversation.**

Prompting a response	Recalling a memory
Do you remember that [1] ________ we … ?	I don't [3] ________ (getting lost).
Don't [2] ________ me you don't remember.	That (whole period's) a bit [4] ________ anyway!
	That [5] ________ a bell!
	It's all [6] ________ back to me now.

C 2.50 **Complete the conversation with expressions from the chart. Listen and check.**

A [1] ________ ________ ________ that time you went to the airport without your passport?

B Oh, come on. I never did that.

A Yes, you did! [2] ________ ________ ________ you don't remember! We had to go back home and get it, and then we spent a fortune on a new flight. You had to ask Mom and Dad for a loan …

B Oh, OK. That [3] ________ ________ ________. We were going to Cancun, right?

A Yes! And we had to wait, like, five hours for the next flight.

B OK, yeah. It's [4] ________ ________ ________ to me now! I don't think I ever paid Mom and Dad back for that. Don't remind them!

2 REAL-WORLD STRATEGY

A 2.51 **Listen to a short conversation. What's the initial memory? What similar memories does the other person share?**

SHARING EXPERIENCES

When you want to share a similar story, or invite others to do so, use these phrases:

That reminds me of a story. … *That's like the time that …*

I had a similar experience once. … *Has that ever happened to you?*

B 2.51 **Read about sharing experiences in the box above. Listen again. Which phrases do the people use?**

C PAIR WORK **Have a conversation in which you share a memory. Your partner then shares a similar or related experience from their own life.**

3 PRONUNCIATION FOCUS: Saying consonant clusters

A 2.52 **Listen. Write the missing letters.**

1 ___ ___ ocked
2 hun ___ ___ eds
3 ___ ___ ashlight
4 camp ___ ___ ound
5 experie ___ ___ e
6 pani ___ ___ ed

B 2.52 PAIR WORK **Listen again. Practice saying the words. Does your partner say each word clearly?**

4 SPEAKING

A PAIR WORK **Do a role play in which two friends recall a memory. Student A recalls the memory and gives details to help Student B remember it. Student B doesn't recall it at first but remembers more as details are given, and adds details, too.**

Don't tell me you don't remember the time we … ?

I don't quite recall that. What happened exactly?

Come on. We were in Hawaii …

B GROUP WORK **Expand the role play with a third person in the conversation. Student C shares a similar experience from their own past. Change roles and add more details each time.**

12.4 MAN'S BEST FRIEND?

LESSON OBJECTIVE
- write a pros and cons analysis about keeping pets

1 LISTENING

A PAIR WORK Look at the pictures. What are the dogs doing in each picture? What kinds of relationship do these animals have with people?

B 2.53 Listen to a debate about people and their dogs. Who mentions the dogs in the pictures, Kenan or Lucia? What do they say about them? Are their opinions positive or negative?

C 2.54 PAIR WORK LISTEN FOR EXAMPLES Both Kenan and Lucia use examples to support their arguments. Listen to the extracts and write the phrases you hear to introduce examples.

1 *For instance, ...*
2
3
4
5
6

D PAIR WORK THINK CRITICALLY Who do you think made a stronger case, the affirmative side (Kenan) or the opposition (Lucia)? Why? What was the strongest point in their argument?

We liked Lucia's argument, but her point about service dogs wasn't relevant. The topic is about pets.

E Think about your culture and its attitude towards dogs. What is their role in society? Do you agree with that role? Why or why not? For ideas, watch Alessandra's video.

REAL STUDENT

Do you agree with Alessandra?

2 PRONUNCIATION: Listening for transitions

A 2.55 **Listen to the excerpts from the debate. Focus on the bold words.**

1 Team A argued that people shouldn't keep dogs as pets and Team B argued that they should. **To finish the debate**, we'll hear a summary of each group's position ...

2 All those jobs help people and they keep the dogs happy and active. So, **in conclusion**, we'd actually be helping dogs a lot more by keeping them as working animals ...

3 So, **to sum up**, there are many ways that dogs and humans help each other.

B **Choose the correct option to complete the statement.**

Speakers often say words with *more* / *less* stress and *higher* / *lower* intonation to mark and transition to a summary statement.

3 WRITING

A **Read one student's summary of Lucia's side of the debate and his own response to it. Does he basically agree or disagree with Lucia's argument?**

Lucia argues that dogs should be kept as pets, and she supports that argument with three points. She says that dogs are more predictable and reliable than people. While this may be true, the company of a dog isn't the same as the company of a person. So despite the fact that dogs are trustworthy, it's not a good argument for why we should keep them as pets. She also says that keeping a dog as a pet is good for children because it teaches them to be caring and responsible; however, there are lots of other ways to teach children responsibility. Finally, she points out that dogs help society as service animals for blind people or as police dogs. Although that is true, those dogs aren't pets. They are working dogs.

B PAIR WORK WRITING SKILL **Identify and circle the words and phrases used to link contrasting ideas in the summary. Then use the phrases you circled to link the ideas below.**

1 Dogs are cute. They should not be kept as pets.

____

2 Most dogs are predictable and friendly. Some dogs are unpredictable and dangerous.

____

WRITE IT

C PAIR WORK **Write your own summary of and response to Kenan's opinion. In your response, be sure to ...**

- mention points that you agree and disagree with.
- use appropriate language to contrast ideas.

D PAIR WORK **Read another pair's summary and response. Did you include the same information? Do you agree with their response? Why or why not?**

The other pair didn't mention how dogs help children. We think that is an important and original idea.

12.5 TIME TO SPEAK
Where were you when ... ?

LESSON OBJECTIVE

- recall and discuss a national moment

A **Read the blog post about a memory. How does the writer describe the memory? Why does she call it a "national moment"?**

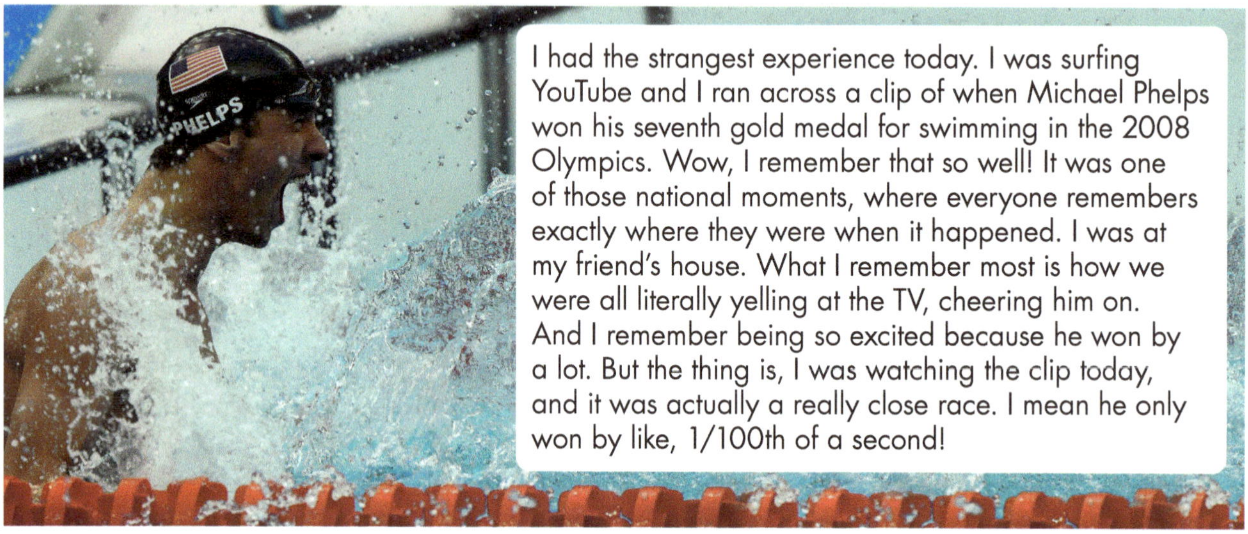

I had the strangest experience today. I was surfing YouTube and I ran across a clip of when Michael Phelps won his seventh gold medal for swimming in the 2008 Olympics. Wow, I remember that so well! It was one of those national moments, where everyone remembers exactly where they were when it happened. I was at my friend's house. What I remember most is how we were all literally yelling at the TV, cheering him on. And I remember being so excited because he won by a lot. But the thing is, I was watching the clip today, and it was actually a really close race. I mean he only won by like, 1/100th of a second!

FIND IT

B **PREPARE** **Think of a "national moment" from your country's history during your lifetime. It could be something from sports, politics, entertainment, or something else. You can use your phone to help you.**

C **DECIDE** **In small groups, share the national moments you thought of. Choose one and discuss your memories of it.**

- Where were you when it happened?
- What do you remember most about the event?
- Does everyone in the group remember it the same way, or are your memories of the event different? If so, how? Why do you think they are different?

D **PRESENT** **Choose someone to present your group's national moment to the class. Describe it but don't say what it was, so the rest of the class has to guess. Does everyone in the class remember the event? Does anyone remember it differently?**

To check your progress, go to page 156.

USEFUL PHRASES

PREPARE

What about when ... ?

Do you remember when ... ?

An event I really remember was when ...

DECIDE

What I remember most about ... was ...

Really? The way I remember it was ...

PRESENT

The things we remembered most about this event were ...

Oh! I know. It was when ...

But I remember it differently. The way I remember it, ...

REVIEW 4 (UNITS 10–12)

1 VOCABULARY

A **Put the words and phrases into the correct categories. There are five items for each category.**

breakthrough	dorm	bring back	stinky	degree	bright	epic fail
phenomenon	fault	freshman	insight	knowledge	tasty	major
misunderstanding	recall	melodic	recognize	remind of	error	research
undergraduate	smooth	confusion	look back on			

1 Discoveries: ______________________

2 Mistakes: ______________________

3 College: ______________________

4 Senses: ______________________

5 Memory: ______________________

B **Add two more words or phrases to each category.**

2 GRAMMAR

A **Complete the conversation with the correct form of the verbs in parentheses ( ).**

A I shouldn't [1] ______________ (buy) this new car. It was way too expensive. I really can't afford it.

B Did you stop [2] ______________ (think) about that before you [3] ______________ (buy) it? You could [4] ______________ (wait) a year or two. Your old car was still in good condition.

A You're right. If I [5] ______________ (not buy) the car, I [6] ______________ (spend) all my savings. And I [7] ______________ (not have to) borrow money from my parents.

B PAIR WORK **What have you done recently that you regret? Talk about it with your partner.**

C **Choose the correct words to complete the paragraph. Then change the underlined parts of the paragraph to make it true for you.**

I'll never forget <u>our family vacations at the beach</u>. Those memories make me [1]*feel / to feel* <u>happy</u>. The thing I liked most <u>about those vacations</u> [2]*was / were* <u>building huge sand castles with my brother</u>. And I remember [3]*to spend / spending* <u>hours in the water with my father</u>. It was <u>so much fun</u>. Of course, there were some negative memories, too. But we all tend to remember only the positive [4]*one / ones*.

3 SPEAKING

A PAIR WORK **What have you done today? What would have happened if things had been different?**

Today I overslept, so I didn't have time for breakfast. I'm really hungry now. If I hadn't overslept, I'd have had breakfast, and I wouldn't be so hungry now.

B **Tell the class what you learned about your partner.**

4 FUNCTIONAL LANGUAGE

A **Use the words and phrases in the box to complete the conversation.**

a good alternative	won't believe	another option	could work	don't tell me
ever happened	I've always had luck	ready for this	that time	amazing

A You [1] ______________ this, but I just washed my phone in the washing machine.

B [2] ______________ you had left it in the pocket of your pants.

A Exactly. And are you [3] ______________ ?

B What?

A The phone's still working. Isn't that [4] ______________ ?

B That's incredible.

A I know, totally! Has that [5] ______________ to you?

B Well, not in the washing machine, but do you remember [6] ______________ when I dropped my phone in the swimming pool? It never worked again.

A You should buy a phone like this. [7] ______________ with this brand.

B But it's pretty expensive.

A [8] ______________ would be a waterproof case for the phone. That's [9] ______________ .

B That [10] ______________ . I guess I'll get myself one.

5 SPEAKING

A PAIR WORK **Choose one of the situations below. Act it out in pairs.**

1 You're looking for a waterproof case for your phone, or another gadget you need. Get recommendations and discuss alternatives.

A I'm looking for a waterproof case for my phone.

B This one is waterproof and it's good up to 30 feet deep in the water.

A I don't need anything that extreme. Can you suggest an alternative?

2 Talk about an event or mistake that had unexpected consequences.

A You'll never guess what happened to me this morning.

B Don't tell me you took the wrong bus again.

A Worse than that. I went all the way to my old job. And you know what? I met my old boss and she asked me to come back to the company!

3 You meet an old school friend and start talking about your days in middle school.

A Do you remember that time you made me skip class and go to the mall with you?

B I don't recall skipping classes in middle school.

A Are you kidding me? Remember we bumped into your aunt and …

B **Change roles and repeat the role play.**

GRAMMAR REFERENCE AND PRACTICE

1.1 TENSE REVIEW (SIMPLE AND CONTINUOUS) (PAGE 3)

SIMPLE TENSES			
Simple present			
I get up at 8. He gets up at 8.	I don't get up at 8. He doesn't get up at 8	Do you get up at 8? Does he get up at 8?	Yes, I do. / No, I don't Yes, he does. / No, he doesn't.
Simple past			
I went to work 8.	I didn't go to work.	Did you go to work?	Yes, I did. / No, I didn't.
Present perfect			
I've done this before. He's done this before.	I haven't done this before. He hasn't done this before.	Have you ever done this before? Has he ever done this before?	Yes, I have. / No, I haven't. Yes, he has. / No, he hasn't.

CONTINUOUS TENSES			
Present continuous			
I'm reading. You're reading She's reading.	I'm not reading. You aren't reading. She isn't reading.	Are you reading? Is she reading?	Yes, I am. / No, I'm not. Yes, she is. / No, she isn't.
Past continuous			
I was eating. You were eating. It was eating.	I wasn't eating. You weren't eating. It wasn't eating.	Were you eating? Was it eating?	Yes, I was. / No, I wasn't. Yes, it was. / No, it wasn't.
Present perfect continuous			
I've been waiting. He's been waiting.	I haven't been waiting. He hasn't been waiting.	Have you been waiting? Has he been waiting?	Yes, I have. / No, I haven't. Yes, he has. / No, he hasn't.

A **Choose the correct form of the verb.**

1 Every day *I'm getting up / I get up* at 7 a.m.
2 Yesterday I *wasn't going / didn't go* to work.
3 *I'm painting / I paint* my bedroom at the moment.
4 *I've been standing / I've stood* here for half an hour waiting for the bus!
5 I was just sitting down to eat dinner when the phone *was ringing / rang*.
6 Have you *ever visited / been visiting* New York in the winter?

1.2 DYNAMIC AND STATIVE VERBS (PAGE 5)

Stative and dynamic verbs

Dynamic verbs describe actions (*go, sleep, talk*). They can be used in the continuous form to describe:

- an action in progress: I**'m working** on a community art project.
- a plan: I**'m interviewing** three candidates tomorrow.

Stative verbs are generally not used with continuous forms. They describe:

- personal qualities (*be*): They**'re** responsible. She**'s** polite.
- preferences (*like, love, hate, want, need*): We **need** someone who's polite. She **wants** to be successful.
- opinions (*believe, think*): I **think** we have the right person.

Most verbs can be dynamic or stative, depending on the context.

Dynamic	Stative
She**'s being** very careful.	She**'s** very responsible.
I**'m thinking** of looking for a new job.	I **think** curiosity is a good quality.
I**'m having** lunch with her tomorrow.	I **have** too much to do.

Stative verbs that describe mental activity *(know, understand, want, need)* are always stative.

A **Check (✓) the sentences that use dynamic and stative verbs correctly. Correct the incorrect ones. Why are they incorrect?**

- ☐ **1** I'm being very scared of snakes.
- ☐ **2** He's being very responsible about his studies.
- ☐ **3** I'm not really seeing what you mean.
- ☐ **4** I'm seeing Jon on Saturday.
- ☐ **5** I'm loving every minute of this holiday.
- ☐ **6** I'm liking to take it easy on the weekend.

2.1 REAL CONDITIONALS (PAGE 13)

Real conditional sentences

Conditional sentences are made up of two parts: the condition (*if* clause) and the result. The clauses can go in either order. When the condition comes first, use a comma to separate it from the result.

If + present, present

Use *if* + present, present to talk about a possible situation and to describe general truths, facts, and habits.

Condition	Result
Even **if** a vegetable **doesn't look** good,	Chef Barber **makes** it taste great.

If + present, imperative

Use *if* + present, imperative to tell someone what to do.

Condition	Result
If it **tastes** good,	**eat** it!

If + present, *will / be going to / might*

Use *if* + present, *will / be going to / might* to talk about possible future results.

Condition	Result
If you **prefer** flavor to good looks,	you**'ll** love his food.
If you **like** good food,	you**'re going to** love Chef Barber's restaurant.
If Chef Barber **serves** it,	I **might** try it.

A **Check (✓) the sentences that are correct. Correct the ones with errors.**

☐ **1** If you like trendy restaurants, you go to Maxine's Bistro.

☐ **2** If enough people start eating quinoa, it is going to be the next big thing.

☐ **3** If a restaurant is "zero waste," doesn't throw away food.

☐ **4** If more people will eat at zero waste restaurants, it will help solve world hunger.

☐ **5** People lose interest if a restaurant will not try something new.

☐ **6** If something is all the rage, it is fashionable.

2.2 CLAUSES WITH *AFTER, UNTIL, WHEN* (PAGE 15)

A **Correct the mistakes in the bold verbs.**

1 Of course, before you**'ll make** the recipe you'll need to go shopping.
2 When the guests **will arrive** at 8, we'll need to have everything ready, so get organized now.
3 The flight takes about three hours, so when we land, it **is** 6:30.
4 When the fog **will clear,** we'll be able to leave.
5 Once you**'ll get** used to the job, it'll be a lot easier.
6 Until you**'re going to have** all the papers, you won't be allowed to apply for the position.

3.1 *TOO* AND *ENOUGH* (PAGE 23)

too* and *enough

	too	***enough***
with nouns	My commute took **too much time.**	We don't have **enough time.**
with adjectives	I was **too busy.**	The suburban lifestyle wasn't **exciting enough.**
with adverbs	I have to work **too hard.**	He doesn't work **hard enough.**
with verbs	My apartment **costs too much.**	I don't **earn enough.**

A **Add *too* or *enough* to the sentences below.**

1 I'm sorry, I can't go out tonight. I have ^too much work to do.
2 Oh no, I don't have money! Can you buy the ticket for me?
3 I'm sorry, we can't serve you. It's late. The kitchen is already closed.
4 Is he old to drive? He looks very young.
5 You work hard! You need to take a break.
6 There aren't hours in the day to do everything!
7 There are many people waiting in line. I'm going to come back later.
8 Is that hot for you or would you like me to heat it up in the microwave?

3.2 MODIFYING COMPARISONS (PAGE 25)

Modifying comparative adjectives.		
It's	**a whole lot** **way** **a bit** **a little**	easier (than something else).
Modifying comparative structures		
It's	**just** **nearly** **almost** **nowhere near**	as expensive as (the other one).
Modifying superlative adjectives.		
It's	**by far**	the (best coffee).

A **Add one word to modify the comparisons in the sentences. Sometimes more than one answer is possible.**

1 Ian is ________ as tall as his older brother James!
2 That was by ________ the hardest test I've ever taken!
3 It's really difficult to choose between them. I guess this one is a ________ cheaper.
4 I'm sorry, but this movie is nowhere ________ as good as the last one she made.
5 I prefer this one. I think it's a ________ nicer.

4.1 MODALS OF SPECULATION (PAGE 35)

Modals expressing certainty	
This **must** be an authentic jersey.	This **must not** be an authentic jersey. This **can't** be an authentic jersey.
Modal expressing uncertainty	
This **may** be an authentic jersey. This **might** be an authentic jersey. This **could** be an authentic jersey.	This **may not** be an authentic jersey. This **might not** be an authentic jersey.

A **Rewrite the sentences with modal verbs so that they have the same meaning.**

1 It's easy to imagine that American football becomes more popular in Europe.
American football could easily become more popular in Europe.
2 I'm sure that Chelsea won't win the league this year.
____
3 It's possible that more NBA teams will put sponsors on their shirts.
____
4 I'm sure that Real Madrid has the most fans of any team in Spain.
____
5 I'm sure that soccer is the world's most popular sport.
____
6 I'm sure that tennis is not as popular as soccer.
____

4.2 SUBJECT AND OBJECT RELATIVE CLAUSES (PAGE 37)

Subject relative clauses

In subject relative clauses, the *relative pronoun* is the subject of the relative clause and is always followed by a verb.

Small stories ***that / which*** **grow into something bigger** are found all over the internet.

The young boy ***who / that*** **made his own Messi jersey** captured the world's attention.

Object relative clauses

In object relative clauses, the *relative pronoun* is the object of the relative clause and is always followed by a noun or pronoun.

He met the man **(*who / that*) he admired more than anyone else.**

Viral stories can be big stories **(*that / which*) we share with the world.**

He got to travel to Qatar ***where*** **his dreams came true.**

In object relative clauses the relative pronouns *that*, *which*, and *who* can be omitted.

A **Read the sentences and circle the relative pronouns. Cross them out where they can be omitted.**

1 She's a filmmaker who I really like. She made a film about robots who control our lives.
2 That's the guitar that I bought in Spain. The little music shop where I bought it was so cool!
3 I have a friend who designs amazing clothes. She's someone that I met in college.
4 LeBron James is an example of an athlete who has become an icon.
5 Comedians are the celebrities that I find most interesting.

5.1 PAST PERFECT (PAGE 45)

Past perfect

To form the past perfect use *had* and a past participle.

She **hadn't shown** her stories to anybody.

Use the past perfect to talk about things that happened before another event in the past.

The previous owners **had died** mysteriously before we moved in.

(The first owners died, then we moved in sometime later.)

When there are two completed events in the past, use the simple past for the more recent event.

I'd never written a novel. I had no idea where to start.

Questions and short answers

Had he ever **written** a novel? Yes, he **had**. / No, he **hadn't**.

A **Complete the conversations with the verbs in parentheses ( ) in the past perfect or the simple past.**

1 A How [1] was (be) your vacation?
B Great! We went skiing. I [2] ________ (never ski) before!
A [3] ________ (you/ever visit) that area before?
B No, it [4] ________ (be) my first time.

2 A [5] ________ (you/ have) a good meeting?
B Not really. When I [6] ________ (arrive) at the office, the meeting [7] ________ (already begin).
A Was the boss there?
B Yes. He [8] ________ (arrive) long before anyone else.

5.2 *WAS/WERE GOING TO; WAS/WERE SUPPOSED TO* (PAGE 47)

was/were going to; was/were supposed to

These forms describe an action that was planned in the past. They are often used to say that a plan didn't happen.

We **were going to** get together, but she texted to say she couldn't come.

We **were supposed to** get together, but she texted to say that she couldn't come.

They are often followed by *but* + an explanation of why the plan didn't happen.

Affirmative	Negative	Question
We **were going to** see a movie (but we didn't).	We **weren't going to** see a movie (but we did).	**Were** you **going to** see a movie?
I **was supposed to** work last weekend (but I didn't).	You **weren't supposed to** work last weekend (but you did).	**Was** he **supposed to** work last weekend?

A **Complete the sentences with the words in parentheses ( ).**

1 My parents ______________ (supposed/move) into their new house last week. They ______________ (going/leave) their old place on Friday, but there was a problem.

2 Some friends and I ______________ (going/visit) some other friends in Florida. We ______________ (suppose/drive) down on Sunday night, but there was a terrible storm and we couldn't leave until Tuesday morning.

3 I ______________ (not supposed/work) this weekend. I ______________ (going/stay) home and relax, but there was an emergency at the hospital, so I had to go in.

4 **A** ______________ (you/supposed/have) a big test this week?

B Yes, we ______________ (going/take) it tomorrow, but they canceled it.

6.1 PRESENT AND PAST PASSIVE (PAGE 55)

Present and past passive

Use passive verb forms to focus on an action, rather than on who or what performs the action.

We use *by* to say who or what does the action in a passive sentence.

The cafés are used by lots of people in the community.

Sometimes we use the passive if the person who does the action is not known or is not important.

These dogs and cats were abandoned in our neighborhood.

The object of the active sentence is the subject of the passive sentence.

Lots of people use these **cafés.** → These **cafés** are used by lots of people.

A **Change the sentences from active to passive.**

1 People usually donate a lot of money to charities that help animals.

____

2 They founded the organization in 1976.

____

3 Licensed professionals train volunteers to help elderly people in the community.

____

4 At first, the charity devoted most of its funds to conserving wildlife.

____

6.2 PASSIVES WITH MODALS (PAGE 57)

A **Change the sentences to passive. Use an appropriate modal.**

1 It's possible that soon the government will introduce new laws about climate change.

____

2 Climate change will alter our behavior.

____

3 It's possible to make positive changes if we all work together.

____

4 They are going to give him an award for all his charity work, it's certain.

____

5 It's probable that people will view this decision in a negative way.

____

7.1 REPORTED STATEMENTS (PAGE 67)

Reported statements

To report and summarize what someone said, we use a past reporting verb. We often report the words in a past tense, too.

"I **feel** much closer to my family." ➔ He **explained** that he **felt** much closer to his family.

"Their use **has multiplied** in recent years." ➔ They **reported** that their use **had multiplied** in recent years.

To report instructions we use a reporting verb + person + (*not*) *to* + verb. We can also use other types of verbs like *persuade* or *convince*.

"Buy a cell phone!" ➔ They **told / persuaded us to buy** a cell phone.

A **Change the sentences from direct speech to reported speech.**

1 "I prefer speaking face to face over texting or sending messages."
He said that ______________________________

2 "Get a new computer!"
She told ______________________________

3 "That's why you should buy a new smartphone, not a tablet."
He convinced ______________________________

4 "We won first prize in the competition."
They explained ______________________________

5 "I will text you when I leave work."
She said ______________________________

7.2 REPORTED QUESTIONS (PAGE 69)

A **Change the questions from direct speech to reported speech.**

1 Why did you buy a new smartphone?
He asked ______________________________

2 Do you prefer to speak on the phone or by text messages?
She asked ______________________________

3 Will you get a new tablet for your birthday?
We asked her ______________________________

4 Can you help me with this computer problem?
I asked them ______________________________

5 How many friends did you meet on Facebook?
She asked him ______________________________

8.1 PRESENT UNREAL CONDITIONALS (PAGE 77)

Present unreal conditionals

Present unreal conditionals refer to imagined present or future situations. They have two parts:

The *if* clause introduces or describes an **imagined situation**		The main clause asks about or discusses **an imagined reaction**
The verb is in the simple past, but it does NOT refer to a past time.		Use the modal verb *would* or *might* + verb for statements, questions, and short answers.
Statement	If I **didn't have** a family, If I **was/were** single, Even if you **paid** me a million dollars	I**'d do** it. I **might do** it. I **wouldn't do** it.
Question	If you **saw** this job ad,	**would** you **click** on the link?
Short answers	Yes, I **would** / **might**.	No, I **wouldn't**.

When the *if* clause comes first, it ends with a comma:
If you wanted a new job, would you look online?
When the main clause comes first, no comma is necessary:
Would you look online if you wanted a new job?
In the *if* clause, you can use either *was* or *were* with *I, he, she, it*:
If he were/was single, he'd do it.
If it were/was a full-time job, I'd take it.
I'd accept the job if I was/were you.

A **Choose the correct words to complete the sentences.**

1 If *I had* / *I'd* more time, *I did* / *I'd take* piano lessons.
2 If *I lived* / *I'd live* in a smaller town, *I can* / *I'd be able* to get to work faster.
3 If my job *had paid* / *paid* better, *I felt* / *I'd feel* happier about it.
4 If *I could* / *I'd be able to* live anywhere in the world, *I chose* / *I'd choose* to live in the Rockies.
5 *Would* / *Had* you move to a new place for a job if you *didn't know* / *hadn't known* anyone there?
6 I don't think I *would agree* / *agreed* to live alone for a long time, even if the place *were* / *had been* beautiful.

8.2 *I WISH* (PAGE 79)

I wish
We use *I wish* to express a desire for something to be different, or feelings of sadness or regret.
Talking about the present: use the simple past. I **don't have** any free time ➔ I wish I **had** more free time.
Talking about the future: use the simple past, the past continuous, or modal verbs *would* and *could*. I **work** every weekend. ➔ I wish I **didn't work** every weekend. I'**m working** this weekend ➔ I wish I **wasn't working** next weekend. I **can't take** time off. ➔ I wish I **could take** time off.
Talking about the past: use the past perfect. I **didn't study** for the exam. ➔ I wish I **had studied** for the exam.

A **Change the statements to wishes.**

I'm leaving tomorrow. ➔ I wish I wasn't leaving tomorrow.

1 I can't speak Japanese. ______
2 I didn't finish my report last night. ______
3 I don't have any free time this weekend. ______
4 I can't go on vacation this summer. ______
5 I have an assignment to finish tonight. ______
6 I spent all my money on a new computer. ______

9.1 PROHIBITION, PERMISSION, OBLIGATION (PRESENT) (PAGE 87)

Prohibition, permission, obligation (present)	
We can use a range of expressions to talk about permission, prohibition, and obligation in the present.	
Prohibition	You **may not / aren't allowed to / aren't supposed to** wear a hoodie. note: *may not* and *be (not) required to* are stronger than *be (not) supposed to*
Permission	You **are allowed to / may** bring your guide dog inside.
Obligation	You **are supposed to / are required to** wear a seatbelt. note: *be required to* is stronger than *be supposed to*

A **Replace the bold words with expressions from the box. Use the negative form where necessary.**

be allowed to   be required to   be supposed to   can   may

1 You **can't** eat or drink in the laboratory. ______
2 You **should** leave your dog outside. ______
3 You **shouldn't** wear outdoor shoes on the squash courts. ______
4 You **can** park your car here for up to half an hour. ______
5 You **must** show your ID when entering and leaving the building. ______
6 You **must not** skateboard inside the building. ______

9.2 PROHIBITION, PERMISSION, OBLIGATION (PAST) (PAGE 89)

Prohibition, permission, obligation (past)	
We can use a range of expressions to talk about permission, prohibition, and obligation in the past.	
Permission	*could, were allowed to*
Prohibition	*couldn't, were not allowed to*
Obligation	*had to, were required to, were supposed to* note: *were required to* is stronger than *were supposed to*

A **Complete the sentences using an appropriate expression from the grammar chart.**

1 When we were kids, we ________________ stay up after 10 o'clock. If we did, we got in trouble.

2 At school, we ________________ wear a uniform at all times. They were very strict about it.

3 When I was in high school, I ________________ play video games on school nights before I did my homework.

4 When I was a teenager, I ________________ come home by nine o'clock on weekends, but sometimes I stayed out later.

10.1 PAST UNREAL CONDITIONALS (PAGE 99)

Past unreal conditionals		
Past unreal conditionals refer to imagined past situations. They have two parts:		
The *if* clause introduces or describes an **imagined situation.**		The main clause asks about or discusses **an imagined result.**
The verb is in the past perfect, but it refers to a hypothetical time, NOT a past time.		Use the modal verb *would* + *have* + past participle for statements, questions, and short answers.
Statement	If I **had studied** more in college, If they **hadn't dug** a well,	I **would have gotten** better grades. they **wouldn't have found** the terracotta army.
Question	If you **had studied** more,	**would** you **have gotten** better grades?
Short answers	Yes, I **would** / **might have.**	No, I **wouldn't** / **might not have.**
When the *if* clause comes first, it ends with a comma: If you had gone with us, you would have seen it for yourself. When the main clause comes first, no comma is necessary: You would have seen it for yourself if you had gone with us. Use *might* instead of *would* when you're not sure about the result: You might have learned something if you had gone with us.		

A **Complete the sentences using the correct form of the verbs in parentheses ( ).**

1 If he ________________ (not have) an accident on the way to the meeting, he ________________ (not arrive) late.

2 If she ________________ (stay) in school and ________________ (get) her degree, they ________________ (hire) her.

3 If they ________________ (not discover) the cause of the infection, many more people ________________ (die).

4 If I ________________ (not go) on vacation to Florida, I ________________ (never meet) my wife!

10.2 MODALS OF PAST PROBABILITY (PAGE 101)

Modals of past probability
We use *should have* to evaluate or criticize past actions. I **should have bought** that apartment. = It was a mistake not to buy that apartment. I **shouldn't have made** that mistake.
We use *could / might have* to talk about something that was possible but didn't happen. You can use *couldn't have* to talk about something that wasn't possible. I **could have worked** harder, but I didn't bother. I **couldn't have caught** that plane. I woke up too late.
We often contract *have* when using past modals in speech but not in writing. "You **should've told** me you were busy." "I **shouldn't've gone** out last night."

A **Rewrite the sentences using past modals.**

I chose not to study medicine in college. ➔ I could have studied medicine in college.

1 It wasn't a good idea to go out the night before the exam. ➔ I shouldn't …

2 I'm sorry that I didn't call you last night. ➔ I …

3 I didn't check the weather forecast and I brought all the wrong clothes. ➔ I …

4 There was a chance of getting that job if I'd really tried. ➔ I …

5 It's not possible for him to come to the U.S. because he doesn't have a visa. ➔ He …

11.1 GERUND AND INFINITIVE AFTER *FORGET, REMEMBER, STOP* (PAGE 109)

A **Choose the correct form of the verb to complete the sentences.**

1 Everyone stopped *talking / to talk* and turned to look at the man who had just walked in.

2 I was feeling hungry, so I stopped *getting / to get* something to eat.

3 I remember *seeing / to see* him for the first time. It was like meeting my twin!

4 I remembered *buying / to buy* a birthday present for my brother this year! He's going to be so happy!

5 Did you forget *locking / to lock* the door? Look, it's wide open!

6 I'll never forget *playing / to play* in the snow at my uncle's farmhouse.

11.2 CAUSATIVE VERBS: *HELP, LET, MAKE* (page 111)

A **Complete the sentences with *help, let, make* and the correct personal pronoun.**

1 My dad's great with engines. He can ____________ ____________ fix your car.

2 My parents were pretty strict. They never ____________ ____________ stay out late with my friends.

3 He's so good with computers. He ____________ ____________ build my own website in, like, an hour!

4 They really love that dog. They even ____________ ____________ ride in the front seat of the car.

5 My big brother used to be a real bully. He used to ____________ ____________ do all his homework for him!

6 We're moving into a new apartment this weekend. Could you ____________ ____________ carry some boxes and stuff?

12.1 ADDING EMPHASIS (PAGE 119)

Adding emphasis

To add emphasis, you can start a statement with a phrase that alerts the listener to the special information about to come. The emphasis phrase usually takes one of two forms:

What I + verb (+ *about*) **OR** *The thing I* + verb (+ *about*)

The verb *be* (in the appropriate form) connects the emphasis phrase with the thing you want to emphasize or point you want to make.

emphasis phrase	***be***	**point/thing you want to emphasize**
What I love about Spanish food	is	all the different kinds of tapas.
The thing I enjoy about running	is	getting outside in the fresh air.
What I didn't know	was	the door was locked!
The thing I liked most about living in California	was	the weather.

A **Rewrite sentences using the expression in parentheses ( ). Make any changes needed to the sentences.**

1 I really liked the smell in that shop. (*What I …*)

2 The food was the best thing about the trip. (*The thing I …*)

3 I remember there was a beautiful beach in that area. (*What I …*)

4 It was a good band, but we especially liked the singer's voice. (*The thing we …*)

5 I really miss my grandma's cooking. (*What I …*)

6 From childhood I remember my first bicycle. (*The thing I …*)

12.2 SUBSTITUTION AND REFERENCING (PAGE 121)

A **Read the paragraph and underline unnecessary repetition. Then rewrite the paragraph using referencing and substitution to avoid the repetition.**

Your podcast on false memories was very interesting. But it really made me question the reliability of my own memories. If my own memories aren't reliable, then how can I learn from my past? I've tried to learn lessons from my mistakes. But what if I can't remember my mistakes correctly? If I can't remember my mistakes correctly, are the lessons that I learn really lessons? Maybe some lessons are based on accurate memories and other lessons are based on false memories. How could I tell the accurate lesson from the false lessons? Just thinking about whether my memories are accurate or whether my memories are inaccurate has gotten me really confused.

VOCABULARY PRACTICE

1.1 DESCRIBING ACCOMPLISHMENTS (PAGE 2)

A **Match the stories to phrases from the box. Some may have more than one correct answer.**

break a record	face your fear	~~get a lot of likes~~
have a sense of humor	run a business	set a goal for yourself
take pride in something	tell a joke	win a medal

1 I posted a funny picture of myself on Instagram and all my friends liked it.
get a lot of likes, ______________

2 I hate speaking in front of people. It really scares me. But last week I gave a short presentation to a room of 70 people, and it went well.
____

3 I'm going to learn to speak German by the end of this year.
____

4 He ran the race in the fastest time ever.
____

5 Matt's new girlfriend is so much fun. She makes me laugh all the time!
____

6 My brother has a small art supplies store in town. He's so proud of it!
____

B **Complete the sentences with the phrases in the box. Change them as needed to fit the sentence.**

~~rise to a challenge~~	run a marathon	run a business
set a goal for yourself	win a medal	work with your hands

1 Your new job sounds difficult, but I'm sure you will *rise to the challenge* .
2 My sister is an artist. She makes sculptures. She really likes to ______________ .
3 My brother loves running. Last year, he ______________ for charity.
4 My grandfather was an Olympic athlete. He once ______________ for swimming.
5 I have always wanted to ______________ . It must be great to be your own boss!
6 I have ______________ of learning a new language. I think I'll try Japanese!

1.2 DESCRIBING KEY QUALITIES (PAGE 4)

A **Choose the correct word.**

1 Tom is so *curious / curiosity* about everything. He never stops asking questions!
2 Her uncle is a very *successful / success* lawyer. He has worked on some very important cases.
3 He isn't very *ambition / ambitious*. I mean, he doesn't want a promotion or a better job or anything.
4 She's an *experienced / experience* actor. She's been working in theater for more than 30 years.
5 I think *truthful / truthfulness* is such an important quality in a person. I hate it when people lie!
6 They're always so positive about everything. I love their *enthusiastic / enthusiasm*.

B **Complete the sentences with the correct form of the words in the box.**

confident	creativity	independence	polite	qualified	responsible

1 Dog owners must be ready to take ____________________ for their pets and always clean up after them.

2 I think it's so important to teach children the basic rules of ____________________, like saying "please" and "thank you."

3 I was really ____________________ as a child. I always wanted to do everything for myself.

4 It takes a lot of ____________________ to start your own business. You really have to believe in yourself.

5 She came up with a really ____________________ solution to the problem. It was so original – and it worked!

6 For this job, we need someone with a college degree, a special certificate, and experience! How will we ever find someone with all the right ____________________?

2.1 DESCRIBING TRENDS (PAGE 12)

A **Complete the sentences with the correct expression. The first word is given to help you. Which sentences do you disagree with? Change them to make them true for you.**

1 The raw diet, where you only eat raw foods, seems to be *on* ____________________, but maybe it will *come* ____________________ in a few years.

2 Food trucks are really *gaining* ____________________. They might *be* ____________________!

3 Nearly everyone loves pizza. It will never *go* ____________________.

4 Have you been to Chef Cesar's new restaurant? It's *all* ____________________.

5 Many diets are just *a* ____________________. They are popular for a while, but then people *lose* ____________________.

B **Choose the correct words to complete the paragraph.**

What is healthy anymore?

Japanese food is suddenly [1]*all the rage / going out of style*. It seems that every restaurant in my town offers a sushi or sashimi now. It's [2]*gaining / losing* popularity because a lot of its ingredients are raw, and they say uncooked food is good for you. Meanwhile, people are [3]*gaining / losing* interest in Argentinian restaurants because cooked meat is supposed to be bad for your heart. But what is healthy anymore? The experts change their minds all the time. You never know what the [4]*old-fashioned / next big* thing will be.

2.2 PREPARING FOOD (PAGE 14)

A **Choose the correct word to complete the sentences.**

1 *Garlic / Mint* has a strong taste – don't kiss anyone after eating it.

2 *Pineapple / Eggplant* makes a really nice dessert.

3 You can add *mint / shrimp* to tea for a refreshing drink.

4 Before you eat any vegetables you should really *stir / rinse* them.

5 It's not a good idea to *fry / boil* all your food, it's very fatty.

6 You can *barbecue / chop* meat or seafood outside on the grill – it's delicious.

B **Complete the paragraph with words from the box. More than one option is sometimes possible. There are two extra words.**

boil	chop	eggplant	fry	garlic
ginger	shrimp	stir	zucchini	

Not sure what to make for dinner tonight? Curry might just be the answer. This Indian dish is both delicious and easy to make. All you need are a few vegetables, a few spices, and maybe meat, fish, or beans for protein. My favorite curries are very spicy and use a lot of [1] __________ . For vegetables, I usually use potatoes and carrots. But you can use [2] __________ or [3] __________ – just be sure to [4] __________ your vegetables in cold water before you [5] __________ them. Most of my curries are vegetarian, but I'll occasionally add some seafood – usually [6] __________ . The actual cooking part is easy – just add everything to a hot pan and [7] __________ it all together!

3.1 TALKING ABOUT TIME AND MONEY (PAGE 22)

A **Complete the paragraph with the words in the box.**

balance	cost of living	lifestyle	salary cut	trade	value	worth

The [1] __________ is generally much lower in smaller towns – big cities are much more expensive! It's also much easier to find a healthy work/life [2] __________ , although you will probably have to take a [3] __________ if you decide to move out of the city. You will also need to [4] __________ the fast-paced city [5] __________ for a quieter life. If you [6] __________ peace and quiet, clean air, and living closer to nature, you'll probably find that it's [7] __________ it.

B **Do you agree with the ideas in the paragraph in exercise A? Complete these sentences about your hometown. Give examples.**

1 The cost of living is generally …
2 The standard of living is generally …
3 It's easy/difficult to find a good work/life balance because …
4 It's easy/difficult to boost your career chances because …
5 I really value the … in my town.
6 I can/can't afford to … because …

3.2 TALKING ABOUT PRICES AND VALUE (PAGE 24)

A **Choose the correct verb.**

1 I know I can *take advantage of / rely on* them to give me great service.
2 I've just *come up with / made the most of* a great idea for a new business!
3 I'm going to *invest in / treat myself to* a trip to a spa next weekend.
4 How much do they usually *charge for / pay a fair price for* a meal for two?
5 I might go with you. It *depends on / has an effect on* how money I can save by then.

B **Complete each question with the correct preposition. Then write answers to the questions.**

1 What has the biggest effect __________ your quality of life, your job or your social life?
2 Do you think it's better to invest __________ property or education?
3 Do you think your quality of life depends more __________ time or money?
4 Do you make the most __________ your free time, or do you waste it?
5 Do you ever treat yourself __________ an expensive meal?

4.1 TALKING ABOUT ADVERTISING (PAGE 35)

A Choose the best option to complete the sentences.

1. The Apple *sponsor / logo* is one of the most recognizable in the world.
2. "Finger lickin' good" is the *product / slogan* of a famous fast food chain.
3. Many smaller companies can't afford to *advertise / sponsor* their products on TV.
4. I only buy one *product / brand* of jeans. They're my absolute favorite.
5. Mike wears the most usual outfits. He says he wants to make a *fashion statement / commercial*.

B Complete the quotes with the words in the box.

advertisement	brand	fashion statement	logo
merchandise	products	slogan	

Nike is my favorite [1] ______ of shoe. I like their swoosh [2] ______ and their [3] ______, "Just do it!" I love wearing their [4] ______. I think it makes a real [5] ______.

Really? Personally, I don't like to wear [6] ______ with the company's logo on it. It's like being a walking [7] ______ for the company.

4.2 TALKING ABOUT PEOPLE IN THE MEDIA (PAGE 37)

A Complete the sentences with words from the box. Some sentences may have more than one correct answer.

audience	celebrity	comedian	designer	DJ	entertainer
filmmaker	hero	icon	model	performer	producer

1. I would never want to be a ______. There's too much attention from the media.
2. Guillermo del Toro is probably my favorite ______. He was the director and the ______ of *The Shape of Water*.
3. We didn't have a band for our wedding. We just hired a ______.
4. Being a professional ______, like a musician, would be hard because they have to travel so much.
5. One of my favorite events in New York is Fashion Week. I love to see all the ______ wearing the latest designs.
6. Ralph Lauren is a famous ______. He founded the clothing brand Polo.
7. My sister really likes that ______ but I don't. His jokes can be a little mean.
8. Steph Curry is more than just an athlete. He's an ______.
9. In most of his films, he plays a ______. But in my favorite film, he's the bad guy.
10. I'd never want to be a ______ on stage. What if the ______ didn't like my act?

5.1 DESCRIBING STORIES (PAGE 44)

A **Read the news headlines and decide which story types they probably are. More than one type is possible.**

coming-of-age story	family saga	feel-good story	hard-luck story
horror story	human interest story	love story	mystery
personal tragedy	success story	tall tale	tearjerker

1 Teenager discovers possible cure for cancer ____________
2 New York couple celebrates 86 years of marriage ____________
3 Dog finds family after 3-day adventure ____________
4 Family loses home in forest fire ____________
5 Panda gives birth to twins in Toronto zoo ____________

B **Read the sentences from different stories. What kinds of stories do you think they are?**

1 He became the first man to climb to the top of Mt. Everest solo! ____________
2 One wrong decision and he had lost everything. ____________
3 As she walked forward to receive her diploma, she looked out at the three generations that had carried her to this moment. ____________
4 Then, out of nowhere, an enormous bird flew down and grabbed the fish right out of my hands! So I can't show you, but it was the biggest fish anyone ever caught in that lake! Really! ____________

5.2 MAKING AND BREAKING PLANS (PAGE 46)

A **Choose the correct verb to complete the sentences.**

1 His parents had *gone ahead / cheered up / split up* the year before, so he lived with his grandmother for a while.
2 It had been a long, hard week, and I was *ending up / looking forward to / making up* the weekend.
3 We were *held up / let down / messed up* in traffic, and we didn't get there in time.
4 He made a terrible mistake, but I wasn't ready to *give up on / look forward to / hang out with* him yet. I'd give him one more chance.

B **Choose the best phrasal verb for each situation. More than one option may be correct. Write a sentence based on the situation and use at least one of the phrasal verbs you chose.**

be held up	cheer up	end up
get together	give up on	go ahead
hang out with	let someone down	look forward to
make up	mess up	split up

1 He called me and said he couldn't play tennis with me this weekend. I was very disappointed.
2 She told me she had an exam next week, but I knew it wasn't true.
3 The lead singer left, and the band stopped playing together.
4 I am so mad at him! He said he wasn't feeling well, but I know he just wanted the day off.
5 I was in a hurry, but as I was leaving the office, the phone rang and I had to decide to answer it or not.
6 My friends and I try to see each other at least once a month if we can.

6.1 DISCUSSING GOOD WORKS (PAGE 54)

A **Complete the sentences with the verbs and verb phrases in the box.**

bring together	connect with	donate	get involved with
help out	join	take part in	volunteer

1 Every year, I ______________ some money to a particular charity.
2 It's good to ______________ a club because it gets you out of the house.
3 I don't like belonging to clubs because I don't easily ______________ other people.
4 I like to ______________ in many different activities.
5 I don't belong to the organization, but I ______________ when I have time.
6 I'd like to ______________ for things more often, but I don't have time.
7 The best way to ______________ groups is through the Internet.
8 This English class ______________ lots of different people with a common goal.

B **Choose the correct words to complete the text about community action.**

In Whitman County, we estimate that there are 14,000 people living in poverty. There are many ways you can help [1]*take care of / take part in* these people. First, with the food banks, you can [2]*connect / volunteer* either to pick up food donations or make deliveries. Then there's emergency housing. In this case, it's important to [3]*bring together / get to know* the needs of local people to identify and design an action plan. After some time, you can [4]*pass on / get involved in* your knowledge to new volunteers. If you're not able to give your time, you can [5]*donate / join* blankets, clothing, and appliances. Whatever you do, you are [6]*passing on / getting to know* the people in your community and making a difference.

6.2 DESCRIBING GOOD DEEDS (PAGE 56)

A **Choose the best adjective to complete the sentences.**

1 Helping people in need can be a very *grateful / rewarding* experience.
2 Most people are very *appreciative / thoughtful* when you do a good deed for them.
3 It's easy to lend someone a *kind / helping* hand.
4 If you don't want to seem *ungrateful / appreciative*, thank a person for what they have done for you.
5 Going to visit someone in the hospital is a very *helping / kind* thing to do.
6 Sending flowers when someone dies is a very *rewarding / thoughtful* gesture.

B **Use words and phrases from the box to complete the conversations. One will not be used.**

appreciate	help	helpful	thoughtful
lend a helping hand		show some gratitude	

1 A If you need some ______________ don't hesitate to call me!"
B Ok, I will! Thanks a lot!
2 A Mike never said "Thank you" after you helped him?
B No! I mean he could at least ______________ .
3 A It's just a small present, nothing big.
B Still, it's very ______________ . Thank you.
4 A This map is in French!
B Well, that's not very ______________ . We'd better ask someone for directions.
5 A I just wanted to tell you how much I ______________ all your help this week.
B Hey, what are friends for, right?

7.1 DESCRIBING COMMUNICATION (PAGE 66)

A **Choose the correct preposition in each sentence.**

1 He never replied *with / to* my email.

2 I was informed *by / of* the problem too late.

3 We had a nice time at the family reunion. It was great to catch up *in / with* all my cousins.

B **Complete the opinions with a reporting verb from the box in the correct form. What other reporting verbs might be possible in each context?**

catch up with	comment	congratulate	contact	criticize
explain	gossip	inform of	keep in touch with	mention
persuade	reply to	report	respond to	

1 "A good thing about social media is that you can read a post and then ________ on it. Other people might then ________ ________ your comments. You get to know a lot of people that way!"

2 "I use social media to ________ people on their birthdays and to ________ ________ ________ my friends, to find out what's happening with them."

3 "I never ________ about people's private lives or ________ people on social media. That's not nice, and it also isn't fair."

4 "It's hard to ________ somebody to use social media if they don't like the idea. You can ________ why you like it, but they probably won't care!"

7.2 COMMUNICATING ONLINE (PAGE 68)

A **Match words from the box with their definitions.**

clickbait	geo-tag	hashtag	lifecaster	lurker
meme	newsfeed	podcaster	profile	status update
tag	timeline	trending topic		

1 part of a website that updates often to show the latest news ________

2 a person who produces audio stories to download or stream online ________

3 the newest information that you post online ________

4 someone who puts everything about themselves on social media ________

5 internet content that encourages people to click on particular links ________

6 a story or news item that has become popular on social media ________

7 biographical information that you post on social media ________

8 add someone's name to your post or photo on social media ________

B **Use the other words in the box to complete the post about online communication.**

Distractions! They're everywhere online. It could be a friend asking for donations to support them in a charity fun run, but then again, it could be a new [1] ________ that everyone is now using in their messages! It might be a really funny [2] ________ that has gone viral overnight. There could be a review that you posted online and now have to [3] ________ to show a location for it. In fact it could be anything – a text, an image, a video that you just have to put on your [4] ________ right now!

This is hard for all of us. Sometimes it's good to disconnect from social media for a while. Or, if that's too hard, just don't post for a while. Be a [5] ________ and enjoy a view of the digital world from a distance!

8.1 DESCRIBING JOBS (PAGE 76)

A Find words in the box to match the definitions.

challenging	desk job	dream job	freelance	full-time
government job	high-paying	main job	part-time	permanent
second job	stressful	temporary	tiring	tough

1 It only lasts a few months. ________
2 This means there are often a lot of problems to deal with. ________
3 You get a good salary. ________
4 You only work a few hours. ________
5 This is what you've always wanted to do. ________
6 This means you work in an office. ________
7 You usually have one of these to get some extra money. ________
8 You don't have a contract with one company, but instead you work for different companies. ________

B Choose the best word to complete the description. Can you guess the job?

The first few years in the job were really [1]*part-time / tough*. I had to work very long hours and it was physically [2]*tiring / freelance*. It's the total opposite of a [3]*desk job / temporary job*. But I loved it! It wasn't very [4]*permanent / high-paying* to start with, but as I progressed through my career my salary grew very quickly. When I got married and had kids I decided to reduce my hours and work [5]*a second job / part-time*. I'm so grateful to the hospital for letting me do that.

8.2 TALKING ABOUT WORK/LIFE BALANCE (PAGE 78)

A Complete the sentences with the words and phrases in the box.

9-to-5	always connected	assignments	busy schedule
family life	seminar	office hours	social life

1 I have such a ________ at the moment. I don't have time for anything but work!
2 I've been traveling a lot for work recently, and it's really affecting my ________ . I hardly ever see my kids these days!
3 Don't call too early. Our ________ are 10 a.m. to 6 p.m.
4 My new job is great, and it's having a really positive effect on my ________ . I go out with my coworkers all the time!
5 I can't believe it. Our professor just gave us three ________ to do over the weekend!
6 I really envy you with your ________ job. I have to work nights and weekends.
7 I love teaching online, but it means I'm ________ . It's really difficult for me to get away from my computer.
8 This is going to be a tough semester. I have five regular classes, but I'm also taking a ________ on business ethics Tuesday nights.

B **Match the words and phrases with their definitions.**

downtime time off commitments seminar chill out shift

1 things that you have agreed or arranged to do ________
2 the period of time a person is scheduled to work ________
3 a time when you can relax ________
4 a meeting of a group of people with a teacher ________
5 a period of time when you do not work due to illness or vacations ________
6 rest, relax, or be calm ________

9.1 TALKING ABOUT PLACES (PAGE 86)

A **Match the places in the box with their descriptions.**

arts center	boardwalk	city hall	construction site	consulate
courthouse	highway rest stop	laboratory	playground	public space
residential area	toll plaza			

1 a park or square or other outdoor place ________
2 a place where children love to go ________
3 where scientists do experiments ________
4 where people live ________
5 where you stop to pay so that you can use the highway ________
6 where you can take painting classes or see a play ________

B **Read the quotes. Use the other places in the box to say where each person is.**

1 "We've been driving a long time and need a break." ________
2 "I'm sorry, but you have to wear a hard hat. It can be dangerous." ________
3 "I've come to get a visa for my trip to Egypt." ________
4 "We'll go swimming later. Let's get some ice cream and walk for a while." ________
5 "Could you tell me if this is the right place to apply for a parking permit?" ________
6 "My mom works here. She's a judge." ________

9.2 TALKING ABOUT RULES (PAGE 89)

A **Choose the correct word to complete the sentences.**

1 Speed limit signs are used to *control / prohibit* traffic within the downtown area.
2 You cannot park your car here unless you have *obligation / permission* from the central office.
3 All guests are required to *limit / register* at reception on arrival.
4 There is a *ban / requirement* on all ball sports in all residential areas.

B **Complete the sentences with the correct form of the word in parentheses ( ).**

1 Swimming in the lake is strictly ________ (prohibit) at all times.
2 You must consider all the legal ________ (require) when starting a business.
3 Click here to start your ________ (register) process.
4 The bus is ________ (limit) to 50 passengers!

10.1 TALKING ABOUT DISCOVERIES (PAGE 98)

A **Complete the sentences with the nouns in the box.**

breakthrough	challenge	connection	discovery	insight
knowledge	phenomenon	research	solution	

1 They have made a great __________ in AIDS research, but there is still no cure.
2 It's a very difficult task, but now I'm ready to take on the __________ .
3 Politicians have discussed it, but they have not provided a __________ to the problem yet.
4 The documentary was fascinating. It provides real __________ into this complex issue.
5 If you get the scholarship, you'll have to carry out your own __________ .
6 The crime rate is rising, and experts are investigating this __________ at the moment.
7 Detectives have noticed the __________ between the crime rate and high unemployment.
8 The internet provided me with the __________ that I needed to complete our report.
9 Like so many others in the past, they made the __________ accidentally.

B **Choose the correct words to complete the sentences.**

1 We *faced / noticed* a terrible challenge, but we achieved our goal in the end.
2 People are *making / finding* new discoveries in the natural sciences all the time.
3 If you *provide / gain* us with the knowledge we need, we'll accomplish the task.
4 Scientists are still *noticing / making* breakthroughs in the world of medicine.
5 Investigators *noticed / faced* this phenomenon, but they didn't know how best to react to it.
6 The program helped me *gain / carry out* vital insights into this problem.
7 A lot of researchers don't realize they've *made / investigated* a breakthrough until much later.
8 They *carried out / provided* the academic research, but they haven't studied the results yet.
9 We'll need to *find / make* a solution soon, or this problem could get out of hand.

10.2 DISCUSSING RIGHT AND WRONG (PAGE 100)

A **Choose the correct words to complete the sentences.**

1 "I'm sorry, it was a complete *confusion / misunderstanding* on my part. I hadn't read the report properly."
2 "I deserve all the *mistake / blame*. I'm the one who broke the vase."
3 "I managed to correct that *fault / error* and now I feel much better."
4 "Rob was reading the wrong page of the instructions, which caused a lot of *blunder / confusion*."
5 "If you can *fail / fix* that little mistake, you'll pass the exam easily."

B **Use the words in the box to replace the underlined words in each sentence.**

~~blunder~~	an epic fail	fault	make this right	mixed up

1 "I can't believe they made such a stupid ~~mistake~~ blunder."
2 "I feel terrible. I have to find a way to correct the situation."
3 "Sorry I missed our meeting. I got the dates switched."
4 "My attempt to cook a fancy dinner for my girlfriend was a complete disaster."
5 "I didn't complete the report on time. It's my responsibility."

11.1 TALKING ABOUT COLLEGE EDUCATION (PAGE 108)

A **Match the words in the box with their definitions. There is one extra.**

dorm	faculty	freshman	grade
major	semester	society	

1 the teachers in a college department ____________

2 a first-year college student ____________

3 a club that is organized by students ____________

4 a building where many students live ____________

5 the main focus of your studies in college ____________

6 a letter or number that shows how good your work is ____________

B **Complete the sentences with the words in the box.**

associations	campus	degree
facilities	professors	undergraduate

1 We have some amazing sports ____________ on ____________ .

2 Our ____________ are awesome! They're so helpful and supportive.

3 I'm an ____________ . After I get my ____________ in biology, I'm going to go to medical school.

4 There are so many different student ____________ . It's really difficult to choose just one!

11.2 TALKING ABOUT SCIENCE (PAGE 110)

A **Match words from the chart to their definitions.**

abstract noun	verb	person	adjective	compound adjective
science		scientist	scientific	scientifically proven
research	research	researcher		research-based
proof	prove		proven	scientifically proven
base/basis	base		based (on facts)	science-based
medicine			medical	medically approved

1 a person who works in a laboratory conducting experiments ____________

2 the set of facts that show something is true ____________

3 the study of the human body and how to repair it ____________

4 the study of natural things ____________

5 a person who studies natural things ____________

6 when doctors say that something is good for their patients ____________

B **Complete the sentences with the correct form of the word in parentheses ( ).**

1 The researchers were not able to ____________ (proof) that cheese gives you nightmares.

2 It is a ____________ (science) fact that carrots can improve your night vision.

3 ____________ (medicine) studies suggest that mosquitoes prefer certain blood types.

4 The fact that honey calms a cough has been ____________ (science) proven.

5 Studies ____________ (base) on a small number of patients are never totally reliable.

12.1 TALKING ABOUT THE SENSES (PAGE 118)

A **Match the adjectives to the nouns. More than one answer may be possible.**

1 stinky ______
2 colorful ______
3 damp ______
4 musty ______
5 melodic ______
6 bright ______
7 tasty ______
8 high-pitched ______
9 deep ______
10 flavorful ______

a trash
b towel
c voices
d clothes
e cookies

B **Choose the correct words to complete the sentences.**

1 I play the bass guitar because I like its rich, *deep / damp* sound.
2 I woke up to the *melodic / high-pitched* scream of the fire alarm.
3 After shaving, my skin feels so *smooth / rough.*
4 The boxes from the basement are so *deep / musty.* Open a window!
5 The omelets at that restaurant are more *bright / flavorful* than you can believe!

12.2 DESCRIBING MEMORIES (PAGE 120)

A **Complete the sentences with the correct form of a word or phrase from the box. More than one answer may be possible.**

bring back	childhood	clear	distant
early	long-term	look back on	recall
recent	recognize	remind	short-term
vague	vivid		

1 We met at Sam's party? Really? I was so tired that night. I only have a ______ memory of the party, but no memory at all of the people there.
2 I don't like to ______ unhappy times from my ______. Best just to move on and forget about it.
3 After all these years, I didn't ______ her face, but I remembered her voice!
4 I have a really ______ memory of the first time we met. I can even remember exactly what you were wearing.
5 That song always ______ me of the summer of 2005.

B **Choose the correct words to complete the sentences.**

1 It was 20 years ago that I lived there, so it's just a *distant / early* memory now.
2 My grandma is losing her *short-term / long-term* memory, but she remembers her childhood very well, so her *short-term / long-term* memory is still great.
3 What's the first thing you can *bring back / recall* about your early years?
4 I have a very *early / vague* memory, but it might be false. I was four, and I was at the zoo with my mother. We were looking at the lions and eating popcorn. I can see it so clearly in my mind. The strange thing is, she doesn't *recognize / recall* this at all.
5 Of all the senses, smell *brings back / looks back on* the most *vague / vivid* memories.

PROGRESS CHECK

Can you do these things? Check (✓) what you can do. Then write your answers in your notebook.

UNIT 1

Now I can …	Prove it
☐ use expressions to talk about personal achievements.	Write five verb + noun combinations to describe someone's achievements.
☐ use a variety of simple and continuous verb forms.	Write five sentences about yourself using five different verb forms.
☐ use nouns and adjectives to talk about key qualities employers look for.	Write three pairs of words to describe yourself in ways that would appeal to a possible employer.
☐ use dynamic and stative verbs to talk about actions, habits, and states.	Complete the sentences: *I love* ____________. *I'm loving* ____________.
☐ make and respond to introductions.	Respond to the introduction in three different ways: *Hey, have you met Simone?*
☐ write a comment in response to an article.	Look at your comment from lesson 1.4. Can you make it better? Find three ways.

UNIT 2

Now I can …	Prove it
☐ use expressions to describe trends.	Write four different ways to refer to something that is currently popular and four more for something unpopular.
☐ use real conditionals.	Write four sentences using *if* clauses: two to refer to a fact that is generally true and two for a future possibility.
☐ use the correct words to describe food preparation.	Describe a dish you can make in six simple steps.
☐ refer to the future with time clauses using *after, until,* and *when.*	Complete the sentences so that they are true for you: *When I finish class today,* ____________. *I won't get home until* ____________. *I'm going to* ____________ *after I leave class today.*
☐ make, accept, and refuse offers in social situations.	Make an offer of food and/or drink, and practice different way of accepting and refusing it.
☐ write the results of a survey that you conducted.	Look at your survey results summary from lesson 2.4. Can you make it better? Find three ways.

UNIT 3

Now I can …	Prove it
☐ use expressions to talk about time and money.	Write five phrases about time and money.
☐ use (*not*) *too* and (*not*) *enough* to talk about quantity.	Write five sentences about yourself using different structures with *too* and *enough.*
☐ use verb phrases to talk about prices and value.	Write three verb phrases, with the correct prepositions, about prices and value.
☐ use modifiers in comparisons.	Make these comparisons stronger: *It's the best movie I've ever seen. Theirs is bigger than ours.*
☐ apologize for damaging or losing someone's property and respond to an apology.	Apologize for losing something that you borrowed. Respond to the apology.
☐ write a product review.	Look at your product review from lesson 3.4. Can you make it better? Find three ways.

PROGRESS CHECK

Can you do these things? Check (✓) what you can do. Then write your answers in your notebook.

UNIT 4

Now I can ...	Prove it
☐ use specific words to talk about ads and advertising.	Choose a product and discuss its brand and the different ways it is advertised.
☐ make different types of speculations using modals.	Write five sentences about something uncertain using different modal verbs for degrees of possibility.
☐ talk about different people in the media.	Talk about some recent viral news or a celebrity of current interest.
☐ use pronouns in subject and object relative clauses.	Talk about a few celebrities and describe who they are and what they do using relative clauses.
☐ exchange and discuss opinions.	Give your opinion about a current movie and then emphatically disagree with it.
☐ write a response to a post about businesses in your community.	Look at your response from lesson 4.4. Can you make it better? Find three ways.

UNIT 5

Now I can ...	Prove it
☐ use specific terms to describe different types of stories.	Name five movies or books and explain what story type(s) each of them is.
☐ order events in the past using past perfect tense.	Write six things that happened yesterday. Connect events using the past perfect tense.
☐ use expressions to talk about making and breaking plans.	Write four excuses for canceling plans at the last minute.
☐ use *was/were going to* and *was/were supposed to* for canceled plans.	Complete the sentence: *I* __________ *make dinner for us, but the electricity is out in my building!*
☐ react appropriately to problems and disappointing news.	Present a situation that involves a problem and react to it. Then resolve it or accept the situation politely.
☐ write a formal apology from a company.	Look at your apology from lesson 5.4. Can you make it better? Find three ways.

UNIT 6

Now I can ...	Prove it
☐ use verbs and verb phrases to describe good works.	Describe one type of volunteer work using different verbs and verb phrases.
☐ use the passive voice in the simple present and simple past.	Write as least five sentences in passive voice to describe a charity or community group.
☐ use expressions and different forms of words to talk about good deeds.	Write six sentences about the value of doing good deeds: three about giving help and three about receiving help.
☐ use the passive voice with the modals *can, might, must,* and *will*.	Complete the instruction: *Requests for shift changes* __________ (approve) *by the manager.*
☐ offer, refuse, and accept help.	Ask for help with something. Respond to the help that is or is not given.
☐ write a report about a community project.	Look at your report from lesson 6.4. Can you make it better? Find three ways.

PROGRESS CHECK

Can you do these things? Check (✓) what you can do. Then write your answers in your notebook.

UNIT 7

Now I can ...	Prove it
☐ use verbs and verb phrases to describe communication.	Write at least five sentences about how and why you communicate with people who are far away.
☐ report statements that were made in different tenses.	Listen to a conversation and make notes. Report what each person said using reporting verbs.
☐ use terms for different types of online communication.	Write six sentences about different aspects of your own online communication habits.
☐ report questions that were asked in different tenses.	Complete the reported question: "Do you prefer one big test or six small ones?" *Their teacher asked* ____________ *one big test or six small ones.*
☐ recount conversations, news, and stories.	Recount something you experienced in story form using appropriate expressions to indicate different speakers.
☐ write an email in both a formal and informal register.	Look at your emails from lesson 7.4. Can you make them better? Find three ways.

UNIT 8

Now I can ...	Prove it
☐ use terms to describe jobs and work situations.	Describe the jobs or work situations of three people you know using the terms from the lesson.
☐ use present unreal conditionals.	Write three questions about what someone might or might not do today.
☐ discuss work/life balance.	Write six sentences about your work/life balance.
☐ express dissatisfaction with *I wish*.	Complete the wishes: I waste so much time playing video games. ➔ *I wish I* __________ *so much time playing video games.* It's so cold outside. ➔ *I wish it* __________ *warmer outside.*
☐ talk through options to reach a decision.	Present and discuss three possible ways to address a situation, and encourage or discourage each of them.
☐ write a response to comments on a podcast.	Look at your response from lesson 8.4. Can you make it better? Find three ways.

UNIT 9

Now I can ...	Prove it
☐ use nouns and compound nouns to name different places.	List five places that have rules and regulations about behavior.
☐ express present prohibition, permission, and obligation.	Write one rule for each place on your list (see previous line) using different structures.
☐ use different word forms to discuss rules.	Write one sentence for each word (in any form): limit, ban, control, permit, require.
☐ express prohibition, permission, and obligation in the past.	Write six sentences about rules and freedoms in your childhood using different structures.
☐ use phrases to make generalizations.	Generalize about your culture or region. Contrast the information with another culture if you can.
☐ write a message registering a complaint.	Look at your message from lesson 9.4. Can you make it better? Find three ways.

PROGRESS CHECK

Can you do these things? Check (✓) what you can do. Then write your answers in your notebook.

UNIT 10

Now I can ...	Prove it
☐ use verb + noun phrases to describe investigation and discovery.	Describe the discovery of microwaves or the terracotta army in your own words but using phrases from the lesson.
☐ use past unreal conditionals to discuss present outcomes.	Write three sentences about how something in your life today would be different if past events had happened differently.
☐ use words for different kinds of mistakes and for corrections.	Use a variety of words to tell the story of a big mistake you or someone you know made and how it turned out in the end.
☐ use modals of past probability to suggest unreal alternatives.	Think of three alternative historical outcomes. For example: *If the U.S hadn't bought Alaska in 1867, it might have joined Canada.*
☐ keep a listener engaged by using phrases to hold their attention.	Tell a story and use phrases to keep your listener engaged. Show interest in someone else's story.
☐ write a comment about things you can and can't live without.	Look at your comment from lesson 10.4. Can you make it better? Find three ways.

UNIT 11

Now I can ...	Prove it
☐ use terms to describe the college experience.	Use your imagination to describe a day in the life of a college student using at least eight vocabulary words.
☐ change the meaning of *forget, remember*, and *stop*.	Write two logical sentences with *forget, remember*, and *stop* followed by a gerund in one sentence and an infinitive in the other.
☐ use different word forms to discuss science and medicine.	Write five sentences using five different vocabulary words, one each for abstract noun, verb, person, adjective, and compound adjective.
☐ use *help, let*, and *make* to indicate cause and effects.	Use *help, let*, and *make* once each to give advice. For example: *If you show your ID card, the guard lets you cut through the building.*
☐ discuss alternatives and give recommendations.	Suggest three alternative routes and present the advantages and disadvantages of each. End with a personal recommendation.
☐ write a comment presenting an argument.	Look at your comment from lesson 11.4. Can you make it better? Find three ways.

UNIT 12

Now I can ...	Prove it
☐ use sense adjectives for descriptions.	Write six sentences using sense adjectives to describe someone else's home, now or in the past.
☐ emphasize something using the structure *What I remember most is ...* or *The thing I liked was ...*	Write three sentences emphasizing particular things about the home you described (see previous line).
☐ use words to describe and share memories.	Write five sentences about an event that you remember differently from someone else. Write from your perspective only.
☐ use substitution and referencing to avoid repetition.	Use substitution and referencing to explain how the other person remembers the event differently (see previous line).
☐ prompt and recall shared memories.	Write three ways to prompt someone else's memory about a shared experience. Write two ways to share a similar experience.
☐ write a summary and response paragraph.	Look at your summary and response paragraph from lesson 12.4. Can you make it better? Find three ways.

PAIR WORK PRACTICE (STUDENT A)

2.5 EXERCISE B (PAGE 20) STUDENT A

Chow Mein Tacos

A small, family-run restaurant specializing in tacos. The idea is a fusion of Chinese and Mexican food, but it is not one thing or another. They don't have the right Mexican sauces or ingredients, and guests don't think the combination works. The decoration and music is also a mixture, so people don't really know what to expect of the food. They find that the tastes interfere with each other: guacamole doesn't go with sweet and sour chicken, for example. The seating area is cramped and hot in summer and the acoustics are not good. However, there is outdoor space that could be used.

GLOSSARY

cramped (*adj*) without enough space

acoustics (*n*) the qualities of a room that make it easy or difficult for people to hear

5.5 EXERCISE B (PAGE 52) STUDENT A

1 **Look at the pictures to learn about his story. Answer the questions.**

1 What plans did the man have?

2 What happened to his friend?

3 What happened while the man was waiting?

2 **Prepare to tell your story to someone from Group B.**

PAIR WORK PRACTICE

6.1 EXERCISE 4A (PAGE 55) STUDENT A

The World Wide Fund for Nature was founded in 1961. It's an international organization whose mission is to help finance other wildlife protection programs. The WWF headquarters is located based in Switzerland, but it has operations worldwide. It receives funding from a variety of sources: governments, corporate sponsors, and private donations.

7.3 EXERCISE 4A (PAGE 71) STUDENT A

Story 1: A person won a prize unexpectedly

Gabrielle (a girl you both know) won the first prize at a school art contest out of twenty candidates. She only started painting a year ago but has a natural talent. You heard she painted a portrait of her father.

Story 2: A birthday party that ended in disaster

Marcus' birthday party ended in disaster. He was blowing out the candles on his birthday cake, and one fell on the floor and set some newspapers on fire. You don't know if anyone was hurt. None of Marcus' presents was damaged, not even his new toy fire truck.

Story 3: Road trouble

Someone told you that the Carter family was driving across the U.S. for their summer vacation. In the middle of the Arizona desert, they got a flat tire. They tried to change the tire, but the spare tire was also flat. Finally, another car came along and took them to a town to get help. You don't know if they are home or still on vacation.

5.5 EXERCISE D (PAGE 52) ALL STUDENTS

She called her own phone. He heard it ring and picked it up. Half an hour later, they met and he gave back her phone. That was the beginning of a beautiful relationship. A year later, to the day, they got married!

PAIR WORK PRACTICE (STUDENT B)

2.5 EXERCISE A (PAGE 20) STUDENT B

Veggie Heaven

A vegetarian restaurant downtown which is both take out and eat in. It's very busy at lunchtime, but people complain about the slow service, the food quality, and the prices. Foods are too heavy, there too many lentil and rice dishes. Many sandwiches and salads are pre-packaged and lose their freshness quickly. There is confusion between vegetarian and vegan dishes, with some take-out meals having the wrong labels. They have great juices, but they take a long time to make and are expensive.

GLOSSARY

heavy (*adj*) large in amount or solid and not enjoyable

5.5 EXERCISE B (PAGE 52) STUDENT B

1 **Look at the pictures to learn about her story. Answer the questions.**

1 Where was the woman at 3:00 p.m.?

2 What happened when she got home?

3 What idea did she have at 4:00 p.m.?

2 **Prepare to tell your story to someone from Group B.**

PAIR WORK PRACTICE

6.1 EXERCISE 4A (PAGE 55) STUDENT B

Médecins Sans Frontières, known as "Doctors Without Borders" in English, is devoted to providing medical care in war zones and in developing countries. The program first began in 1971 and now operates in over 70 nations. Although it does not have a headquarters, the program's international council meets in Geneva, Switzerland. Doctors Without Borders in almost entirely funded by private donations.

7.3 EXERCISE 4A (PAGE 71) STUDENT B

Story 1: A person won a prize unexpectedly

Gabrielle (a girl you both know) won first prize at a school painting contest. At just 13, she was the youngest person in the competition. This was the first time she had entered the competition. You heard she painted a landscape of the area near her house.

Story 2: A birthday party that ended in disaster

Marcus' birthday party ended in disaster. There was a fire at the house, but you don't know what started the fire. They had to evacuate the house, but nobody was hurt.

Story 3: Road trouble

Jane Carter told you last month that they were going to drive somewhere for their summer vacation, but you don't remember where. You saw Jane Carter at the supermarket just yesterday, and she told you that they had had some car problems, but they were all fine and very happy to be home.